THE SOCIETY OF ANTIQUARIES
OF NEWCASTLE UPON TYNE

MONOGRAPH SERIES

General Editor: John Philipson, M.A., F.S.A.

THE SOCIETY OF ANTIQUARIES
OF NEWCASTLE UPON TYNE

MONOGRAPH SERIES No. 1

THE ROMAN FORT AT SOUTH SHIELDS

Excavations 1875–1975

J. N. DORE and *J. P. GILLAM*

NEWCASTLE

Society of Antiquaries

1979

ISBN 0 901082 16 3

Filmset in 'Monophoto' Times by
Northumberland Press Ltd, Gateshead, Tyne and
Wear
Printed in Great Britain by
Fletcher and Son Ltd, Norwich

To the Townsmen of South Shields whose representatives early showed an appreciation that the remains of their Roman Fort were something to investigate and preserve, and to our sister society, *The South Shields Archaeological and Historical Society*, whose members have greatly contributed to the investigation of the site.

CONTENTS

LIST OF ILLUSTRATIONS

FOREWORD

For most of the papers that the Society wishes to publish *Archaeologia Aeliana*, with its periodical appearance and its established channels of distribution, is a wholly satisfactory medium of publication. Inevitably, however, there are upon occasion reports, for example of excavations extending over many years, which are too large for inclusion in *Archaeologia Aeliana*, and for such we need an alternative format.

To meet this need the Council of the Society decided to begin publication of a Monograph Series and has been encouraged in this project by generous aid from the Department of the Environment towards the cost of the first volume.

The report by John Dore and John Gillam, covering as it does not only recent excavations, but a series of early excavations which required recapitulation and review, exemplifies the kind of necessarily extended report for which the Series is designed. The Series, indeed, has come very opportunely to facilitate the appearance of this comprehensive report upon a site which has not hitherto received adequate publication.

CHARLES M. DANIELS, *President*

ACKNOWLEDGEMENT

The thanks of the Society are due to the Department of the Environment whose generous financial aid has enabled us to print and publish this report.

SUMMARY OF CHRONOLOGICAL CONCLUSIONS

Period I

First half of Hadrian's reign; small cohort fort facing south; reduced garrison during Roman occupation of Scotland.

Period II

Early in the reign of Marcus Aurelius; fort reoccupied and possibly enlarged, axially, south-wards. Internal buildings largely rebuilt.

Period III

Latter part of the reign of Septimius Severus; possible enlargement now if not before; fort largely rebuilt internally as supply-base for the Severan campaigns in Scotland.

Period IV

Severus Alexander; fort reoccupied by a cohort; Headquarters building rebuilt facing south; many granaries converted to living quarters.

Later Third Century

Evidence for non-military activity within the defended area and neglect of defences; cohort probably removed and place taken by occupants of now abandoned *vicus*.

Mid-Fourth to Early-Fifth Century

Evidence for increased use of site though little of new structures; garrison: *Numerus Barcariorum Tigrisiensium*.

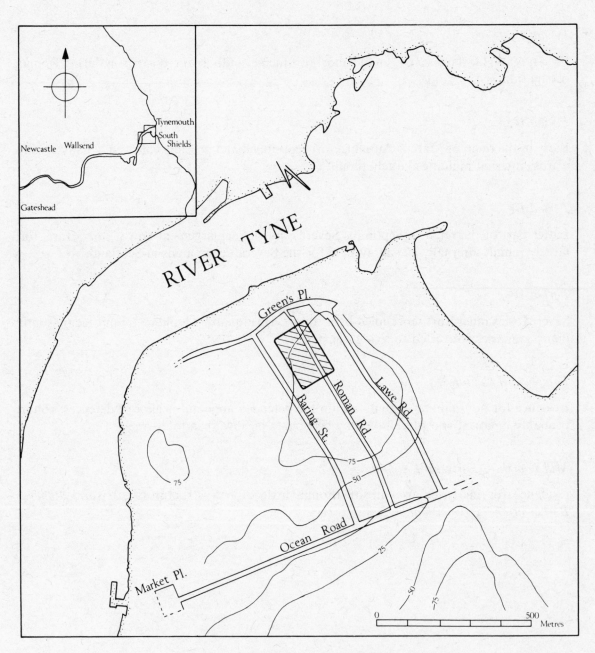

Fig. 1. The location of the Fort.

INTRODUCTION

The Roman Fort at South Shields is situated on the south side of the mouth of the Tyne, at the head of a promontory formed by a bend in the river. It lies on the north slope, just below the crest, of the area of higher ground known locally as the Lawe, a position which, without the obstruction of modern buildings, gives it a commanding view over the north bank of the river, from modern North Shields to Tynemouth Priory, and all the water in between. Across the neck of the promontory, between the Lawe and the modern town centre further inland, is a narrow channel where modern Ocean Road runs. Before 1816, when Newcastle Corporation filled it in, the Mill Dam stream flowed through this channel, and Bruce records that, "…. the memory is still preserved of occasions when the tide had risen so high as to insulate the promontory." (Bruce, 1884, p. 293.) A map of the time of Henry VIII, in the Cotton collection, (published: Savage, 1898) shows that at high tide alternative passage was afforded by this channel, known then as the "Gut". A similar state of affairs probably existed in Roman times. Even now the Lawe has an air of isolation, with the sea to the east, the river to both north and west, and a steep slope to the south.

There are certain problems concerning the exact dimensions of the fort. The plan obtained in the first excavations of 1875 shows the fort as measuring $c.$ 188 m (616 feet) by $c.$ 112 m (367 feet) and enclosing an area of $c.$ 2·1 ha. (5·18 acres), (Hooppell, 1878, pl. VIII, Bruce, 1884, p. 230). On the site today, the distance between the centre of the Headquarters building and the outer face of the west wall is 56 m, and this doubled (assuming the Headquarters building to be in the centre of the fort) gives a width the same as that above. However, in 1961, a small trench was dug by members of the South Shields Archaeological and Historical Society behind Pearson Street on the east side of the fort, and what appeared to be the inner defensive ditch and the fort wall were located. These results give the fort a width of $c.$ 116 m. Uncertainty must remain until a larger section of the east rampart is again uncovered and accurate dimensions can be obtained. It is hoped to achieve this in a programme of further excavation, at present under consideration.

The fort was connected to the Roman road system of north-eastern Britain by a special branch, known locally as the Wrekendyke, which led off the Durham to Newcastle road at modern Wrekenton, $3\frac{1}{2}$ miles south of Newcastle. The road kept to a single alignment north-eastward until close to South Shields, where it turned more to the north to reach the fort, (Margary, 1967, p. 442, no. 809). It can be traced for much of its length but the last stretch from Jarrow to the fort is lost beneath modern buildings.

The Name of the Fort

There is no mention of South Shields in the Antonine Itinerary as it was not on a through route but on a branch road, and the equation of South Shields with the *Ostia Vedra* of Ptolemy's geography was effectively disproved by Richmond (1958, p. 138). Probably the earliest reference to South Shields is in the *Notitia Dignitatum* where a *Praefectus Numeri*

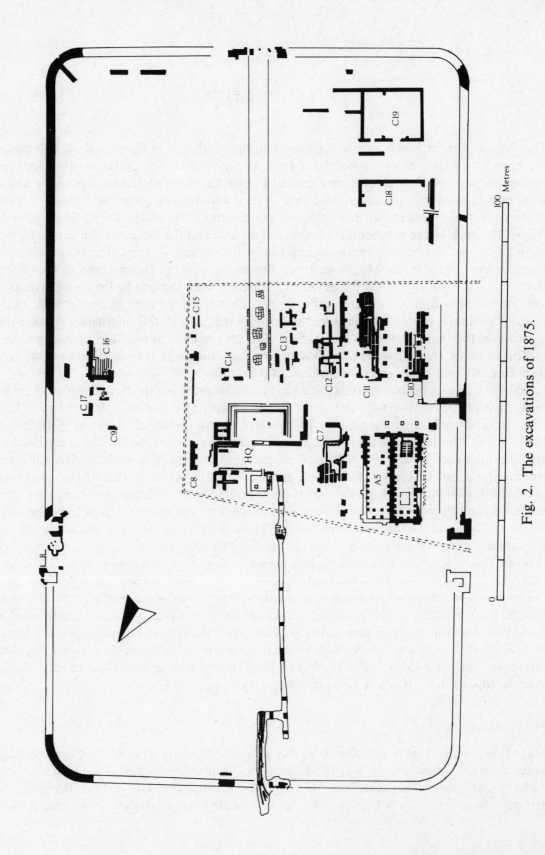

Fig. 2. The excavations of 1875.

Barcariorum Tigrisiensium is recorded at *Arbeia*, (Seeck, 1962—Not. Dig. Occ. XL, 22). That *Arbeia* was South Shields seems highly likely. From Leland it appears that the post-Roman name of South Shields was *Caer Urfa*, (Leland 1715, ii, p. 290). *Urfa* could be taken as a phonetic transmutation of *Arbeia*. Leland twice says that *Caer Urfa*, which he places at the mouth of the Tyne opposite Tynemouth, leaving little doubt that South Shields is meant, was the birthplace of King Oswin and that it was a city sacked by the Danes, so there was evidently a sizable post-Roman settlement there, (Leland, *ibid.* and iii, p. 43).

Excavations 1875–1975

Before 1874 the land on which the fort is situated was owned by the Dean and Chapter of Durham and given over to tillage owing to the fact that only twenty-one-year leases were granted and no-one would build on it. In about 1874 the Ecclesiastical Commissioners obtained both the freehold and leasehold of the land and began to lay it out for building purposes. During the laying out of the streets, which was keenly watched by local antiquaries, quantities of samian and other finds turned up. A public meeting was held and it was decided that the fort should be archaeologically examined before building proceeded. This admirable decision, revealing a judgement and a sense of values remarkable at that date, was only the first of a long series. The funds were raised, the permission of the Ecclesiastical Commissioners sought and, on the 15th March, 1875, work began. The excavation was published both by the Rev. R. E. Hooppell and by Dr. J. Collingwood Bruce (1878 and 1884, respectively). For the time, the standard of publication was high, notwithstanding the fact that the excavators were under the mistaken impression that they were dealing with a town and not a fort. Both reports include descriptions of the structures found, plans, lithographed plates of drawings made from photographs of excavated structures, coin lists and many woodcuts of the pottery and small-finds.

The parts of the fort excavated in 1875 were as follows:

1) Portions of the fort wall including a long stretch of the east wall. The excavators did not realise that the wall had been backed with an earth rampart.

2) Portions of all four gates. The east gate was the most thoroughly excavated and seems to have had twin portals, with the south portal blocked and converted to a room at some time.

3) The Headquarters building which Hooppell calls the "Forum and Praetorium" and notes that it appeared to have been destroyed by fire. He also shrewdly observes that a portion of the south wall of the cross-hall, which had fallen intact on to the courtyard, must have collapsed after the desertion of the fort on account of the build-up of soil underneath it.

4) The large granary (now known to be primary), interpreted as a church.

5) Parts of about eight other granaries (now assigned to the third period).

6) Parts of two buildings at the southern end of the fort, which Hooppell suggests were barracks, as they may well have been.

The finds from the excavation are deposited in the Museum of the Roman Fort at South Shields, as are most of the finds from all the excavations at the fort, the remainder being in the Joint Museum of Antiquities of the University and the Society of Antiquaries of Newcastle upon Tyne.

After the excavation an area of some 0·45 hectares, which later proved to include most of the central portion of the fort, was kept clear of modern buildings and reserved to display the older structures. This became known as the Roman Remains Park.

In the years between 1875 and 1949 no further excavations were undertaken though in 1934 Richmond published a reconsideration of the results of the excavations of 1875. He was the first to realise the function of the surviving stone buildings and to assign them to the time of Septimius Severus. In 1893 the dedicatory inscription to Severus Alexander (RIB 1060) was found when the boiler room for the Baring Street Schools, which overlay the southern portion of the fort, was being built. The two finest sculptured and inscribed stones from the site, the tombstone of Victor, a Moorish tribesman (RIB 1064), and of Regina, freedwoman of Barates (RIB 1065) (Smith 1959), together with other tombstones, were found to the south-west of the fort, indicating that the cemetery area lay along the road running south from the fort.

In 1949 South Shields Borough Council financed the re-excavation and consolidation of the area of the fort within Roman Remains Park. This work was directed by the late Sir Ian Richmond who was able, with the assistance of Mr. J. P. Gillam and Dr. D. J. Smith, and in collaboration with members of the South Shields Archaeological and Historical Society, to undertake further examination and interpretation of the stone buildings first excavated in 1875, as well as of newly discovered buildings from earlier phases of the fort's history. The results are summarised in Richmond's Guide to the fort.

Among the discoveries made by Richmond in 1949 were that the visible south-facing Head-quarters building, assigned by him to the Severan period, had two predecessors which faced north. The site of the cross-hall was common to all three phases. Below the visible granaries, also assigned to Severus, and in part below the Headquarters buildings, were found three buildings all with an east–west axis. Two were taken by Richmond to be barracks, the third a workshop. Two seemed to be contemporary and were built, where masonry survived, of a pinkish-purple micaceous sandstone. The third, which was "double ended" was built of white magnesian limestone. The existence of two successive stone forts, previously unknown, was thus demonstrated. The earlier was assigned to the time of Hadrian, the later to that of Marcus Aurelius, partly from ceramic evidence and partly on general grounds. All the granaries south of the central range were assigned to Severus while that to the west of the Headquarters building was assigned to Marcus Aurelius, owing to the fact that it contained an abnormally high proportion of the pink micaceous sandstone which is so often found in structures of the second period. Tile kilns of the late third or early fourth century were in-vestigated within the linked pair of granaries. The later subdivisions within two of the Severan granaries, previously discussed by Richmond in print (1934), were investigated afresh. They were assigned to the time of Constantius Chlorus but without evidence other than that they were post-Severan.

Between the years 1959 and 1962, the South Shields Archaeological and Historical Society undertook excavations in the area immediately surrounding the fort. In 1959 the discovery of an altar and bases for others outside the north-east angle of the fort indicated the approxi-mate site of the parade ground (Thornborrow, 1959). In 1960 a section was cut across the outer defensive ditch, in modern Beacon Street, at a point between the north gate and the north-east angle (Thornborrow, 1960). In 1961 and 1962, two sections were cut across the inner ditch: the first, behind modern Pearson Street, was at a point between the east gate and the south-east angle; the second was behind modern Baring Street at a point between the west gate and the south-west angle (Thornborrow, 1961 and 1964).

In 1966 and 1967 further areas were excavated within the fort, under the direction of Mr. J. P. Gillam and Mr. J. Tait with the assistance of Mrs. B. Charlton and Dr. D. J. Breeze, on behalf of the Ministry of Public Buildings and Works, as it then was, and South Shields Borough Council. In 1966 the southern ends of the granaries in the western half of the area to the north of the central range, as well as further pre-Severan buildings were discovered, and the north guardchamber of the west gate was excavated. In 1967 the north gate and the north-west angle tower were uncovered and selective trenching in the remainder of the area revealed the size and character of the recently discovered granaries, as well as further remains of pre-Severan barrack blocks or similar.

Shortly before his untimely death in 1970, Mr. Tait directed a small scale excavation outside the north-west corner of the fort and, in 1973, Mr. Gillam and the South Shields Archaeological and Historical Society directed excavations, financed by the Department of the Environment and the Borough of South Shields, in advance of the erection of new school buildings, in the area of the suspected civil settlement to the west of the fort. In spite of the large area stripped in 1973, and the large amounts of pottery recovered, no structures of Roman date were discovered and one can only conclude that heavy post-Roman and modern disturbance had removed all trace of them. Finally, in 1975, Mr. J. N. Dore, with the assistance of Mr. R. Miket and Mr. B. Whitaker, directed small scale excavations on behalf of the Museum Service of Tyne and Wear and the Department of the Environment, in advance of consolidation of the north gate, to remove material unexcavated in 1967.

Today various portions of the site are on display under the care of the Museum Service of Tyne and Wear, and it is hoped to excavate and display more of the fort in the future. As already mentioned, the area containing the buildings disengaged in 1875 was surrounded by railings and became known as Roman Remains Park. This was consolidated for display between 1949 and 1953, and a site museum was built. The Park encloses a length of the fort wall, the south guardchamber of the west gate and many of the buildings of the central and southern portions of the fort, including the primary granary, the Headquarters building and parts of eight of the later granaries. For ease of identification, and because it would have been difficult to display them in the condition in which they were excavated, the foundations of the earlier buildings have been marked out in modern concrete: white for primary and pink for second period.

To the north of the central range all the structures excavated in 1966 and 1967 were reburied after excavation. The north gate, the north-west angle tower and the north guardchamber of the west gate were subsequently disengaged afresh and, in December, 1975, were consolidated for display.

Various kinds of stone were used, at different times, in the construction of the fort. In all periods the main component of the foundations was river washed cobble, probably dredged from the mouth of the Tyne, bonded with clay. The builders of the primary structures used mostly buff coloured sandstone for the defensive circuit but seemed to prefer magnesian limestone, obtainable from the Trow Rocks near South Shields, for the internal buildings. In the second period it would seem that pink micaceous sandstone from the Deans, between South Shields and Tyne Dock, was preferred. The later buildings contain much re-used material from both the preceding periods and also the buff coloured sandstone, obtainable from Billy Mill near South Shields, and from Gateshead Fell. As for roofing material, many tiles, the clay for which probably came from the Lawe itself, were found.

The primary aim of this report is to describe the results of the excavations of 1966 and 1967, but in formulating conclusions it is necessary to refer frequently to buildings within the fort, excavated at other times. For the sake of clarity, it has been decided, therefore, to describe all the known structures in the fort in chronological order, and where these have previously been published, to present summaries, with full references, and, in some cases, reconsiderations.

THE DEFENCES (figs. 3 and 4)

The defences of the fort consisted of a stone wall, reinforced at the rear by an earthen ramp; in front two parallel defensive ditches are known.

The Inner Ditch

This has been tested in four places. In the Pearson Street trench, on the east side of the fort, it was *c*. 7 m wide and *c*. 1·7 m deep. A slight dip in the original surface had been used to advantage at this point. A small ditch, with steep sides, had been dug at the centre and the upcast used to increase the height of the outer bank, the end-result being a ditch with gently sloping outer edges and a deeper, more steeply sided centre. In the filling of the ditch was found a building stone of the Sixth Legion (cf. Thornborrow, 1961).

On the west and north-west sides of the fort, the ditch had more of the classic V-shaped profile. In the Baring Street trench it was *c*. 7 m wide and *c*. 2·3 m deep. It had a thin lining of clay and both banks had been raised, by 0·4 m, with dumps of clay. In the bottom was a layer of silt, *c*. 300 mm deep. In both the above trenches the inner slope of the ditch was found covered with stones, almost certainly fallen from the core of the fort wall. Under the material in the Baring Street trench was found pottery dating to *c*. A.D. 200–280 and a silver denarius of Septimius Severus, dating to A.D. 98–200 (cf. Thornborrow, 1964).

In the trenches outside the west gate and the north-west angle tower, the inner ditch did not appear to have been strengthened or renewed. In both places it was *c*. 5·5 m wide and *c*. 1·9 m deep, the bottom being covered by a thin layer of grey silt. The filling contained some mortar and small, loose stonework but there was no concentrated mass of stone upon the inner face, as there had been in the Pearson and Baring Street trenches.

The Outer Ditch

This has been tested in three places and appears to have been of about the same depth as the inner ditch, but with a flatter bottom. Outside the north-west corner of the fort it was *c*. 5·6 m wide but the depth could not be ascertained. Outside the west gate it was *c*. 2 m deep, the bottom being covered by a thin layer of grey silt, but the width could not be ascertained. At both these points it was separated from the inner ditch by a space *c*. 4·5 m wide.

In the Beacon Street trench, only the outer half of the ditch was excavated, as the inner half lay under the modern street. It was *c*. 1·5 m deep, and its outer lip was *c*. 11·4 m from the fort wall. The bottom was covered with a layer of blue, anaerobic clay, which indicated that it had probably been under water in Roman times (Thornborrow, 1960).

Although the evidence was looked for, in none of the seven sections was there any indication that a ditch had been intentionally filled, re-cut or otherwise substantially altered, although a simple cleaning out, followed by further natural weathering, might well have left no trace. Thus, as far as can be ascertained, the ditches were in use throughout the fort's history, and filled naturally after its desertion.

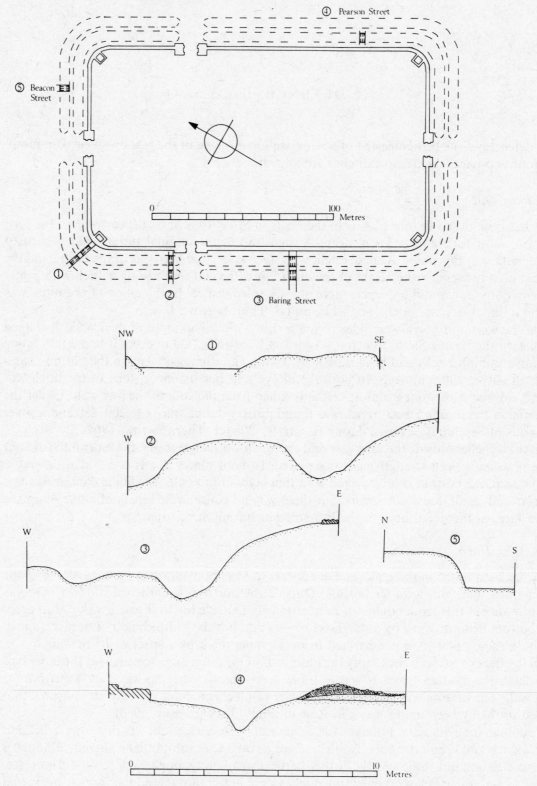

Fig. 3. The sections through the Fort ditches.

The Fort Wall

The fort had a stone wall from the beginning and this survived, with little change, throughout the Roman period. At the end of the excavations reported on here, though there seemed to be puzzling differences between the fort wall in the southern part of the fort, recorded in the nineteenth century, and that more recently investigated in the northern part, there was no direct evidence that the defended area had been at any time contracted or enlarged. Mr. R. Miket has however recently produced evidence that the original fort was enlarged southwards, on the same axis, from 140 m to 188 m. In 1875 at least 80 m of the east wall, the northeast and south-east corners, and short lengths of the other three sides were exposed. In 1967 three sections through the wall and its backing were obtained, one on either side of the north gate and one in a long trench about half-way between the north gate and the north-west angle tower. At these points the foundations of the wall were 2·5 m wide, of heavy clay and cobbles, *c.* 200 m thick, set in a shallow trench in the natural subsoil. To the east of the gate the wall had been completely robbed down to the foundations but, in the other sections, several courses of buff sandstone facing stones and a core of rubble, mortar and irregularly shaped blocks remained *in situ*. Here the wall was *c.* 1·9 m thick but, when compared with the much better preserved south-east corner (Hooppell, 1878, pl. VIII), it would appear that what survived were basal courses which had supported a, now vanished, chamfered plinth, and the wall proper, which must have been some 100 mm narrower.

Extending at least 4 m behind the wall was the earth backing composed of mixed layers of sand, and grey, orange and yellow clay. That the backing had been banked up against the wall can be clearly seen in fig. 4 where the edge of it is flush with the inside of the wall, and where the bottom layers slightly overlie the inside edge of the bottom course. Underlying the backing was a layer of mason's chippings clearly derived from the inside face of the wall, which had been properly finished. To the west of the gate, some of the backing material had already been dumped before the masons had finished their work, as the layer of chippings overlay the lowest clay level of the backing. Thus the mason's chippings were always overlain by at least some of the material of the backing, which fact, taken together with the close contact already remarked upon between backing and wall face, leaves no doubt that wall and ramp were part of a single concept and operation, and that there can be no question of the wall having been added to a previously free-standing rampart.

In the sections to either side of the north gate, the different levels of clay could be taken as evidence for the repair and renewal of the backing during the fort's history but, in the long trench, (fig. 4.3) definite evidence for a renewal was found. The turf kerb at the base of the primary backing can clearly be seen. Over this was a dump of yellow sand sealing the first backing and the north side of the earliest *intervallum* road. Resting on this road surface, under the tail of the first backing, was found a small sump or drain constructed of magnesium limestone.

The coarse pottery from the lower levels of the backing, by the north gate, is all of a Trajanic to early Hadrianic date (nos. 1–7). While no vessel of any type which first reached the region in the course of Hadrian's reign was found in this deposit, vessels of such types were found elsewhere in the fort, in the same structural level. The small fragment of Domitianic samian (no. 1) must be regarded as a survival.

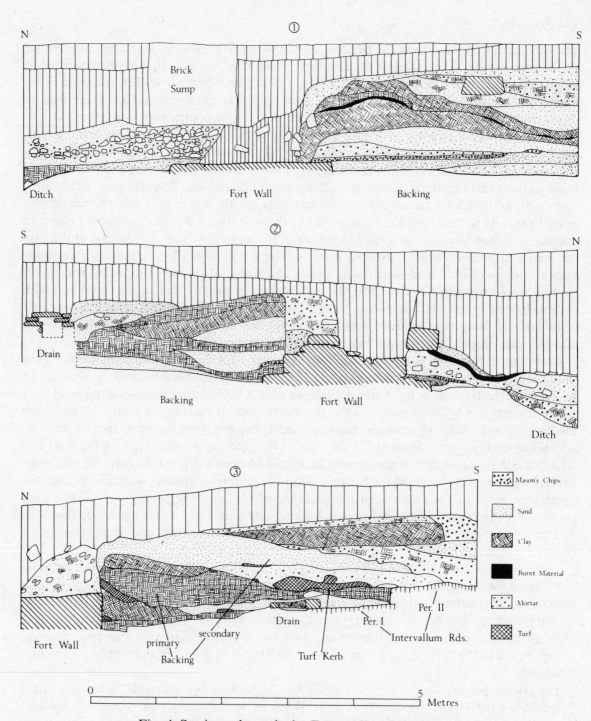

Fig. 4 Sections through the Fort wall and backing.
1 and 2: On either side of the North Gate.
3: Between the North Gate and the North-West Angle Tower.

The Intervallum Roads

A complete cross-section of the *intervallum* roads, in the north-western portion of the fort, was obtained in two places in the excavations of 1966 and 1967: 1) by the north guardchamber of the west gate; 2) about half-way between the north gate and the north-west angle tower, in the long trench dug between granaries C2 and C3.

By the north guardchamber of the west gate, the earth backing extended *c.* 5 m behind the fort wall, its tail resting on a footing of clay-bonded cobbles. Behind this and the main drain which ran along the west ends of the buildings was the earliest *intervallum* road, *c.* 2·4 m wide. It was metalled with gravel on top of small cobbles which, in turn, lay on top of sand. Where the backing ended, at the north wall of the guardchamber, the road widened to cover the area immediately to the east of the guardchamber. The kerb stones of the west side of the drain had been laid on a thin layer of this road gravel, the higher part of the road having been banked up against the kerb. Over this road had been built the extension to the north guardchamber and slightly to the east of this was the west kerb of the second *intervallum* road. By the guardchamber this road was *c.* 1·7 m wide, dipping, at its east side, to the kerb of the drain. Further to the north it was slightly wider and spilled over into the earlier drain. The third road was *c.* 3 m wide, slightly wider than its predecessor. At its west side it ran right up to the wall of the guardchamber extension and at its east side it overlay the drain. To the north of the guardchamber it was bedded on a layer of small stones and sand; where it overlay the drain it was founded on flat slabs. In effect, as time went by, the drain became more and more submerged beneath road surfaces, although it would still have functioned perfectly well.

In the long trench the earliest *intervallum* road was found to be *c.* 3 m wide, between the drain or sump at the tail of the earth backing and the northernmost of the earliest buildings. The second road was the same width but, as mentioned earlier, the earth backing had been renewed at this point, which meant that the road had to be laid further to the south, thus sealing a construction trench of the earliest period. When the early third century granaries were built the alignment of the buildings was changed, through 90°, which left a much larger space between the buildings and the fort wall than hitherto. It would appear that the whole area, some 8 m wide, was gravelled over but, as this surface was much higher than the preceding ones, much of it had been removed by post-Roman disturbance.

The North Gate (figs. 5 and 6)

The North gate was excavated in part in 1875, the main intention of the excavators being to find the fort wall. The gate was almost completely excavated in 1967. The structural alterations made to the gate during the occupation of the fort are complex, and interpretation has not been made any easier by the disturbance caused by the nineteenth-century excavation trenches.

The First Gate

In its original state the gate had two portals each *c.* 2·5 m wide, with twin projecting guardchambers. The west guardchamber measures *c.* 5·3 m north–south and *c.* 4·4 m east–west.

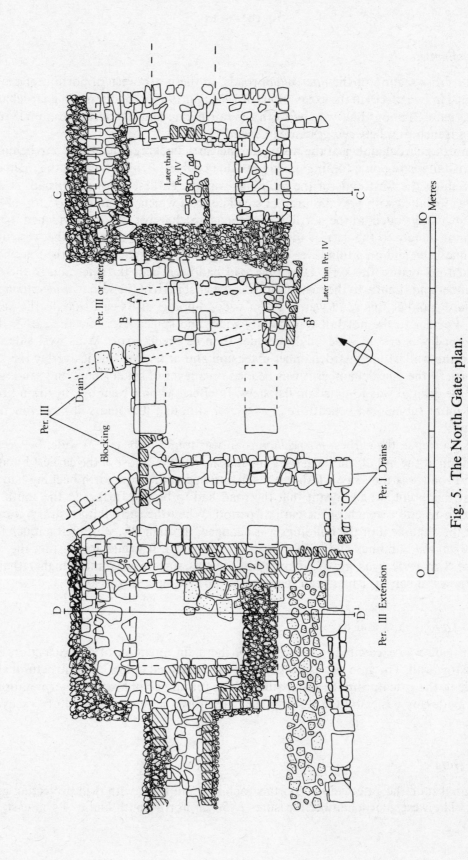

Fig. 5. The North Gate: plan.

The precise dimensions of the east guardchamber could not be ascertained, owing to heavy robbing, but they are assumed to have been the same as the west. They projected *c.* 1·7 m in front of and *c.* 1·9 m behind the fort wall.

The main walls of the west guardchamber had been extensively robbed. About half the length of the east wall, from the south-east corner, survived to a maximum of four courses high, and a short section of the west wall, where it joined the south face of the fort wall, survived two courses high. These sections of the wall were *c.* 1 m thick constructed of magnesian limestone blocks with a core of rubble, mortar and irregularly shaped blocks. They rested on a footing course of similarly sized limestone blocks and larger sandstone blocks, a single course everywhere except at the outside face of the north wall, where a double footing course, doubly offset was used. There was no offset on the outer face of the east wall, presumably so as not to impede passage through the west portal. The foundations on which the footings rested were of heavy cobbles set in clay and laid in a trench *c.* 150 mm deep, in the natural subsoil.

Of the responds for the arch over the west portal, only the southern one survived. This was a sandstone block, 0·9 m × 0·65 m and 0·4 m high, chamfered along its upper east edge, placed at the south end of the east wall of the guardchamber and slightly set into the face of the wall. It was supported on a flagged footing and a foundation of clay and cobble. The flagged footings for the second pier were found 2·35 m to the north of this. Immediately to the south of these was the pivot stone of the gate containing the rusted remains of an iron collar.

The east guardchamber appears to have been constructed in the same way as the west, with the walls resting on a footing course, double at the inside face of the east and south walls, laid on a foundation of heavy cobble set in clay. The level of the natural sand rose slightly from north to south and consequently the foundations of the south wall were laid in a shallow trench, while those of the north wall simply rested on the natural subsoil. The walls had been extensively robbed, however, and only a short length of the inside facing of the east wall remained above the footings. The west wall had been robbed almost completely down to the foundations apart from five stones of the footings and the pivot stone of the gate.

The piers of the *spina* had been constructed of large chamfered blocks of magnesian limestone. The north pier was found almost complete whereas only one block of the south pier remained and this was found tipped on edge, an attempt having been made at some time to remove it. Both were built on a footing course of flat slabs laid on a foundation of heavy cobble. These overlay a thin spread of mason's chippings which indicated that enough had been built of the guardchambers for the masons to have started work on finishing the stonework before the piers were built.

The main feature of the west portal was the large drain which ran north, straight through the portal, until it reached the line of the outer arch, where it turned north-west to run out of the fort. It was well made, of blocks of the same size as those used to construct the guardchambers. It was set in clay, had a water channel 0·45 m wide and was covered with large flat slabs. It was laid in a trench *c.* 150 mm deep in the natural subsoil. To the south of the portal, a small portion of a branch running in from the south-east was found. On the west side of the drain a thick layer of mason's chippings lapped over its kerb stones. This and the fact that part of it was overlain by the footings of the north-east corner of the west guardchamber, indicated that it was laid down before the guardchamber was built. On the east side

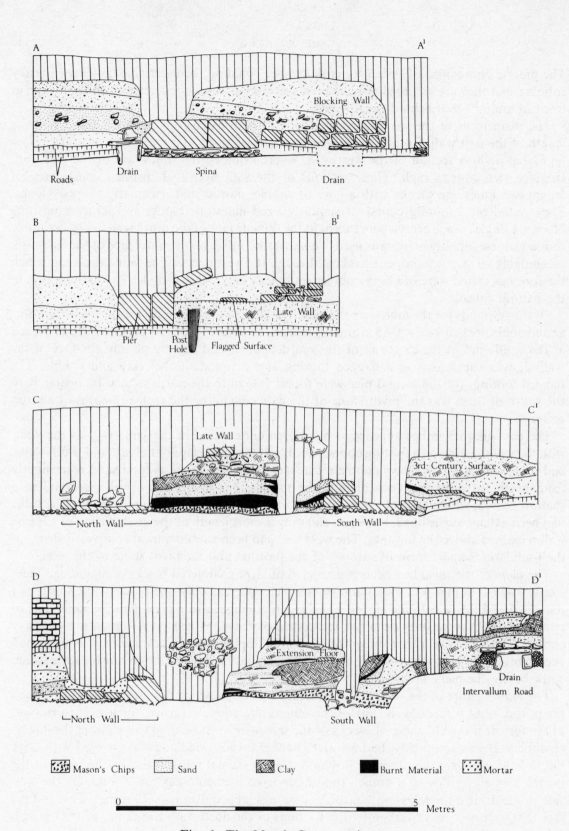

A   A¹

Roads   Drain   Spina   Blocking Wall   Drain

B   B¹

Late Wall

Pier   Post Hole   Flagged Surface

C   C¹

Late Wall   3rd Century Surface

—North Wall—   —South Wall—

D   D¹

Extension Floor   Drain   Intervallum Road

—North Wall—   South Wall

Mason's Chips   Sand   Clay   Burnt Material   Mortar

0   5 Metres

Fig. 6. The North Gate: sections.

of the drain was a much thinner spread of chippings. Immediately above the chippings was a road surface composed of small cobbles and gravel, *c.* 80 mm thick, and this would seem to have been the only road surface in the west portal. In places there was evidence that it had been repaired at some time but nothing was found to indicate a completely new surface laid over the original one, although the nineteenth-century excavation trench through the west portal could have removed most of it. In the east portal there were two road surfaces, the lower corresponding with that in the west portal. The significance of the upper remains to be discussed. To summarise, in the initial phase of construction in the fort, the building sequence of the north gate was as follows: 1) Main drain constructed. 2) Guard-chambers built to the point where the masons could complete the dressing of the stone. 3) *Spina* constructed. 4) Road surface laid down.

Joining the main drain through the west portal, another drain constructed of medium sized stones, with a water channel *c.* 200 mm wide, and covered with large slabs, was found. This ran along the tail of the earth backing and behind the west guardchamber. It was probably an early modification to cope with the drainage problems of the north-west corner of the fort, in modern times the most waterlogged part of the site. It was cut into the tail of the earth backing and into the levelling for the *intervallum* road which, in its turn, filled the construction trench for the south wall of the west guardchamber. It is then evident that much building had been done before the drain was constructed but the *intervallum* road was banked up around it implying that, basically, it belongs to the initial phase of construction in the fort. Three coarse-ware vessels were recovered from the filling (nos. 8–10).

Inside the east guardchamber evidence was found suggesting small scale industrial activity at an early period and probably continuing into the latter half of the second century. Modern disturbance, while sparing a column of Roman material in the middle of the chamber had, unfortunately, isolated it. The material was removed in 1975, in advance of the consolidation of the gate by the Department of the Environment (cf. Dore, 1976). This material was composed of two successive clay floors each covered by a layer, *c.* 100 mm thick, of black earth, charcoal, unburnt coal and clinker. Both floors had been exposed to heat and the concentration of the effects of burning indicated that each had supported a small hearth. The lowest floor rested directly on the mason's chippings associated with the building of the guardchamber and must, therefore, date to a time immediately following the building of the gate. Trampled into the upper floor was a fragment of Trajanic/Hadrianic samian (no. 25) and coarse-ware dating to *c.* A.D. 160–180 (nos. 62–6). In 1967 three small crucibles (nos. 257–9) were found at the bottom of the disturbed soil surrounding the hearths and had almost certainly been associated with the floors.

Subsequent Modifications

The first major structural alteration to the gate occurred when the west portal was blocked and the west guardchamber extended southwards. The original south wall of the guardchamber was demolished and the east wall extended with a well-built wall running from its south-east corner. Where it crossed the drain it was built directly on top of it though elsewhere it had a foundation of sandstone slabs and, just to the south of the original east wall, it rested on a large sandstone block. Inside, as in the east guardchamber, much of the Roman stratigraphy had been removed by later disturbance but what was left showed that the level of the original guardchamber floor had been raised by *c*. 0·4 m to that of the new extension. Layers of sand and clay had been dumped over the original south wall and a new floor of sandstone flags, incorporating the earlier drain, had been laid down. The exact dimensions of the modified guardchamber are not known as the excavation did not extend far enough to pick up the south wall and no traces were found of the west wall.

The west portal had been blocked with a wall which appeared to have been faced only on the north, that is the outer, side. It was constructed of magnesian limestone blocks backed with rubble and mortar. It had been built directly over both the drain and the road, between the *spina* and the north respond of the guardchamber. In places it survived two courses high, though it had been robbed at its western end, presumably when the north respond was removed.

There is some evidence that the south end of the west portal was paved over at the same time. Presumably the paving and the blocking of the portal were contemporary as there would have been little point in paving this area if the portal was still open to traffic. Pottery from under these flags (no. 102) and from under the floor of the guardchamber extension (nos. 97–100) dates to the late second or early third century. An *As* of *Lucius Verus* was found over the flags of the guardchamber extension (no. 7). The area to the south of the east guardchamber was also levelled up and covered with flagstones. Pottery from under these flags dates to the late second or early third century, (nos. 103–10).

The west portal having been blocked, a second road surface was laid down in the east portal. However, it appears that something, possibly the modifications to the west guardchamber, had caused structural damage to the arch over the west portal, and a timber post had to be put in to support it. A large, square post-hole, more than half a metre deep, was found in the centre of the portal. It penetrated both road surfaces and the rotted remains of the post survived for 280 mm above the second road surface. At the same time a new drain was built in the portal. Presumably the builders had originally intended to have the drain running straight through the portal but, because of the vault-supporting post, had to build it running diagonally. Only a short length, constructed of pitched stone slabs with irregularly shaped cover slabs, survived near the north pier of the *spina*, but the silt filling could be traced running south-east across the portal. It used the earlier road surface as a bottom and must have been laid before the second road as this extends up to it and is not cut by it. The timber post must have proved inadequate, however, because it was removed, probably only a little later, leaving *c*. 280 mm of stump above the road. It was replaced, slightly to the north, by a much more substantial sandstone pier, the massive basal blocks of which survive today sitting on the road surface. This action necessitated the re-positioning of the drain, probably as there was a danger of the pier subsiding into the old drain which ran close to its corner. A new drain was built on the second road surface, to the east of the pier, and this ran straight through the portal to discharge through a hole in a large sandstone slab pitched between the pier and the guardchamber wall.

It was quite apparent at the time of excavation, and can be seen in fig. 6, that the vault-supporting pier had been built directly on top of the second road with no accumulation of debris underneath, and must have replaced the timber post within a short space of time. This means that shortly after the blocking of the west portal, passage through the north gate was reduced to the narrow gap between the vault-supporting pier and the *spina* and this could only admit pedestrian traffic. The gate had, in fact, ceased functioning as a gate and the extended west guardchamber was, presumably, utilised for some purpose other than the housing of sentries.

Only two fragments of any later structure were found in the north gate. Over the second road in the east portal was found a thick layer of brown sandy soil containing much animal bone and roofing tile. This was probably an intentional levelling rather than a natural accumulation of debris. The only pottery vessel from it (no. 165), though not closely datable, was certainly not of a date earlier than the third century. Over this soil was found a short length of wall, the upper courses of which were offset from and on a slightly different alignment from the lower, probably indicating work of two periods. Inside the east guardchamber a similar levelling-up was found over the second-century hearths, and over this was found another short fragment of wall surviving two courses high in places. Both lengths of wall had been isolated by later robbing but they could have formed part of the same structure, namely a small building or shed erected over the remains of the earlier guardchamber. To the north of the wall over the east portal, the area had been covered with flagstones. Pottery from over these flags and from over the wall inside the east guardchamber was, apart from obvious survivals, of the later fourth century.

Dating

Primary: The masonry of the north gate is homogeneous with that of the fort wall adjoining it. There seems little doubt that the gate formed part of the primary defensive circuit, the Hadrianic dating of which is derived from pottery from beneath the backing of the fort wall and from beneath the mason's chippings of the north guardchamber of the west gate.

Stratigraphic reasons for dating the drain behind the backing within the primary phase have already been advanced. The coarse pottery from the filling (nos. 8–10) tends to confirm this dating. It is admittedly only a small group but two out of the three pieces are of a Trajanic to early Hadrianic date.

At the least the lower clay floor inside the east guardchamber must date to a time immediately following the building of the guardchamber and it could possibly fall within the primary building phase. From the pottery evidence (Decorated samian no. 25 and coarse-ware nos. 62–6) it is not possible to date the second floor closely beyond saying that it is probably of the middle or latter part of the second century.

Later: Pottery evidence (nos. 97–100 and 102) dates the modifications to the west portal and west guardchamber to the early years of the third century. Structurally, the sequence of events in the east portal would seem to follow on directly from these modifications. The suggestion that the modifications led to damage to the east portal, while not provable, seems reasonable and the relative stratigraphy of the post, the stone pier and the successive drains in the east portal shows that the building of these took place within a fairly short space of time.

Pottery from material overlying the surfaces of the gate in its modified form is of predominantly third and fourth century date. The material overlying the floor of the west guardchamber extension and the flagging at the south end of the west portal contained no pottery later than the mid-third century, and it is possible that these deposits represent occupation debris. The significance of this will be discussed in general conclusions at the end of the report. The material overlying the modified east portal and the area to the south of the

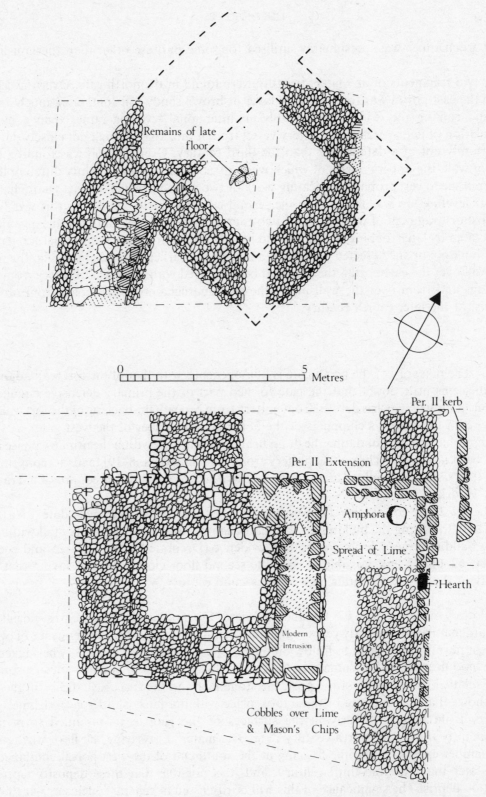

Remains of late floor

Per. II kerb

Per. II Extension

Amphora

Spread of Lime

?Hearth

Modern Intrusion

Cobbles over Lime & Mason's Chips

0   5 Metres

Fig. 7. The North-West Angle Tower and the North Guardchamber of the West Gate.

east guardchamber and portal could be regarded as intentional levelling for the later structure over the east guardchamber.

It is impossible to give a firm *terminus post quem* for the building of this late structure as the only piece of pottery stratified in the deposit below it is not closely datable. But, in view of its general level, above deposits containing fourth-century pottery, it is unlikely to be earlier than the fourth century.

The West Gate (fig. 7)

Lying, as it does, under the north fence of Roman Remains Park the central area of the west gate has never been excavated. Thus it is not known for certain whether the gate had a single or double portal. The latter seems more likely, however, as the distance between the guardchambers is the same as that for the north gate (7 m).

The south guardchamber was first explored in 1875 and conserved inside Roman Remains Park. The north guardchamber was totally excavated in 1966. The chambers measured 7 m east–west and 5·6 m north–south, externally, with walls *c.* 1·3 m thick. What survived of the main walls was mostly of magnesian limestone on a roughly dressed footing course of red micaceous sandstone and a foundation of clay and cobble. The foundations of the north guardchamber were not as deeply set as those of the fort wall at this point, but those of the west wall of the guardchamber were deeper than those of the east, to cope with the slope of the ground surface. No trace was found of a floor over the mason's chippings inside the north guardchamber. Pottery from beneath the mason's chippings was of Hadrianic date (nos. 21 and 22).

To the north of the north guardchamber, behind the fort wall, the earthen backing was *c.* 5 m wide. Its tail rested on an underpinning of clay bonded cobbles. To the east of this was the earliest *intervallum* road. To the south of the point where the backing stopped at the north wall of the guardchamber, the *intervallum* road widened to cover the area immediately to the east of the guardchamber. In this area, over the earliest *intervallum* road, an extension had been built on to the east wall of the guardchamber. Its walls were *c.* 0·6 m thick of red micaceous and other sandstone. These survived three courses high in places. No trace could be found of a south wall and it is assumed that the structure was open-ended. Inside it had been floored with lime mortar and, sunk into this in the north-east corner, was the bottom half of a globular amphora containing stones and fragments of pottery (nos. 70–2). This had probably been used as a urinal. About half-way along the inside face of the east wall several of the stones had been blackened by fire, suggesting that a small hearth had been built against the wall.

The clay and cobble foundations, both of the guardchamber and the fort wall, penetrated deeply into the natural subsoil. In the course of the excavations in 1966, the whole area of the guardchamber and its immediate environs was steadily cleared down to a level below the top of the natural subsoil. No trace was encountered of any structure, of any material, earlier than the guardchamber and fort wall. The foundations of the fort wall and of the north wall of the guardchamber were structurally homogeneous. They go together and both are primary. An absolute *terminus post quem* is provided by the pottery already mentioned. Both fragments are of a ware which, it is generally accepted, reached northern Britain in the early years of Hadrian's reign.

By definition the extension is later than the primary structures and is either contemporary with or slightly earlier than the second *intervallum* road as its presence necessitated a reduction in width of this road. Its kerb was found 0·3 m east of the extension built on top of the earliest road. The third *intervallum* road incorporated this kerb in its surface and extended right up to the east wall of the extension.

The East Gate

The east gate was explored in the excavations of 1875 but no subsequent work has been done on it as it lies under modern Henry Street which is still standing. Hooppell mentions it only in passing (p. 11) but Bruce's account and J. H. Morton's plan provide a certain amount of information (Bruce, 1884, pp. 230 and 233). The gateway appears to have had twin portals and to have had the same dimensions as the north gate. The north guardchamber certainly and, in all probability, both guardchambers projected *c.* 1·9 m beyond the line of the outer face of the fort wall. The south portal seems to have been blocked at some time and converted into living quarters. Hypocaust *pilae* and red and blue plaster, coating the walls, were found (Hooppell, 1878, p. 11).

The South Gate

Similarly the south gate has not been explored since 1875. Morton's and Oswald's plans, though unintelligible in detail, suggest that it had twin portals (Bruce, 1884, p. 230, Hooppell, 1878, pl. XIII). It is not clear from the plan whether or not the guardchamber projected, though on general grounds it seems likely that they did.

The Angle Towers

Two out of a probable total of four angle towers have been excavated at some time or another. One wall of the south-east tower was found in 1875 and, in the angle formed by it and the fort wall and thus presumably under the earth backing, were found the fragments of five swords and four enamelled belt mountings (Hooppell, 1978, p. 41, pl. VIII). One of these swords is by now well known, as it has, inlaid on either side of the blade, figures of Mars and an Eagle between standards. Stylistically the sword dates to the third century so how it, apparently, came to be under the earth backing which, as has already been shown, dates to the early second century, is difficult to explain.

The north-west angle tower was almost completely excavated in 1967 (fig. 7). Immediately to the south west of the tower a short length of the inside facing of the fort wall was found, standing five courses above the foundations. The walls of the tower itself had been completely robbed down to the foundations, apart from some stones of the first course at the inside east and west corners but, from the foundations and the position of the robber trenches, the dimensions of the tower could be gauged with a fair degree of accuracy. It measured 5·9 m by 4 m externally with walls *c.* 1·3 m thick. Its foundations had obviously been laid at the same time as those of the fort wall. Inside the tower, *c.* 250 mm above the foundations, were found the remnants of a flagged floor resting on a layer of mixed sandy clay soil which in turn overlay the mason's chippings from the construction of the tower. Pottery from under these flags (nos. 135–7) dates to the late second or early third century. No trace was found of any floors of an earlier date.

THE HEADQUARTERS BUILDING (fig. 8)

The Headquarters building was first uncovered during the excavations begun in 1875, and was subsequently re-examined by Richmond during the consolidation of Roman Remains Park in 1949 and 1950. The site was thoroughly cleared during the original excavations with the result that very few stratified datable finds are known. All that can now be attempted is a consideration of the extant structural remains assisted where necessary by Richmond's plan and earlier photographs. These indicate a minimum of three separate structural phases on the site. The first two buildings faced north. The third was a re-building, in part, of the second to face south. In places structures additional to and later than the third building are known.

The First Building

The only surviving portions of the first building, apart from the well in what had been its courtyard, were clay and cobble foundations, c. 0·9 m wide, for the walls of its rear range; no masonry survived. The foundations were undoubtedly earlier than structures both of the courtyard of the third building and the rear range of the second building. The central room, the *aedes*, measured 5·4 m by 4·3 m internally, and projected southwards beyond the line of the rear wall to a distance of c. 1·4 m. To the west was found part of the rear wall. To the east were parts of the wall between the cross hall and the administrative offices, and the wall separating these two offices. There are no remains of the first building elsewhere and it seems as though, except in the rear range, it may have had exactly the same plan as the second building. In this case it must be asked why any change of structure was made at all. One possibility is that the cross-hall and courtyard structures of the first building were of timber, subsequently replaced by stone to precisely the same plan, in such a way that the post-holes were covered or obliterated by the new cobble foundations. There is an exact parallel at Corbridge where the timber Headquarters building of fort III was replaced, to the same plan, by a part stone, part timber structure of fort IVa, (cf. Richmond and Gillam, 1952). The rear range of the first building at South Shields was clearly either stone or part timbered. This too was replaced but with some change in plan; the earlier structure was not entirely obliterated.

The Second Building

The remains of the second building are more substantial, although it is often difficult to distinguish them from later work. This is particularly so for the cross-hall whose site was retained for the third building. Based on a surviving portion of masonry which was not subsequently incorporated in the third building (viz. at the east end of the main rear wall) the characteristic masonry of the second building would seem to have been composed of a high proportion of pink micaceous sandstone in neatly finished blocks of average dimensions 0·25 m long, 0·25 m wide and 0·15 m high.

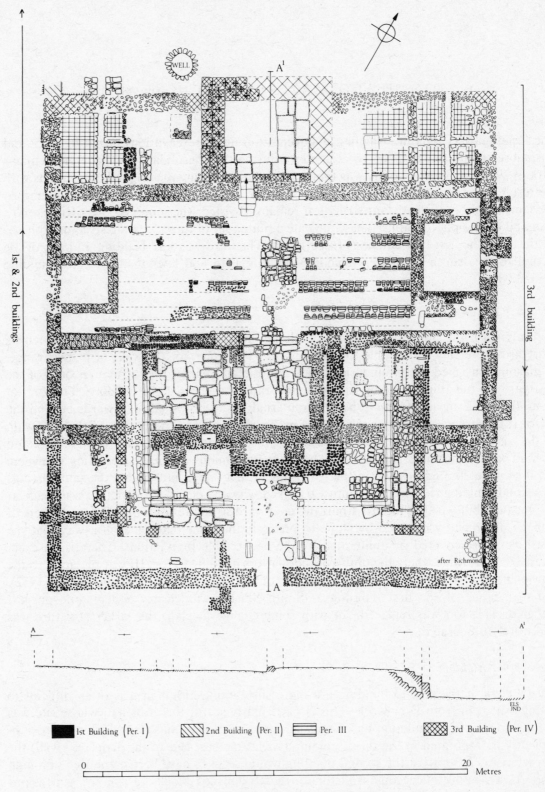

WELL.

A¹

1st & 2nd buildings

3rd building

well

after Richmond

A

A

A¹

ELS
JND

◼ 1st Building (Per. I)   ▨ 2nd Building (Per. II)   ▤ Per. III   ▩ 3rd Building (Per. IV)

0   20
|___|___|___|___|___|___|___|___|___|___| Metres

Fig. 8. The Headquarters Building.

The building measured 28 m by 24 m externally. The cross-hall measured 24 m by 8·4 m. The portions of the cross-hall as it survives today which would seem to have been original to the second building are as follows:

1) The whole of the west end wall. This is 0·82 m wide, standing two courses high. Projecting from its inner face are the footing courses for a tribunal measuring 3 m square. Where the tribunal abutted the wall it was faced with pitched sandstone slabs.

2) The central portion of the east end wall which survives to a maximum of three courses high. The main wall is 0·8 m wide resting on an offset 0·15 m wider.

3) Possibly the east and west ends of the north wall up to where the strong-room of the third building was inserted. The wall is between 0·8 m and 0·9 m wide and survives two courses high.

4) The extreme east and west ends of the south wall, though the footing course which these rest on is continuous throughout the whole length of the south wall. At the west end the dimensions of the surviving fragment are 4·7 m long by 0·85 m wide; it stands to a maximum of three courses high. At the east end the fragment measures 4 m long by 0·85 m wide and stands to a maximum of two courses high. The fragments end precisely where the walls which divide the rear range to either side of the *aedes* are situated.

On the south side of the cross-hall little of the rear range of the second building survives apart from the foundations. It comprised the usual five rooms: a central *aedes* flanked on either side by two rooms. The south wall of the range, the rear wall of the building, was 0·9 m wide with surviving fragments of upstanding masonry at its east and west ends. Along the outer face of the south wall were found the cobble foundations of five buttresses. The central three were spaced at intervals of *c.* 2 m. If we assume this spacing to have been regular, then there was probably originally a total of eight buttresses along the wall. There had also been an external buttress on each of the main side walls of the rear range. That on the west was situated at the south corner while that on the east was set back slightly from the corner. It is difficult to be certain whether these buttresses formed part of the original plan of the second building or whether they were later additions. The partition walls of the range were 0·7 m wide. The *aedes* measured internally 3·6 m east–west by 3·8 m north–south. To the west the outer room was 4·3 m by 3·8 m and the inner was 3·4 m by 3·8 m. To the east the outer was 3·8 m by 3·8 m and the inner was 3·6 m by 3·8 m.

The coincident end of the surviving fragments of the south wall of the cross-hall at the point where the partition walls between the rooms on either side of the *aedes* are situated would suggest that the *aedes* and the inner rooms were open-fronted. The continuous footings would have supported the piers for a three-opening arcade, the openings being filled with metal or wooden grilling, possibly supported on low stone sill walls. A similar arrangement is known in the Headquarters buildings at Chesters, Housesteads and Chesterholm-Vindolanda (Chesters: Collingwood-Bruce, 1966, p. 89; Housesteads: Bosanquet, 1904, p. 217; Chesterholm-Vindolanda: Birley, Richmond and Stanfield, 1936, pp. 221–5).

To the north of the cross-hall almost nothing survives of the courtyard of the second building. Much of it lies outside the boundary of Roman Remains Park, and the portion which lies inside was almost certainly obliterated by the rear range of the third building, in particular by the deep foundations of the strong-room. The robbed foundation trench of the main west wall of the courtyard was observed continuing north from the rear range of the third building. In a small trench, in 1966, clay and cobble foundations which were, in all probability, those of the north wall of the courtyard were found 13 m north of the cross-hall. The only other feature remaining from the courtyard was the well which had been retained in use from the first building and continued in use for the third.

Modifications to the Second Building

In the cross-hall the foundations and ill-preserved remains of stone sleeper-walls, running from east to west, were discovered and recorded in 1949. If the record is reliable, there were seven walls to the west of the paved pathway between the strong-room and the entrance from the courtyard, and six to the east. As the site had been completely disengaged before 1949 there was no evidence for their date except that of their relationship to surviving structures. The walls are later than the cross-hall of the second building, and this is all that can be said for certain. Their relationship with the third building is difficult to ascertain, for the remains of the sleeper walls were removed during consolidation to make the site easier for visitors to understand, and the only record is a single simplified plan. On this the sleeper walls appear to have run up to the tribunal at the east end of the cross-hall and to either side of the pathway; they certainly did not run over them. It is not impossible that the sleeper-walls had been removed by the insertion of these structures, and their foundations covered by them; both structures belong to the third building. Richmond assigned the sleeper-walls to the time of Count Theodosius, A.D. 369, and actually used them as evidence for late fourth-century conditions on Hadrian's Wall. It seems more likely that as they are certainly later than the second building, and possibly earlier than the third, they are to be dated to the time of Severus, and represent yet another granary. Administrative tasks could still have been conducted in the offices of the rear range.

The Third Building

The 180° change in orientation of the third building did not necessitate a complete re-building. The site of the cross-hall was retained; the position of the courtyard and the rear range exchanged. A certain amount of alteration was necessary in the cross-hall. In the south wall the large spaces which had been the openings into the *aedes* and inner rooms of the second building were filled in around the much narrower opening into the new courtyard. The new wall was built on top of the pre-existing footings from the second building. This can quite clearly be seen on the site where the new walls are narrower (0·65 m) than and make clear straight joints with the originals, and the masonry is of quite different character. The new entrance was *c*. 3 m wide. The threshold stones survive much worn as do two blocks, possibly re-used, comprising the west jamb. In the report of the excavations of 1875, Hooppell describes (pp. 6 and 7) how the south wall of the cross-hall was found where it had collapsed flat on the surface of the courtyard. He estimates it to have been at least 30 feet high originally and thought he could discern "a window at the south-east portion as it lay on the ground, and a door towards the north-west portion." From the build-up of soil between the wall and the courtyard flags he concluded that it must have stood for some time after the final desertion of the building. Near the eastern end of the collapsed wall was found the keystone of an arch with the head of a bull in relief on its front.

It has already been mentioned that the well-built central portion of the east wall is thought to be associated with the second building. The north and south ends of the wall are filled by masonry of an inferior standard to the central section and at both these points on the outside face of the wall are the remains of a small buttress. It is conceivable, though by no means certain, that there were small doorways at these points in the second building and that these were blocked up in the third building.

It is possible that the whole of the surviving north wall of the cross-hall dates to the time of the third building. Certainly the central section must, on account of the fact that its foundations are unusually deep because of the sunken strong-room to the north. The foundations of the east and west ends of the wall have not been examined and it is impossible to do so at the present time.

At the eastern end of the cross-hall a new and larger tribunal was built.

To the north of the cross-hall a massive sunken strong-room was built. This is interesting architecturally as it is a completely self contained unit. None of its walls is party with any of the structures surrounding it. Its south wall, built flush with the north wall of the cross-hall, is composed of large oblong blocks, the largest of which is some 0·8 m by 0·35 m by 0·2 m. It is one course thick and survives four courses high. In one of the plates of the original excavations (Hooppell, 1878, pl. VII) two blocks forming the base of a window between the strong-room and the cross-hall can be seen on the topmost surviving course. The window had deeply splayed jambs and a chamfered sill with holes in it for three upright iron bars. The window does not survive today. Of the other walls only the west and about a third of the north survived above the foundations. The lowest course was composed of a double row of blocks 0·6 m square and 0·25 m high originally tied together with dove-tail cramps. Richmond inferred that the cramps had probably originally been of wood since there was no trace of metal in the holes. The second course was composed of dressed stone across the full width of the wall, with no rubble or mortar core. In the same plate as mentioned above, three large cramped blocks of similar dimensions to those of the first course, can be seen forming the third course. Only one of these survives today and this is almost certainly not now *in situ*. Two of the blocks of the second course have a slightly splayed surface ending in a prominent check. Richmond was of the opinion (1934, p. 91) that these had originally served as springers for a barrel-vaulted ceiling to the strong-room and that this in turn, taken with the evidence of the third course, implied a re-building of the strong-room. It seems equally possible, however, that the blocks were re-used from elsewhere. The strong-room had been floored with large rectangular paving stones and must have had a tendency to dampness as there was a square sump near the north-east corner. The floor was 1·35 m below that of the cross-hall and entrance was gained down a narrow flight (*c.* 0·8 m wide) of five stone steps. In the excavations of 1875 the strong-room was found to contain "a great mass of stones and rubbish". This included the capitals of some pilasters, the moulded base of a pillar which was probably an altar, and the greater part of a human skeleton (Hooppell, 1878, p. 9).

On either side of the strong-room were the administrative offices. In this area little upstanding masonry of the main walls survives and the internal arrangement of the rooms has been completely obscured by modern consolidation. The main side walls of the rear range were on the same line as the side walls of the courtyard of the second building and almost certainly re-used the earlier foundations. In the west wall the small fragment of upstanding masonry at the junction with the cross-hall would seem to have been original to the second building as it is a continuation of the west wall of the cross-hall. The upstanding remains of the east wall are wider than, and obviously later than, the east wall of the cross-hall and thus, presumably, original to the third building. The rear wall of the rear range, and of the building as a whole, of which only foundations survive, must be original to the third building as its position is within the courtyard of the second building. On the site today the inner walls of the administrative offices, built flush with the east and west walls of the strong-room, stand nine courses high. In the plate of the original excavations (Hooppell, 1878, pl. VII) and Richmond's photograph of the building in *c*. 1949 (unpublished) these walls cannot be seen and it is clear that as they stand today they are the product of modern consolidation. It is assumed that at the time of consolidation there was some original structural evidence on which to base the reconstruction, although none of the photographs are sufficiently detailed to show actual foundations.

As mentioned earlier, modern consolidation has obscured all the internal details of the administrative offices. On his plan of the building Richmond marks one lateral partition wall between the western rooms and this can be seen on his photograph though exact structural relationships cannot be discerned. In the absence of evidence to the contrary, Richmond's view that this wall belonged to the third building must be accepted.

To the south of the cross-hall a paved courtyard had been laid over the remains of the *aedes* and adjacent rooms of the first and second buildings. In building the walls of the courtyard the main east and west walls of the earlier building had been incorporated and their line continued. The entrance to the courtyard was through a gap *c*. 1·4 m wide in the middle of the south wall. The courtyard had been surrounded on three sides by a colonnaded portico, *c*. 3 m wide on the east and west sides and *c*. 1·6 m wide on the south. Many of the stones comprising the sill wall for the columns remained in position. Fragments of three columns were found on the west side of the courtyard. The one complete, though broken, example was 2·1 m high, monolithic, with a double torus moulding at the top and a single torus moulding at the base. Today this has been re-erected on the sill-wall at the south-east corner of the courtyard. Richmond reckoned the height of the portico to the eaves to have been *c*. 12 feet.

About 1 m in front of the colonnade was found much of the eaves-drip gutter for the pent roof of the portico, composed of lines of small square and oblong blocks of sandstone with a channel cut into them. Underlying the paving, in between the gutter and the sills, on either side of the courtyard, had run a small stone-lined drain leading from the gutter. Much of this had been lost on the east side but on the west side it drained the gutter just before its eastward turn, then ran north to turn along the north wall of the courtyard and debouch through an opening in the west wall. The courtyard had been surfaced with sandstone flags of which many still survive. At the east side a small table altar surrounded on three sides by dry stone walling was found (Hooppell, 1878, pp. 14 and 15) though the association of this with the third building is uncertain.

Modifications to the Third Building

In the rear range underfloor heating was installed in three or possibly all four of the administrative offices. These arrangements cannot be fully examined today owing to modern consolidation but Richmond's plan gives the details. He shows further lateral dividing walls subsequent to the one original to the third building. Around these the floors had been raised with dumps of earth and stones, revetted with stone walls to form channels for the hot gases. This mass had been covered with stone flags, of which a few still remain, and these in turn by red concrete (*opus signinum*) which, although it had been removed by 1949, still survived in 1875 as Hooppell reported: "On each side of the chamber are the red concrete floors of rooms on a level with the floor of the great hall, but parted from it by a substantial wall, and heated apparently by flues. . . ." On the north side of the westernmost room were found the remains of a stokehole and a flue had been cut through the main north wall at this point. Nothing is known of the stokehole for the two rooms to the east of the strong-room as this lies outside the boundary of Roman Remains Park, but a flue through the wall was noted in a corresponding position to the stokehole on the west side.

The Wells

There was a small well (*c*. 0·7 m diameter) in the south-east corner of the east portico of the courtyard, which was partially excavated in 1875. "In the forum there is a well or pit built round with stone without mortar, which the explorers excavated to a depth of several feet. When I saw it, soon after it was opened out, it was quite dry." (Hooppell, 1878, p. 8.)

A much larger well was situated behind the strong-room of the third building. This appeared to have been in use from the initial construction of the fort and thus would have been situated in the courtyard of the first and second buildings.

The excavation of the well was undertaken by members of the South Shields Archaeological and Historical Society during 1949 and 1950 as part of the programme of excavation and consolidation supervised by Richmond. Excavation proved difficult, even with the help of steel bars to pin the sides, and, following a collapse, work was suspended at a depth of *c*. 7 m. What follows is based on an unpublished written report submitted to Richmond by two of the Society's members, T. Walsh and J. Kershaw.

The well had a diameter of *c*. 1·22 m. To a depth of *c*. 4·9 m the sides were of regular masonry courses. Below this to the bottom of the excavated area, the sides were revetted with an open framework of timber planks, pinned at the corners with timber uprights. To the bottom of the stonework the filling consisted of earth, some stone, both dressed and undressed, and other debris. Below this, for another 1·8 m, was a concentration of stone, roofing tiles, mortar and silt. From this level came the pottery and stamped tiles here illustrated. At the bottom limit of the excavation was a concentrated mass of dressed stone and large boulders.

Dating

Only a small number of stratified datable finds are known from the site of the Headquarters building.

A *denarius* of Julia Domna dated to A.D. 207–211 was found in the cobble foundations of the west courtyard wall of the third building, (cf. Coin Report, Richmond Excavation, no. 1). This coin was in extremely worn condition and Mr. Casey is unwilling to see its date of deposition placed much earlier than *c*. A.D. 220.

The pottery from the filling of the well spans the Roman period of occupation of the fort and shows that the well must have been in use throughout this period, (Samian stamp no. 29, Coarse Ware nos. 486–9). In particular no. 29, a Dr.18/31 stamped by the potter *Cracuna* and dated to A.D. 130–155, was complete and in good condition and cannot have seen much wear at the time of deposition.

THE OTHER INTERNAL BUILDINGS

The Earliest Period (fig. 20)

Building A5—the Granary (fig. 9)

Excavated in 1875 and 1949—cf. Hooppell, 1878, Bruce, 1884, Richmond, Guidebook.

Well to the west of the Headquarters building was the granary, the only substantial building of the earliest period still to be seen on the site. It was a buttressed stone building 23·1 m long and 15·7 m wide, with a single longitudinal dividing wall, effectively making it two single granaries with a party wall. The walls have a rubble and mortar core and are faced with magnesian limestone. They rest on a flagged footing course which in turn rests on a clay and cobble foundation laid the full width of wall and buttresses. Little now remains of the walls and buttresses above the first course. There were ten buttresses along the east and west walls, four on the south and two on the north, the end buttresses on all four walls being set in from the corners. Against the outside face of the west end of the north wall was the loading platform, of which only the pitched stone supports now remain. They were 2·1 m apart, and as this is too great a distance to be spanned by a single stone slab, which would have had to endure quite considerable loads, the superstructure must have been of timber. There was doubtless a loading platform at the other end of the north wall for the eastern half of the building, but this has been obscured by a modern wall. At the southern end of the building there was a portico, supported on four columns of which three chamfered base blocks of gritstone, and the cobble foundations for a fourth, were found. It is strange that the loading platform should be at one end of the building and the portico at the other. In the Severan granaries at Corbridge loading platforms and porticos are at the same end (cf. Richmond and Gillam, 1950). One possibility is that the purpose of the south portico, possibly matched by a similar portico on the north, was purely decorative. Another possibility is that the south portico dates to the time of the later granaries when there was more room to the south of the granary; timber loading platforms may have vanished without trace.

The floors had been supported on a regular series of low stone pillars, four rows of fourteen in the eastern half and four rows of fifteen in the western. The outside rows in each half abutted the main walls. Of most of them only the foundations and footings now remain, and in places even these have been removed. Since the space between the pillars is too great to have been spanned by a single flagstone, the floors must have been of timber, as at Housesteads (cf. Bosanquet, 1904), with the joists running across, and the planking along, the building. The outer walls did not survive high enough to show evidence of vents communicating between the underfloor space and the open air.

At some time the floor and the central rows of supporting pillars in the western half of the building had been removed and two tile kilns inserted. They were both of conventional oblong type, the best parallel, though considerably earlier in date, being kiln no. 6 at Brampton (cf. Hogg, 1965).

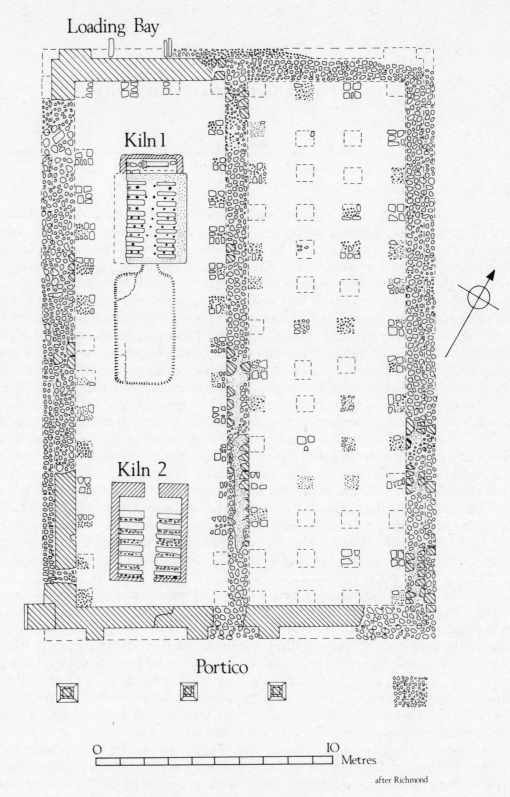

Loading Bay

Kiln 1

Kiln 2

Portico

O   IO
                        Metres

after Richmond

Fig. 9. Building A5 (drawing by K. Lawson).

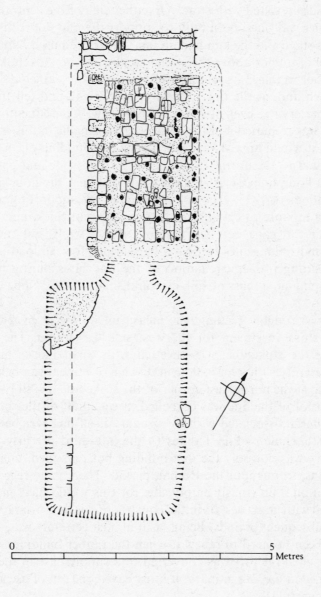

0   5
Metres

after Richmond

Fig. 10. Kiln 1 (drawing by K. Lawson).

Kiln 1, at the north end of the building, measured *c.* 3·7 m by 2·9 m. Kiln 2 measured 3·8 m by 3 m. Both appeared to have been constructed in the same way: a square pit had been dug, and its sides revetted with stone. On either side of the central line of the pit a row of short stone sleeper walls had been built to support the kiln floor. In kiln 2 work had not proceeded past this stage and the kiln had, in fact, never been used. No ash was found in the flues, nor any trace of a floor above the sleeper walls, and no stokehole had ever been dug. As there was no floor in kiln 2 its remains were excavated completely. Kiln 1, on the other hand, had been used and, at the time of excavation, Richmond felt that the largely intact floor was worth preserving, even if hidden from view. Consequently, the floor was not removed. The kiln was re-buried and turfed over, and remains in this state today. From this partial excavation, it would appear that kiln 1 was a re-building of an earlier kiln of which a fragment was found to the north. It had been *c.* 2·2 m wide and part of a column shaft had been used as a floor support. At the west side of kiln 1 the floor had been removed in the original excavations of 1875, exposing the ends of the supporting walls. The floor itself was composed of a mixture of clay and stones, *c.* 100 mm thick, and baked hard, pierced by vent holes over the gaps between the underlying walls. Set into the surface were numerous square and oblong tiles to give a flat surface for the load and to raise it above the vents, thus ensuring proper circulation of the hot gases during firing. The sides had been sealed by heaping up a mass of soil, clay and small stones. None of the superstructure survived.

The stokehole was roughly rectangular, measuring *c.* 4·3 m by 2·6 m and about 1 m deep. Part of the stone revetment for the west side was found. The main flue, *c.* 0·4 m above the floor of the stokehole, was revetted with small blocks and an oddly shaped re-used stone, apparently with a lewis-hole in it. This revetment ran behind a curved section of dry stone walling at the north-west corner of the stokehole, possibly built after a collapse at this point. The roof of the flue was corbelled; it was built of tiles bonded with clay.

No stratified material associated with the granary itself has ever been recovered, though pottery from the stokehole of kiln 1 dates to the late-third or early-fourth century (nos. 172–5). The granary was not only the first building but remained, unaltered except for the insertion of the kilns, throughout the Roman period. There is no reason to suppose that it was a late insertion on a previously empty site, for this would have meant that the earliest fort was unprovided with granaries. Its initial construction is then primary by definition and its use continued in subsequent periods. Being, as it almost certainly was, of stone throughout, there would have been no need to renew it when the timber buildings of the earliest period were replaced and when the fort was converted to a supply base in the early third century, it was simply retained in use as a granary. It must have gone out of use as such shortly before the tile kilns were inserted.

Building A6 (fig. 11)

Excavated in 1949—cf. Richmond, Guidebook.

To the south of the Headquarters building and granary were found the foundations and a little of the first masonry course, in white magnesian limestone, of a building *c.* 42 m long with its long axis running from east to west. The central section of the building was *c.* 34 m long and 7·5 m wide with one longitudinal medial subdivision which ran the full length of the

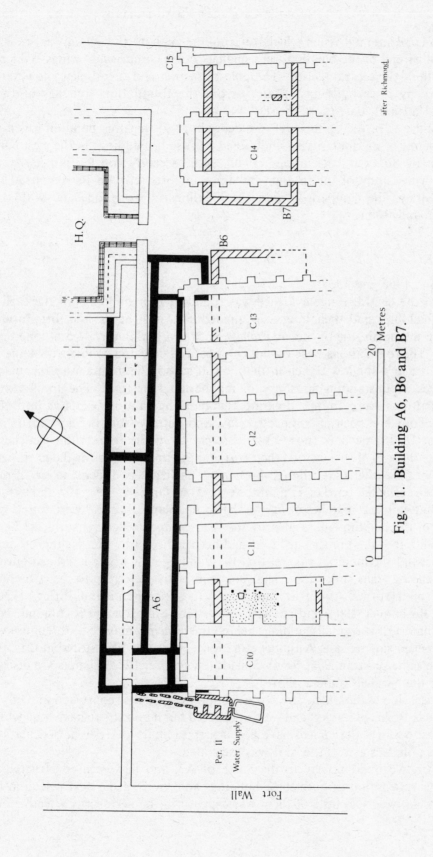

Fig. 11. Building A6, B6 and B7.

after Richmond

H.Q.

Fort Wall

Per. II
Water Supply

A6

C10   C11   C12   C13   C14   C15

B6   B7

Metres

0   20

section, and one lateral division which ran from the main north wall only as far as the medial wall. At either end of the building were smaller rooms comprising "wings" which projected to the south of the central section. The plan of neither end is complete, however, owing to disturbance by later buildings. Pottery from the foundation trenches of the building was all of Hadrianic date (nos. 55–61).

Richmond was of the opinion (cf. Guidebook, p. 9) that this building was a workshop, on the grounds of its similarity to undoubted workshop buildings in the west compound at Corbridge (cf. Birley and Richmond, 1940). More recently von Petrikovits has supported this view in his study of the internal buildings of forts (cf. von Petrikovits, 1975, p. 93). He again draws the comparison with the buildings at Corbridge and with buildings at Novaesium and Bonn.

Buildings A1, A2, A3 and A4 (fig. 13)

Excavated in 1966 and 1967.

North of the central range evidence was found of four buildings of the earliest period. All these buildings had their long axes aligned east–west across the fort. Inside the west gate, along the north side of the *via principalis*, was a building *c.* 41·5 m long and *c.* 4·5 m wide (A3). The foundations were found, composed of clay and cobble with some magnesian limestone, set in a shallow trench in the natural subsoil with, in a very few places, one or two courses of upstanding masonry in magnesian limestone. The foundations of two lateral partitions were found, dividing the building, almost exactly, into three equal areas. The floor had been of compacted clay, and pottery from in and under this was of a Trajanic or Hadrianic date (nos. 23–7). Pottery from the foundation trenches was of a similar date (nos. 11–17). Towards their east end the foundations for the north wall had cut into a pit of an earlier date, though how much earlier it is difficult to say. From this pit came a small carinated bowl of Trajanic or early Hadrianic date (no. 18), and a small crucible (no. 19). In two places patches of fire-hardened daub and charcoal were found lying on the clay floor of the building and sealed by the later compacted gravel surfaces. These suggest the possibility that the timber partitions had been removed by fire. Neither in quantity, nor in character did the material suggest that the building as a whole had been burnt down.

This building falls into the class conventionally referred to as storehouses, and paralleled on Hadrian's Wall at Birdoswald (cf. Richmond and Birley, 1930), Housesteads (cf. Bosanquet, 1904) and possibly Benwell (cf. Simpson and Richmond, 1941), where the westernmost of two small buildings behind the *principia* may be a storehouse with its two halves arranged side by side. A timber storehouse may now be restored at Carrawburgh, in exactly the same position as at South Shields (cf. Breeze, 1972. Thanks are also due to Dr. Breeze for the parallels quoted above).

On the east side of the *via praetoria* was a building of similar construction. Only the cobble foundations for part of its west end were uncovered but it appears to have been wider than the A3, (at least 6·8 m wide) and to have had a longitudinal subdivision. Speculation as to its function is pointless as so little of it was excavated.

The other two buildings lay to the north of A3, and had been constructed entirely of timber. The restoration of both these buildings and those of the next period in this area is highly speculative, as so little of them was exposed in the necessarily selective trenching of

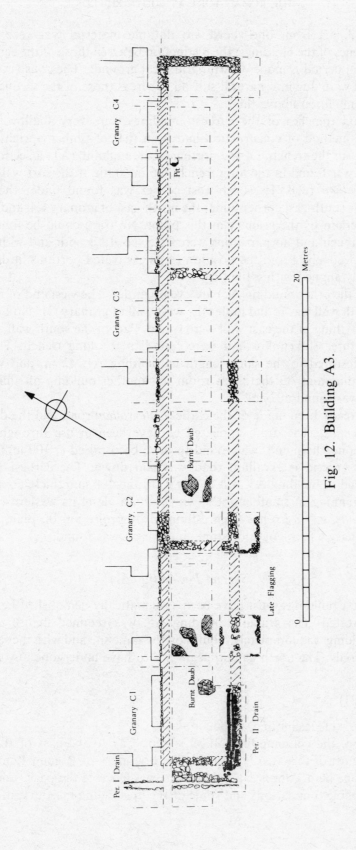

Fig. 12. Building A3.

Granary C4

Pit

Granary C3

Granary C2

Burnt Daub

Late Flagging

Granary C1

Burnt Daub

Burnt Daub

Per. I Drain

Per. II Drain

0   20
Metres

1966 and 1967. Apart from one sherd, no datable material was recovered from the construction trenches of the buildings; the distinction between those of the earliest period and those of the second period is made on stratigraphical grounds. The construction trenches of the earliest period were dug into natural subsoil, whereas those of the second period were in the layers of accumulation above this.

The construction trenches of the earliest buildings were very shallow, *c*. 50–100 mm implying that the method of construction had been that of timber uprights slotted into a base plate laid flat in the trench. Of the northernmost building (A1) a section of the trench for its north wall was found in the long trench, 6·6 m south of the fort wall, and sealed by the second *intervallum* road. Its south-west corner was found under the north wall of granary C1, and its south-east corner under the north-east of granary C4, and the drain of the second period overlain by the granary at this point. No trace could be found of the south wall in the long trench and no partitions were detected. Its length and width were *c*. 42 m and *c*. 10·5 m respectively. From the position of its excavated portions, it does not seem to have been squarely aligned within the fort.

The remains of the other building(A2) are even scantier. The west end of the construction trench for the north wall was found under the west wall of granary C1. No other trace of the north wall, nor anything of the east wall were found. Part of the south wall and a trench for a partition with three stakeholes in it were found in the long trench. The building has been tentatively restored to the same length as building A1, 42 m, and was 10 m wide. Between this building and A3 there was room for another building of similar dimensions, though no trace was found of one.

Mention has already been made of the earliest *intervallum* road and the drain at the west side of the *praetentura*. The drain appeared to have been in use throughout subsequent periods and, at its northern end, was found to have been raised *c*. 100 mm, or one stone's depth, before the second intervallum road was laid down. The earliest *via praetoria* as measured at the end of building A3, was *c*. 3 m wide and 100 mm thick, composed of gravel laid on an underpinning of small cobbles, with a drain along its western edge. The width of the *via principalis*, *c*. 7·8 m, has been estimated by projection on plan. At its southern end, north of granary C8, a length of stone-lined drain was found.

Second Period (fig. 21)

Most of the earliest buildings must have been systematically demolished before subsequent buildings were erected. The granary, building A5, was retained in use unchanged. The Headquarters building was completely rebuilt, on the same site and with the same orientation, but in fresh materials. The north gate appears not to have undergone any change.

Building B5 (fig. 21)

Excavated in 1949—cf. Richmond, Guidebook.

In all likelihood, the commanding officer's house lay to the east of the Headquarters building but, as most of this area lies outside the boundary of Roman Remains Park, little work has been done here. Almost up against the east fence of the park, under granary C8, were found the cobble foundations and some of the upstanding masonry, in pink micaceous

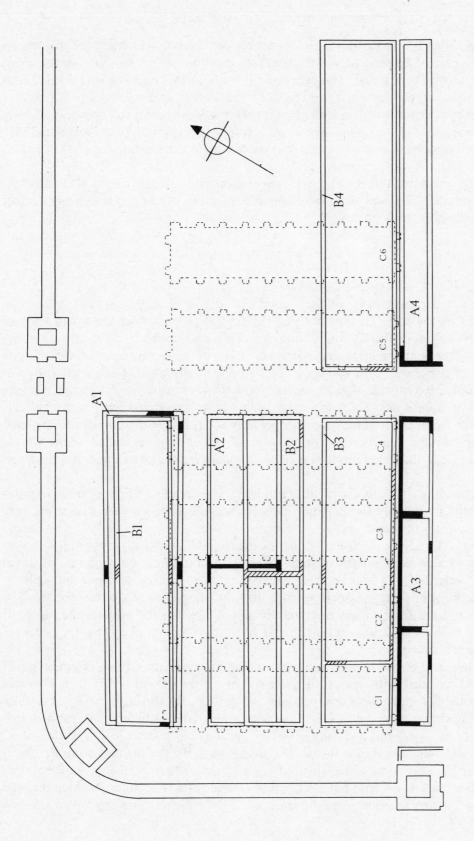

B1
A1
A2
B2
B3
C1
C2
C3
C4
A3
B4
C5
C6
A4

0   50 Metres

Fig. 13. North end of Fort, buildings of Periods I and II.

sandstone, of building B5. These foundations were bedded directly on natural subsoil and no trace was found here of an earlier building, implying that the earliest buildings in this area, must have lain further to the east. The excavated portion of this building was divided into two sections. The southern section appeared to be the western end of a room, or range of rooms, running east. From the north wall of this room a wall ran north and turned east along the southern end of the *via principalis*. The length, from north to south, of the excavated part was *c*. 28 m. A fragment of mortarium (no. 80) was found in the binding material of one of the walls.

Richmond suggested that this building was a workshop with an enclosed yard (Guidebook, p. 9), but it could equally well have been the commanding officer's house. Only further excavation could solve the problem.

Buildings B6 and B7 (fig. 11)

Excavated in 1949—cf. Richmond, Guidebook.

Like the earliest barracks, those of the second period had their long axes running from east to west across the fort. To the south of the central range, under the north ends of granaries C10–C15, were found foundations, of clay and cobble, together with some upstanding masonry of pink micaceous sandstone, of two of the second period barracks, one on either side of a narrow *via decumana*. The barrack to the west of the road (B6) was *c*. 43 m long and *c*. 9·5 m wide. Under the alleyway between granaries C10 and C11 were found a series of square post-holes for the uprights of internal partitions which, at this point, divided the building into three rooms, or possibly two rooms with a corridor in between. The two rooms (or room and corridor) on the north side had been floored with lime mortar and, at the east side of the larger room, was found a square slab much cracked and reddened by heat.

Of the other building (B7) only the western end was found. A short length of stone foundations for a partition, possibly the partition between the officer's and men's quarters, was found projecting from the south wall.

Like buildings A1 and A6, the use of stone for the foundations of these buildings implies that their walls were, at least in part, of stone. While they could have been entirely of stone, it seems more likely that they had a timber superstructure supported on stone sill walls.

Only one fragment of pottery associated with these buildings was recovered (no. 81). The dating of them as later than primary rests mainly on the fact that the western one was built rather too close to the foundations of building A6 for it to have been likely that the two were standing at the same time.

Outside the west end of building B6 and partly underlying granary C10 was found a structure which had been part of the system of water supply for the second period fort. This was a stone tank, roughly rectangular in shape and *c*. 1·5 m deep, fed through a series of settling tanks or aeration chambers *c*. 0·9 m deep. The pipe which fed the chambers from the north was, presumably, of wood and had long since disappeared but a short length of the stone-lined duct, in which the pipe sat, was found. The chambers of the settling tank were separated from each other by short stone walls which projected from the east wall. The gaps between their ends and the west wall would have held timber sluice gates. The point at which the pipe discharged into the first chamber would have been slightly higher than the top of the first timber gate, and the other gates would have been successively slightly lower. The first chamber would have filled slowly, until water spilled over the top of the gate into the next chamber. There the process was repeated, and so on through the third chamber and into the storage tank. Care would have had to be taken to equalise the system so that delivery was sufficient to keep water moving through the chambers, but not so much as to flood the system. In this way a gentle convection current was maintained in each chamber so that sediment settled out to the bottom while the topmost levels of water flowed on through the chambers. A fragment of mortarium from the core of the settling tank wall dates to the second century. Pottery from the fill of the settling tank is all of a mid-late second century date (nos. 82 and 83–94).

Buildings B1, B2, B3 and B4 (fig. 13)

Excavated in 1966 and 1967.

To the north of the central range evidence was found of four buildings of the second period, one built entirely of timber (B2), and the other three having at least stone sill walls. Immediately to the north of building A3 were found parts of the south wall of building B3. These were constructed of pink micaceous sandstone, standing three courses high in places, on a foundation of cobbles, one stone thick, capped with a layer of clay. The wall could be traced to a point *c.* 10 m short of the west end of building A3. The foundation trench could be traced for a further 2 m but if, as seems likely, the building ran right up to the *intervallum* then the western end of this wall had been removed completely. This is curious for, where it survived, it had been incorporated in the foundations of granaries C2, C3 and C4, and thus there should have been no need to remove it completely at its western end. Part of the foundations of the east wall were found, again incorporated in the later granary foundations. The only trace of the north wall was a short length of robbed out foundation, partly obscured by modern disturbance, located at the southern end of the long trench. Part of a shallow foundation trench for a timber partition was found under the alley between granaries C1 and C2. The only pottery recovered from the foundations was a fragment of a lid (no. 78) not closely datable, though there are Antonine parallels.

One reason for thinking that this building and building A3 were not contemporary, apart from their proximity, was the difference in the construction of their foundations. The foundations of building A3 were thicker, two or three stones thick, and truly clay bonded. They were a general mixture of clay and cobbles. The later foundations were only one stone thick and the clay had been spread over them rather like margarine on bread. As excavated the building was *c.* 9·5 m wide and *c.* 34 m long but, as we have seen, it is highly probable that it occupied the full width of the western half of the *praetentura* and was originally *c.* 42 m long.

The area where building A3 had stood was never again built on but was gravelled over and left as open space. Two successive layers of gravel were found overlying the floor of the building. Pottery from under the lower layer was of Hadrianic or early Antonine date (nos. 73–7). Various post-holes, contemporary with or later than the upper gravel were found, but they formed no coherent pattern.

Almost all the evidence for the other two buildings of the second period in the western half of the *praetentura* came from a long trench cut between granaries C2 and C3. The northernmost (B1) appears to have been constructed in the same way as building B3.

Short lengths of the foundations of its north and south walls, of cobbles, and a little up-standing masonry, of pink micaceous sandstone, were found. The building had a width of *c*. 8 m. The foundations for the north wall lay at the southern edge of the second intervallum road. Those of the south wall seem to have served both for the wall of the building and for a gutter of rectangular blocks, with a water channel *c*. 80 mm deep cut into them, which had run along the south side of the building. Nothing of the east end of the building was located. At the west end it appeared that the foundations of granary C1 incorporated earlier foundations which, on plan, lined up with those of the south wall of building B1, but the actual west end wall was not located. The section obtained in the long trench showed that the building had been floored with clay, as much as *c*. 0·55 m thick at the north side, where the level of the natural subsoil sloped away. Some of this clay had spread over the foundations after the building had been demolished and the north wall removed.

The other building (B2), in between the two with stone foundations, had been constructed entirely of timber and, like its predecessors, had shallow construction trenches, *c*. 100 mm deep, which had been dug into the slight accumulation of material overlying the construction trench for the south wall of building A2. Short lengths of the trenches for the north and south walls were located in the long trench, giving the building a width of *c*. 8·2 m. Further lengths of the trench for the south wall were found between granaries C1 and C2 and inside and under granary C4, giving the building a minimum length of 33 m. A fragment of a bowl, in BB2 fabric, dated to A.D. 160–180, was found in one of the construction trenches (no. 79).

In the eastern half of the *praetentura* a small part of a building of the second period was found on the north side of the *via principalis* (building B4). Mainly on the grounds of symmetry, this has been restored with the same dimensions as the buildings in the western half of the *praetentura*. A length of the cobble foundations of the west wall, associated with the gravel surface of the second *via praetoria*, was found to the north of and running underneath the south-west corner buttress of granary C5. The area had been quite heavily robbed but the approximate line of the south wall of the building was marked by the edge of the rubble build-up for the second *via principalis*, at a higher level than the foundations of building A4.

The position of the second *intervallum* road has already been mentioned, as has its relationship to the earliest drain at the west side of the *praetentura*. The drain along the west side of the earliest *via praetoria* was subsequently replaced by another drain immediately to the west of the original. That this was the sequence is clearly shown by the fact that the second drain overlies the construction trench for the east wall of building A1. The eaves drip gutter running along the south side of building B1 presumably connected with the drains at either end of the buildings. A short length of a drain running between buildings B2 and B3 was located at its junction with the drain at the east end.

The second *via praetoria* was slightly wider than its predecessor (*c*. 4 m). At its east side, by building B4, it ran right up to the wall foundations, while a little further to the south, where it was clear of the building, it was bounded by a kerb. The second *via principalis* was considerably wider than its predecessor, the total width of the surface being *c*. 16 m. On its north side, as already mentioned, it extended to the south wall of building B3, while its south edge ran up to the north wall of building B5. It is doubtful, though, whether its full width was used as a thoroughfare. From the position of the east kerb of the *via praetoria*, south of building B4, it would appear that traffic was kept off the area where buildings A3 and A4 had stood.

The nature of the excavations, with limited endowment, meant that, in 1966 and more especially in 1967 when the area was greater, all investigation of the *praetentura* had to be selective, and that only fragments of the plans of the buildings in this area, apart from A3, were recovered. From the reconstruction attempted at present, it can be seen that they must have been either barracks or stables, but lack of knowledge of internal details makes it impossible to decide which.

Third Period (fig. 22)

The fifteen granaries, so far located, were all so nearly identical in construction that there can be no doubt that they were all erected at the same time. Each was a single separate unit, oblong in shape, with ten buttresses on each of its side walls and two on each end wall. The walls and buttresses were mostly of buff sandstone but with some pink micaceous sandstone and a little magnesian limestone. They had a rubble and mortar core and rested on a foundation of clay and cobble with, in places, a footing of small stone slabs. The variety of shape and type of stone indicated much re-use of material from earlier buildings. The walls were all between 1·1 and 1·3 m thick, and the buttresses, which were of one build with the walls, had average dimensions of 0·8 m by 0·7 m, with the end buttresses on the side walls possibly slightly wider. Depending on where the easiest access was, each granary had a loading bay built between the buttresses at one end. Inside, the original stone flagged floors were supported on a series of short, low, stone sleeper walls, as in the still visible Severan granaries at Corbridge (Richmond and Gillam, 1950). The sleeper walls were all *c.* 0·6 m wide and, where they survived to their original height, *c.* 0·9 m high. Vents through the lowest courses of the main side walls, between each buttress, connected the underfloor area with the open air.

It was in the arrangement of the internal sleeper walls and the end buttresses of the main side walls that there was some difference between the granaries. In granaries C1, C2, C3, C4, C11 and possibly C5 the end buttresses were placed in line with the corners of the building, but in C8, C12, C13, C14 and C15 they were set back from the corners by *c.* 0·5 m. In C7, C10, C11, C13, C14 and possibly C6 the sleeper walls were in rows of four across the width of the building and the outside ones in each set were separate from the main walls. In C12 and possibly C1 they were in rows of six and the outside ones abutted the main walls. There seems, however, to be no meaningful correlation between the different methods of buttressing and the different arrangements of the sleeper walls.

These granaries conform to the widespread type of Roman buttressed granaries. The walls will have been of stone to the eaves apart from wooden-louvred shutters set high up. The buttresses counteracted either the sideways thrust of the grain against the inside of the walls or, possibly, though there is no evidence from the site for this, the thrust of a vaulted roof. The roofs, if not vaulted, would have been of simple gabled timber frame construction. The bins which contained the corn on either side of a central alleyway and which were presumably rectangular and used the outer wall of the granary as a support, may also have been of wood, resting on the stone floor and probably tied to the roof cross-beams. It has long been widely accepted that something like this was the usual method of corn storage, though other possible methods could be envisaged.

Of the fifteen granaries excavated, several show evidence of having been later modified for habitation purposes. The vents, where they survived, of granaries C2, C8 and C10–14 were found to have been blocked and in all except C8 and C10 there was evidence for re-flooring and the erection of stone sills for new partition walls. In granaries C11–14, the original sleeper walls still remained under the new partitions but in C2 they had been removed and the level made up with a dump of earth and stones before the new floor was laid.

The south ends of the six granaries, nos. C10–15, to the south of the central range lie south of the extreme limit of Roman Remains Park, while the north ends of granaries C7 and C8, in the central range, lie north of the former northern limits of the park. In 1934 Richmond restored these as a mere 23·4 m long. In 1966 the north-west corner of granary C8 was discovered and a length of 27·8 m established for it. In 1967 the position of the north and south ends of granaries C1 and C4, to the north of the central range, was established, giving lengths of 30·4 m and 29 m. These figures are of the same order as each other, though somewhat greater than that for granary C8. They presumably indicate the approximate lengths of most of the granaries. It is possible that all the granaries in the central range, including C7 and C8, were shorter than the rest, as space for them was restricted by, on the one hand, the line of the earlier but still functioning *via principalis*, and on the other, by the wall which divides the fort, if this indeed be contemporary. The widths of ten of the known granaries have been measured, and prove to vary between a minimum of 6·5 m and a maximum of 6·95 m.

Granaries C2, C3 and C4 re-used the foundations of the north wall of building A3 and the remains of the south wall of building B3 for the foundations of their south walls and buttresses.

Granary C1

Excavated: 1966 and 1967.
Length: 30·4 m   Width: 6·6 m.

At the north-west corner of the building, the foundations of the north and west walls were 1·2 m and 1·6 m thick, respectively. The west buttress of the north wall overlay the flagged floor of building B2. Inside the granary, at this point, were two sleeper walls, 0·4 m apart, and measuring 2·6 m by 0·5 m. The foundations of the westernmost sleeper wall and the main west wall were one and the same, and the sleeper wall was not faced on its west side. The north ends of the next set to the south were also located.

The south wall was 1·3 m thick and the foundations no wider. The east buttress of the south wall had been completely robbed out. As mentioned earlier, for some reason, the south wall of building B2 which, further to the east, was re-used for the foundations of the south walls of granaries C2, C3 and C4 had, at this point, been completely removed.

Most of the west wall, between buttresses 3 and 4, had been removed by the foundations of a modern water tank. Inside, at this point, were found the fragmentary remains of sleeper walls.

All the excavated buttresses of the west wall, where they survived, overlay the east side of the earliest drain. Outside the south-west corner, the drain was overlain by the second *intervallum* road, and the build-up for the third road, but must have remained in use, for a

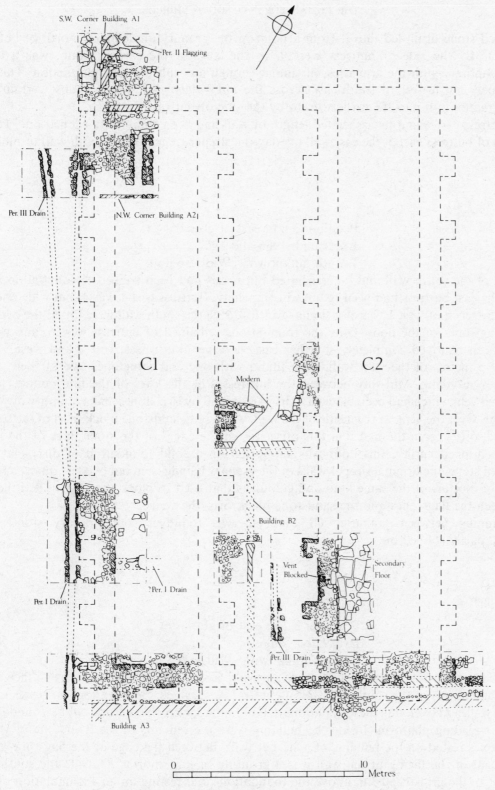

Fig. 14. Granaries C1 and C2.

covered stone drain led into it from a point in the granary immediately north of buttress west 1. By the side of buttress west 9, to the west of the earliest drain, was a drain contemporary with the granaries, of similar though less substantial construction. This ran obliquely north-west to south-east across the *intervallum*. What was almost certainly its continuation ran into the earliest drain by the side of buttress west 4.

Buttress east 6 and its associated length of wall had been completely robbed out. To the south of buttress east 5, the east wall overlay the sleeper trench of the south wall of building B2.

Granary C2

Position: 3·6 m east of granary C1.
Excavated: 1966 and 1967.
Length: unknown.   Width: 6·6 m.

Most of the south wall and its associated buttresses had been robbed to foundation level, and the east buttress had been removed completely. Buttress east 1 was 1·2 m wide and the robber trench of west 1 was of a similar width. Inside the south wall were found the edges of the flagstones of the floor. Only the foundations remained of buttress west 6, and west 5 had been removed completely. Further east, however, buttresses west 2 and west 3, and about 5 metres of the west wall, were found with one and sometimes two of their upper courses surviving. Mid-way between the buttresses at the level of the first course, was a tapered vent which had been blocked at its narrow end by two stones and a quantity of yellow mortar. Over the vent, at the inside of the wall, was a buff sandstone block, part of the second course, offset from the first. On this offset rested the edges of the stone flags of the floor. As mentioned earlier, this floor was supported on a solid foundation of dirty clay and broken stone, the original sleeper walls of the granary having been removed. A quarter-round fillet of mortar, of the same kind and colour as that used to block the vent, sealed the gap between the flagstones and the sandstone block over the vent.

Running between granaries C1 and C2 was found a contemporary stone lined drain, partly robbed out.

Granary C3

Position: 3·2 m east of granary C2.
Excavated: 1966.
Length: unknown.   Width: 6·5 m.

Apart from buttress west 1, which was 1 m wide, and a few stones of the inside face, only the foundations of the south wall and its buttresses survived. Between the buttresses of the south wall, and overlying the foundations of building A3, were the clay and cobble foundations for the loading platform. Inside the building were the remains of the floor, one of whose flagstones rested on the remains of a sleeper wall. Between the edge of the flagstone and a fragment of the facing of the wall was a grouting of lime mortar. Outside the south-east corner of the granary, 0·3 m above the foundations and resting on an accumulation of soil and rubble, was a later flagged surface.

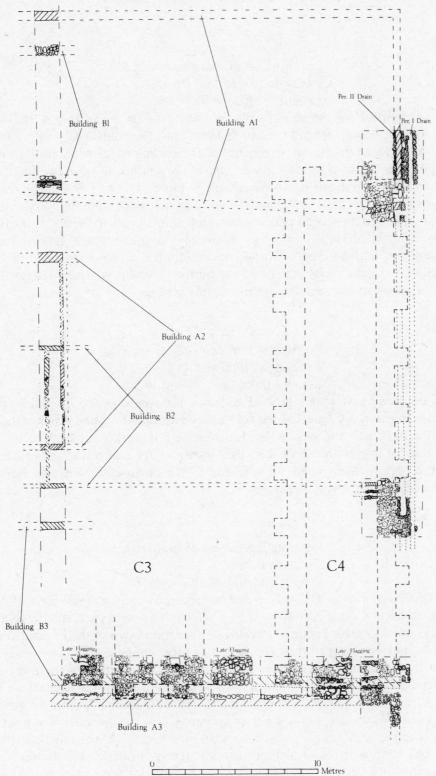

Fig. 15. Granaries C3 and C4.

Granary C4

Position: 2·6 m east of granary C3.
Excavated: 1966 and 1967.
Length: 29 m.   Width: 6·6 m.

Apart from fragments of the south wall, and buttress east 1 and east 4, the walls in the excavated areas had been robbed to their foundations. The south wall was 1·3 m wide, and between its buttresses were found the remains of the loading bay, its core resting on a foundation of cobbles and gravel. Inside the west end of the south wall were two flagstones of the floor. In two places, to the west of foundations of buttress west 1, and partly overlying one of the flagstones of the south wall, flagstones of a later surface were found. The foundations of buttress east 4 filled the second period drain, and, immediately to the north, the foundations of the east wall filled the drain which had run along the south side of building B2. Further north, at buttress east 10, however, the drain had not been filled, but had been covered with large slabs which supported the buttress. As this was near the north gate, this section of drain may have remained in use in this period.

Granary C5

Position: 4·6 m east of granary C4.
Excavated: 1966 and 1967.
Length: unknown.   Width 6·5 m.

Buttress west 1 and east 4 were located and they survived one and, in places, two courses high. As in granaries C2, C3 and C4, the builders had utilised the foundations of the two earlier buildings for the south and west walls. Buttress west 1 overlay the kerb of the second *via praetoria* and the robber trench of the west buttress of the south wall indicated that it had overlain the edge of the second *via principalis*. The north-east corner of buttress east 4 overlay the edge of a roughly square pit.

Granary C6

Position: 2·8 m east of granary C5.
Excavated: 1967.
Length and width: unknown.

The alley between granaries C5 and C6 had been surfaced with a single layer of cobbles laid directly on the natural subsoil. Buttress west 4, which survived in part, and the foundations of the west wall were located. Inside the west wall were found two of the internal sleeper walls, 0·66 m wide, and surviving to their full height of three courses, *c*. 0·6 m.

Between the south ends of granaries C4 and C5, the contemporary road was 4·4 m wide and had been laid right up to the buttresses. The area to the south of granaries C1–C6, over buildings A3 and A4 and right up to the north end of granary C8 received a new surface. Associated with this surface, to the south of granary C1, was found part of a drain which had connected with the earliest drain which was still functioning. At the junction the drain had been dug and lined with stone slabs in the usual way. Further east, however, the water had been carried in a narrow channel cut in large rectangular stone blocks, of which two and part of a third were found.

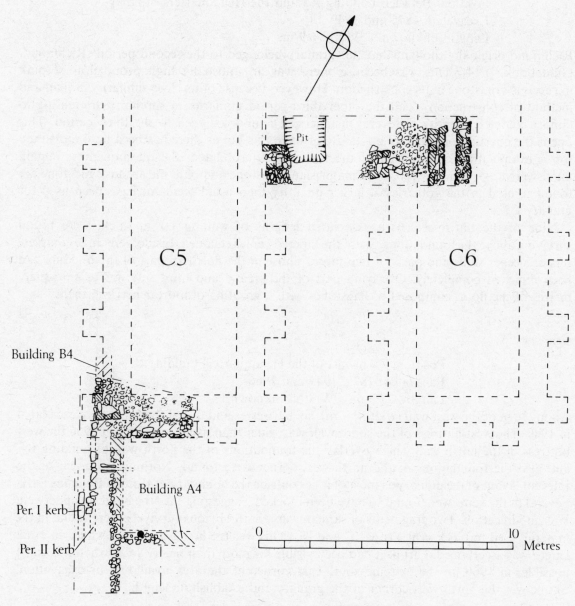

Fig. 16. Granaries C5 and C6, and Buildings A4 and B4.

Granary C7

> Position: Between building A5 and the Headquarters building.
> Excavated: 1875 and 1949.
> Length: unknown.   Width: 6·9 m.

Richmond originally thought that this granary belonged to the second period (Richmond, Guidebook, p. 4). This was because there was an unusually high proportion of pink micaceous sandstone in its construction. However, because of its close similarity in plan and method of construction to all the other third-period granaries, a similarity amounting to almost complete identity in several instances, it is now assigned to the third period. This opens the question of what lay on its site prior to this but as there has been no opportunity for re-examination of any part of the fort now consolidated, the question must remain unanswered. As we have seen, both magnesian limestone and pink micaceous sandstone are found re-used in the granaries; a larger quantity than usual seems to have been used for granary C7.

Nine of the buttresses, with associated lengths of walling 1·1 m thick, were found surviving above the foundations. Six of the tapered vents remained. Inside were three complete sets of sleeper walls and parts of two more. Those in the northern part of the building had been removed completely. Overlying part of the second and third sets was *c*. 4·6 square metres of the floor, composed of flagstones with a grouting of mortar between them.

Granary C8

> Position: 7·4 m east of the Headquarters building.
> Excavated: 1875, 1949 and 1966.
> Length: 27·8 m.   Width: unknown.

About 16 m of the west wall (width 1·1 m), six buttresses and five of the vents were excavated in 1949. The west buttress of the south wall was wider than usual, *c*. 1·7 m. In 1966 the west buttress of the north wall which overlay the foundations of the north wall of building B4, and also the foundations of the north-west corner were found. Nothing is known of the internal layout of the granary as most of it lies outside the boundary of Roman Remains Park. Several of the vents were found to have been blocked, suggesting that the building underwent later modification. Two fragments of samian ware, both obvious survivals, were found in the material used to block vent 4 (nos. 22 and 29). This was the first granary for which an exact length was ascertained. Part of it had been visible for more than ninety years when it became possible, in 1966, in the extreme south-east corner of the area available for excavation, to uncover the north-west corner of the granary and establish its length.

Granary C9

On the plan of the excavations of 1875 is shown a small fragment of walling about 26 m to the east of the Headquarters building (Bruce, 1884, p. 230). This is of the right shape and in exactly the right place, given that the granaries were regularly spaced in this area, which there is every reason to suppose that they were, to be the south-west corner buttress of a further granary of this period.

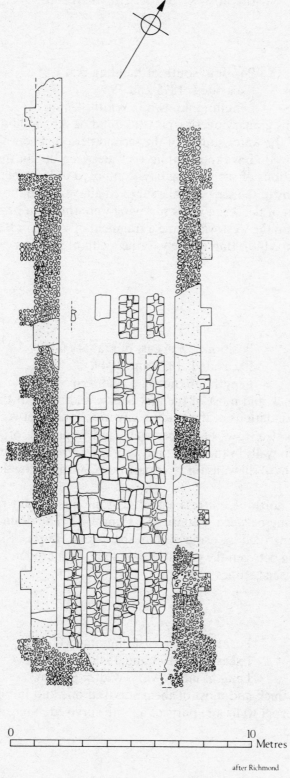

0   10
                                         Metres

after Richmond

Fig. 17. Granary C7 (drawing by K. Lawson).

Granary C10

> Position: south of building A5.
> Excavated: 1875 and 1949.
> Length: unknown.   Width: 6·6 m.

The northern end of this granary overlay parts of building A6, building B6 and the west side of the settling tanks of the water supply of the second period. The walls were 1 m thick and a total of *c*. 20 m survived above foundation level. Between the buttresses of the north wall were found the foundations of the loading bay, composed of large blocks and pitched slabs. Inside the building many of the sleeper walls survived above foundation level. Nothing of the floor survived but most of the seven vents surviving were found to have been blocked. From the blocking of vent 1 on the west wall came a fragment of a dish in BB2 fabric dating to not earlier than A.D. 180 (no. 140). Immediately to the south of buttress east 7 was a small stone lined trough.

Granary C11

> Position: 2·5 m east of granary C10.
> Excavated: 1875 and 1949.
> Length: unknown.   Width: 6·5 m.

The walls were 1 m thick and most of the first course and some of the second survived. As in granary C10, the foundations of the loading bay were found between the buttresses on the north wall. Seven complete rows of sleeper walls and fragments of one more were found. Of the easternmost two walls in the third and sixth rows from the north end of the building were found short lengths of sill walls for later partitions. Many of the thirteen vents found had been blocked.

Immediately to the north of buttress east 7, a stone lined drain ran out of the granary to join the drain running between granaries C11 and C12. The drain from the granary was of quite substantial construction, using well finished stone. Three of its capping stones were found *in situ*. The drain between the granaries was somewhat cruder, constructed of a variety of small blocks, unfinished stones and flags.

Granary C12

> Position: 3·4 m east of granary C11.
> Excavated: 1875 and 1949.
> Length: unknown.   Width: 6·95 m.

The walls were 1·1 m thick and most of them survived one and in places two courses high. All of eight rows of sleeper walls and parts of a ninth survived. Nine of the vents were found, many of them blocked.

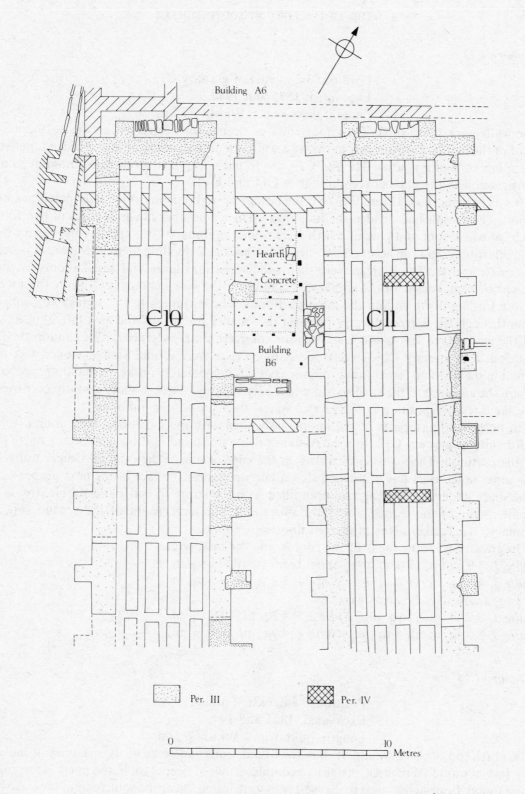

Building A6

C10

C11

"Hearth"

"Concrete"

Building
B6

Per. III   Per. IV

0   10
                                           Metres

Fig. 18. Granaries C10 and C11 (drawing by K. Lawson).

Granary C13

> Position: 3·3 m east of granary C12.
> Excavated: 1875 and 1949.
> Length: unknown.   Width: 6·85 m.

The walls were 1·1 m thick. Only four rows of sleeper walls survived, in the northernmost third of the building. Four vents in the west wall were found, many of them blocked. Between the south ends of granaries C12 and C13 was found a length of stone lined drain of similar construction to the one between granaries C11 and C12.

It was in granaries C12 and C13 that the best preserved remains of the later partitions were found. These walls had divided the buildings up into a number of small suites of two rooms each, of which four and part of a fifth were found in granary C12, and five in granary C13. Main partitions had run across the width of the buildings, dividing them into areas of roughly 16 square metres. These areas were then subdivided into large and small rooms by walls which ran from the east wall, in granary C12, and from the west, in granary C13, into the interior before turning north to join the main partitions. The entrances to the suites had probably been through the narrow passage between the smaller rooms and the next lateral partition. At the entrance to this passage, in the four complete suites in granary C12, and in the first and fourth in granary C13, large stone slabs on edge were found. Similar stones were also found in the first and fourth suites of granary C12, immediately inside the building, probably where the entrance to the smaller room had been. Though these stones regularly occurred in the same relative position in the several suites, their purpose is unknown.

In both buildings, parts of the floors, associated with the partitions, were found. In the third suite of granary C12, four large flagstones were found laid up against the north wall of the partition. Their west ends rested on the edge of one of the original sleeper walls, but the other rested on a line of pitched stones laid up against the face of the next sleeper walls. The space under the flooring had been filled with a mixture of earth and rubble. Inside the small rooms of the second and third suites, and the large room of the second suite, in granary C13, further areas of flagged floor were found.

In granary C12, the areas of the rooms, smaller first, were:

Suite 1, 3·9 sq. m, 10·4 sq. m.   *Suite 2*, 5·6 sq. m, 13 sq. m.
Suite 3, 4·3 sq. m, 11·2 sq. m.   *Suite 4*, 5·8 sq. m, 12 sq. m.

In granary C13 the areas were:

Suite 1, 3·9 sq. m, 11 sq. m.   *Suite 2*, 3·4 sq. m. 10·8 sq. m.
Suite 3, 5·9 sq. m, 10·6 sq. m.   *Suite 4*, 4 sq. m, 11·4 sq. m.

Granary C14

> Position: 8·7 m east of granary C13.
> Excavated: 1875 and 1949.
> Length: unknown.   Width: 6·5 m.

The north end of this building overlay the foundations and some of the masonry of building B7. Its walls were 1·1 m thick; inside two complete rows of sleeper walls and parts of two others were found. Four of the vents in the west wall were found. Near the south end of the excavated area, one lateral partition wall was located.

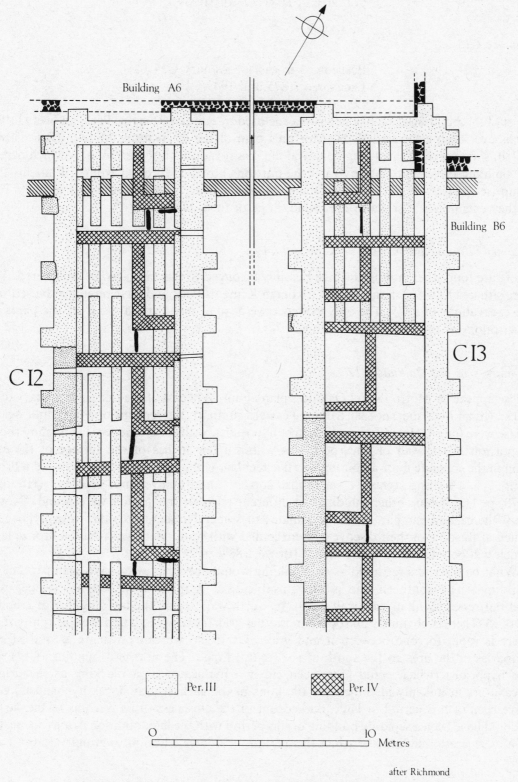

Building A6

Building B6

C12

C13

Per. III

Per. IV

O 10 Metres

after Richmond

Fig. 19. Granaries C12 and C13 (drawing by K. Lawson).

Granary C15

> Position: 4 m east of granary C14.
> Excavated: 1875 and 1949.
> Length and width: unknown.

Most of this building lies outside the area enclosed by Roman Remains Park, and very little of it has ever been excavated. J. H. Morton's plan of the excavations of 1875 (Bruce, 1884, p. 230) shows several small lengths of walling, but it is difficult to be sure now which parts of the building these were. At any rate, the portions now preserved in Roman Remains Park comprise most of the west wall and the north-west corner. The walls were 1·1 m thick. Four of the vents in the west wall were found, none of them blocked.

Granary C16 and Buildings C17, C18 and C19

There are four other buildings which possibly belonged to this period to be considered. They were situated to the east and south of Roman Remains Park and have remained buried since the excavations of 1875. The only evidence we have at our disposal now are the plans and descriptions of the original excavators.

Granary C16 and Building C17

These appear on Morton's and Oswald's plan about 20 m east of the eastern boundary of the park. "In another spot, not far from the eastern rampart, the remains of a large and wealthy house were found. Here was a very perfect hypocaust, with sooty flue, coal and many rooms. A portion of the wall of one room was within a few inches of the surface of the earth though the concrete floor adjoining was five feet below the surface. Here was found a bronze lamp, ... a writing stylus, ... a bronze cup, ... and many minor articles." (Hooppell, 1878, p. 11.) "Some other buildings in different parts of the station were found. 'Not far from the eastern rampart were the remains of some chambers provided with hypocausts, which at the time of their discovery, were coated with soot.' Here was found a bronze lamp, which will be referred to afterwards." (Bruce, 1884, p. 247.)

What both writers regarded as one building would appear now to have been parts of two buildings. The southern one is recognisable as a granary with internal sleeper walls and buttresses along its east wall (C16). Its north wall lies on the building line of granaries C10–15. There is obviously no room for another granary between it and the east rampart, but there is room for one between it and granary C15, so we can postulate a total of eight granaries in the area to the south of the central range. The northern building (C17), with the hypocaust (which could have been either a hypocaust or a tile kiln, as the original excavators mistakenly identified the tile kilns in the earliest granary as hypocausts) could have been of this period or later, on account of the closeness of its remains to the surface. It could have been a separate building of this period with the later addition of a hypocaust/tile kiln, a separate building later than this period, or a later addition to granary C16.

Buildings C18 and C19

The two other buildings lay to the south of the park, under what are now the Baring Street schools. "On the southern side of the station many walls still many feet in height have been excavated. There were evidently numerous large buildings in this direction. In several cases the doorways are plainly visible. It has been suggested that these edifices were barracks. Their walls were probably those standing above the ground in Leland's time, for the explorer found some of them within a few inches of the surface of the soil. In the neighbourhood of these buildings and in other localities of the station, large well-made drains were found." (Hooppell, 1878, pp. 12 and 13.) "On the southern side of the station, Dr. Hooppell also tells us, several large buildings were found. All traces of them are now removed, but they are shown on the plan." (Bruce, 1884, p. 247.)

From the plans we can gather the following: Both the buildings had their long axes aligned east-west. Of the southern one (C19) about 24 m of its length was excavated. It was *c.* 13·5 m wide and had three lateral partitions at intervals of *c.* 3·5 m. In the north wall were two gaps, presumably the doorways mentioned, which gave access to two of the rooms. From the easternmost of the lateral partitions a longitudinal partition ran east. The other building (C18) lay about 10 m north of the first. The excavated part was rectangular, *c.* 17 m long and 7 m wide, with one longitudinal and one lateral partition. Around the two buildings were several unrelated fragments of walling.

The most likely explanation is that these buildings were either both barracks, as suggested a century ago, or that one was a barrack and the other a kit store. That they belonged to the third period is based mainly on the fact that they were found so close to the surface, and, with the exception of the granary of the primary period, all the substantial stone remains so far discovered in the fort belong to the third period.

Taking into account the extant structural evidence, various suppositions have been made concerning the areas about which little or nothing is known, and a simple restoration of the third period fort attempted. Two granaries have been restored to the east of granary C6; one has been restored between granaries C8 and C9 and another between granaries C15 and C16. Thus, including building A5, there could have been as many as twenty-two granaries in the third period fort.

Dating

The pottery associated with the granaries (nos. 111 to 134 and samian nos. 22 and 91) naturally includes material which survives from earlier periods but most of it dates to the later second or early third century. The latest piece from a securely stratified context, and that which provides the *terminus post quem* is no. 132.

The Dividing Wall

Finally, mention must be made of the wall which apparently divided the fort in two at some time later than the first period. Little of it is left now apart from a 4·8 m length projecting from the fort wall at a point *c.* 37 m south of the west gate, and two smaller fragments 1·2 m and 1·8 m long respectively, situated further into the interior of the fort. The foundations are of clay and cobble. The upstanding masonry, two or three courses high, is mostly of buff sandstone, with a little magnesian limestone and pink micaceous sandstone. The wall is 1 m wide and, in the largest and middle fragments, the upper courses are offset from the first course, on the north side, by *c.* 150 mm. Whether the wall extended the full width of the fort cannot now be ascertained. The projected line of the extant fragments joins the west wall of the courtyard of the third Headquarters building, though no traces were found at this point. No traces were found on the east side of the Headquarters building. That the wall was later than the fort wall is apparent, for although the upper courses stop short, the foundations can clearly be seen to form a butt-joint with those of the fort wall. The wall is clearly later than the end of the earliest period for the east end of the largest fragment overlies the foundations of building A6. Apart from building A6 the wall does not interfere with any other building of any period, so it is impossible to establish further direct structural relationships.

Later Remains

Little structural evidence of occupation at a date substantially later than the granaries has been found. The tile kilns and the structures in the north gate have already been mentioned. The only other evidence is in the form of several small patches of paving around the southern ends of granaries C1–C4. Two small areas occurred over the topmost of the two gravel surfaces which overlay building A3. Of the other three, one was outside the south-east corner of granary C2, one was outside the south-east corner of granary C3, and the third overlay the dilapidated south wall of granary C4. The paving did not rest directly on top of the earlier surface or structures, but upon a build-up of soil *c.* 100–150 mm in depth. This build-up resembles closely that directly below the late fourth century structures at Haltonchesters and Rudchester, and less closely a build-up at the corresponding level at Wallsend; it is natural to think of a phrase on a fourth-century inscription from Birdoswald (RIB 1912) describing ruined buildings as being covered with earth. From beneath the paving, over the gravel, came a small group of pottery (nos. 176-8) including a flanged bowl in grey Crambeck fabric, dated to the fourth century. All the paving was at the same general level, which would seem to indicate that the whole of this area immediately inside the west gate was paved over at some time in the fourth century.

EXTRA MURAL ACTIVITY

The Vicus

It is highly likely that the *vicus* extended over much of the area to the west of the fort. In 1970 Mr. J. Tait directed excavations outside the north-west corner of the fort. Unfortunately since his untimely death in the same year, most of the records of this excavation have disappeared, and although it is reported that structures of Roman date were found, no further information is now available.

In the excavations of 1973 much of the area immediately outside the west gate of the fort was examined. Although no structures of Roman date were found, the large amount of pottery recovered indicates that there was almost certainly quite intensive occupation in the vicinity. The date of the pottery spans the period from the early second century to the latter half of the third century but, in contrast to the interior of the fort, there was very little of fourth century date.

The Cemetery

The cemetery of the fort and *vicus* lay to the south of the fort. Excavation has been impossible in this area since the nineteenth century, but the publications of the excavations of 1875 provide a certain amount of information. "The burying ground of the station was to the south-west, probably stretching along each side of the great road leading from the fortress in that direction. The southern side only has thus far been explored. Many graves and skeletons have been disclosed." (Hooppell, 1878, p. 16.) Both cremation burials and extended inhumation burials were found. Plate XII, in Hooppell, shows one of the graves, a long narrow pile of stones, some of them finished, isolated by the excavation, with the skull of the skeleton protruding from one end. It would appear that the corpse had been buried in a stone lined grave, more stones then being piled on top. The text accompanying the plate says, ".... many others were found thus buried in this place: many urns also, with calcined ashes within, and marks of fire around." (Hooppell, 1878, p. 42.)

It is certain that the cremation burials were Roman. Many of the pots containing the ashes are in the Museum of the Roman Fort, and are illustrated here (nos. 334–42). It is possible that the inhumation burials were of post-Roman date, though there is no way, at the moment, of being certain on this point.

In addition to the actual graves a number of inscribed tombstones have been recovered from this area (cf. RIB 1062–1066).

The Parade Ground

As mentioned earlier, the South Shields Archaeological and Historical Society undertook excavations at the east end of Beacon Street *c.* 36 m outside the north-east corner of the fort.

Here was located a shrine area probably associated with the parade ground of the fort. At the northern corner of the excavated area were found cobble foundations, *c.* 1·8 m square and 0·9 m high, for a platform or dais, possibly that for the commanding officer who would have presided over regimental ceremonies here. Close by this was found the head and torso of a sandstone statuette, of native workmanship, probably representing Mars. In the area surrounding the platform were found the following: two smaller patches of cobbles; three altar bases and, close by, what was almost certainly the accompanying altar for the westernmost of these; fragments of a large altar and three fragments of an uninscribed sandstone panel. The coins found were mostly of Hadrian and Antoninus Pius with one of Domitian, and one fourth-century minim. (Cf. coin report.) For a detailed account of the excavation cf. Thornborrow, 1959.

DATING AND CONCLUSIONS

Period I

In the past, even the recent past, South Shields has appeared on maps illustrating the Agricolan advance. In fact, it is as certain as evidence can make it that South Shields was not the site of the station of one of Agricola's *praesidia*. A careful search over a wide area for post trenches earlier than the stonework of period I produced the clearest possible negative results. Only five pieces of decorated samian of markedly pre-Hadrianic date are known from the site (nos. 1–5), less than 4 per cent of the decorated ware assemblage, and these must be regarded as survivals. The three pieces of Trajanic date (nos. 6–8) could still have been on the market in the next reign. Coarse pottery vessels of types which emerged before Hadrian were found exclusively in the rampart backing (nos. 1–7) and in the groups from the foundation trench and beneath the clay floor of building A3 (nos. 16, and 23 and 24) but they were types which are also found surviving in use in Hadrianic contexts elsewhere and are not evidence for an earlier occupation. Neither are they evidence for a pre-Hadrianic date for the stone founded fort of period I, for this is dated by the presence of undoubtedly Hadrianic pottery from the foundation trenches of buildings A3 and A6 and from beneath the mason's chippings of the north guardchamber of the west gate. The first Headquarters building and the other internal buildings from which no independent dating evidence is known (A1, A2, A4 and A5) have been assigned to period I by virtue of their occurrence at the same structural level as, and their position relative to, the dated buildings. The dated group from the west gate is important as it means that the part of the defensive circuit known in the north-west corner of the fort, including the west and north gates with their externally projecting guardchambers, must be Hadrianic; the occurrence of such projecting guardchambers at so early a date has often been remarked upon. The evidence from the west gate does not necessarily imply, however, that the whole of the rest of the defensive circuit is Hadrianic. Indeed, Richmond was of the opinion that the Hadrianic fort was smaller and subsequently extended to the now familiar size and shape. It has been discovered, since this report was written, that he was entirely correct in his inference.

Thus the first fort at South Shields is Hadrianic and the pottery suggests that it was founded in the first half of the reign. Hadrian's legates would hardly have left the four and a half mile stretch of the river down-stream from Wallsend without any kind of protection, when one considers the heavy flank protection given to the west end of Hadrian's wall and the fact that on the Antonine wall there was some degree of protection on both flanks. South Shields should then be thought of as a Wall fort; and possibly one of the first series of Wall forts, whose twelve forts are spaced at fairly regular intervals of 7·3 Roman miles. This in turn suggests that it might be contemporary with them and be dated between *c*. A.D. 124 and A.D. 128.

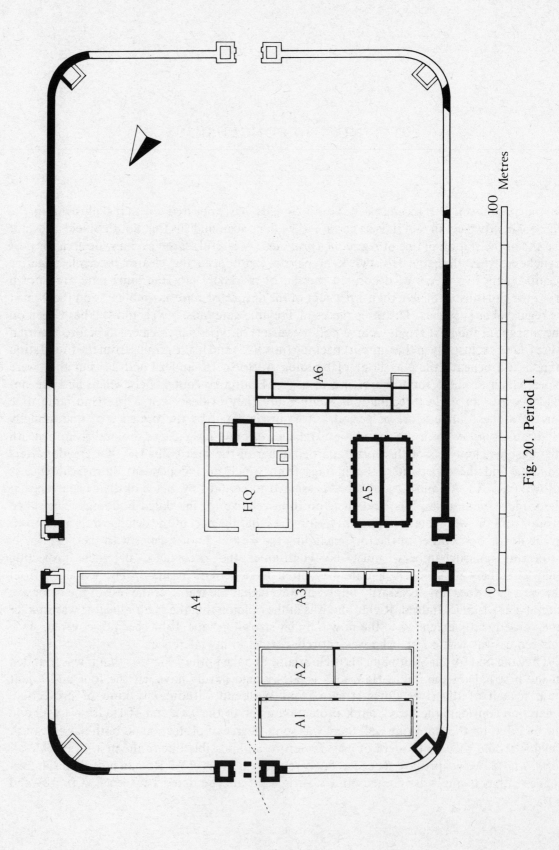

HQ

A6

A5

A4

A3

A2

A1

0   100   Metres

Fig. 20. Period I.

Period II

The evidence of the coins and pottery, in particular of stamped and assignable samian, suggests that occupation of the fort followed the same pattern as that of the other forts on Hadrian's wall during the first period of occupation of the Antonine wall; that is, during the period A.D. 140–160 the fort was either abandoned or operated with a much reduced garrison.

The discovery of a fragment of BB2 in the construction trench of building B2 (no. 79) adds further weight to the argument. While BB2 began to be made and distributed from centres in Essex and Kent over much of south-east England as early as the beginning of the reign of Hadrian, it never appeared in any part of northern Britain until the Antonine occupation of Scotland. It did not, however, appear in northern England until after the withdrawal from Scotland, in A.D. 163. It is absent, for example, from the deposits of forts IVa and IVb at Corbridge. It then began to appear in turrets on the eastern end of the wall, at Corbridge, Haltonchesters and elsewhere. The stratified piece from South Shields should give a *terminus post quem* of *c.* A.D. 160 for the beginning of period II. A word of caution is, however, needed. As the ware, and even the precise type had been in existence for forty years, and in use in Scotland for twenty, it is possible that odd vessels might have reached an east coast site, such as South Shields, at a date earlier than its coming into general use in northern England.

A date early in the reign of Marcus Aurelius is likely enough on general grounds. Hadrian's wall had just been brought back into commission and South Shields, a wall fort under Marcus as well as under Hadrian, doubtless shared in the general re-furbishing. This date also allows close on forty years for the Hadrianic timbers to have shown signs of age.

The second Headquarters building is to be assigned to this period by simple virtue of the fact that it is the second building on its site. The extension to the north guardchamber of the west gate is dated to period II on the grounds of relative stratigraphy. The second phase of small scale industrial activity in the east guardchamber of the north gate is certainly no earlier than this period, a late-Antonine *terminus post quem* being provided by the pottery (nos. 62–9).

In the *praetentura* of the period II fort there were fewer buildings than in the previous period; the area where building A3 and probably A4 had stood was not built on. Pottery from beneath the earlier of the two gravel surfaces over the site of these buildings was of predominantly early-Antonine date.

Period III

South Shields, like Wallsend, seems to have escaped the violent destruction which left dramatic traces at Benwell, Rudchester, Haltonchesters, Corbridge and elsewhere. It matters little whether this took place in A.D. 180 or A.D. 197, so far as South Shields is concerned, for there occupation was, apparently, continuous and peaceful, until the fort was modified to perform a different function.

The date of the multiple granaries can be in no doubt. There is a little stratified pottery, the crucial piece being no. 132 which indicates an approximate third-century date. Once this is

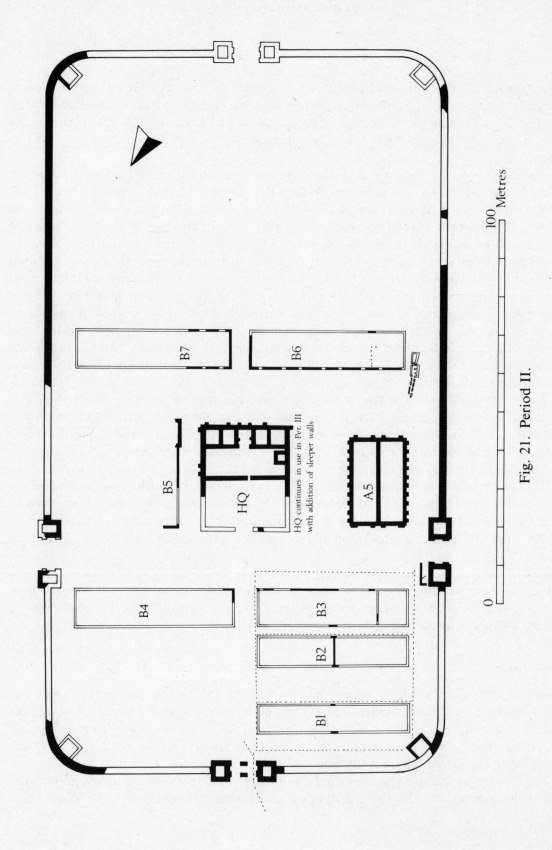

HQ continues in use in Per. III
with addition of sleeper walls

B5

HQ

B7

B6

A5

B4

B3

B2

B1

Fig. 21. Period II.

0   100 Metres

established, a consideration of the character of the site and its position at the river mouth leaves no doubt that the granaries belong to the time of the northern campaigns of Septimius Severus. Richmond was, of course, the first to see this (cf. Richmond, 1934). He was able to work out the date and function of the visible remains knowing nothing of earlier structures and with only an incomplete tally of the granaries. Further evidence that the site was linked with the campaigns is provided by the lead seals (nos. 1–8 on p. 164). These bear three heads and the inscription *AVGG*, that is three emperors of whom only two were *Augusti*. They can only be Severus, Antoninus and Geta, at a time after A.D. 198 when Antoninus became *Augustus* alongside Severus, and before A.D. 209, when Geta became *Augustus*.

At the same time as the granaries were being built, it would seem that modifications were made to the north gate: the west portal was blocked, the areas to the south of this portal and to the south of the east guardchamber were flagged over and the west guardchamber was extended southwards. Pottery sealed by the flags of the extension and by the flags to the south of the portal and guardchamber gives a *terminus post quem* of the later second century. It is believed, however, that the modifications carried out in the east portal, and the construction of the third Headquarters building date to a time subsequent to the Severan campaigns, and this will be dealt with shortly.

Whether or not the structures in the most southerly area of the fort were barracks contemporary with the granaries, it is evident purely from the space available that the garrison at this time must have been small: only a force large enough to guard and administer the supplies would have been necessary. Nothing is known about the commanding officer's house at this time. It was certainly not situated in the usual position, to one side of the Headquarters building, but as the role of the fort was atypical one should not necessarily look for typical arrangements. It is possible that the commander's residence was situated in the as yet unexplored southern part of the fort, alongside the barracks. It is indeed possible that there was no commanding officer's residence at all at this time; that the garrison was too small to merit a separate residence for the commander or that it was more expedient to build granaries than a residence, an argument which is strengthened if one considers the possibility that the cross-hall of the period II Headquarters building was converted to a store-building at this time. This somewhat circular argument cannot be stressed overmuch, but nevertheless, when considering the date of the sleeper-walls in the cross-hall one can only argue in general terms, and a Severan date makes better sense than any other.

In all, counting the Hadrianic linked pair as two on this occasion, as many as sixteen granaries, possibly seventeen if one includes the Headquarters building, are known from their remains, whether fragmentarily or almost completely. Simple extrapolation suggests that, were the fort to be completely uncovered, the remains of twenty-three in all would be found. This is an extremely large number, probably greater than in any fort of its size in the whole Roman empire. As Richmond perspicaciously saw in the 1930's the site was a supply base for the Severan campaigns. South Shields handled expendable supplies, corn in particular, in contrast with the contemporary depot at Corbridge which handled arms.

South Shields is sometimes spoken of as if it were a supply base for Hadrian's wall. In fact, the garrison of some 16,000 on Hadrian's wall, probably less than a third of the size of the army which campaigned with Severus in Scotland, was probably able to live, up to a point, on local supplies. Even as late as the eighteenth century, in a good season, corn was exported from Northumberland to countries which had had a bad season. The balance of the Wall's requirements would be met from further south in England, and the corn would quite certainly come by sea, and not by land, which in ancient times was an extremely expensive method of transport. The corn would not be offloaded at South Shields; there would be no point in this. Even before the Tyne was dredged, at the beginning of the nineteenth century, ocean-going ships could sail as far inland as Newcastle, though the journey was slow as they could not negotiate the shallower stretches at low tide. There is no need to suppose that Roman ships had any greater difficulty, and it is of course known, from epigraphic evidence, that troop-ships sailed right into Newcastle. The South Shields base has nothing to do with imports and exports; it is a staging post and reservoir on the journey from the richer corn-growing lands further south in England, to the Severan theatre of war in Scotland. The reservoir was doubtless topped-up from local supplies which would be the more readily available as the sedentary garrison was at that time so much reduced. So far from being a supply-base for Hadrian's wall, South Shields was linked least strongly with the Wall when it was a supply-base, and, when its links with the Wall were strongest, it was a perfectly ordinary fort.

Several other supply-bases are known in Britain, or may be inferred, quite reasonably, to have existed. At Richborough, in north-east Kent, a supply-base is dated from very shortly after the Claudian conquest to about the time of the close of Agricola's northern campaigns. About a dozen timber granaries are known, from their remains on the site, and there may well have been more, as the full extent of the supply-base is unknown. As the base was in existence for quite a long period of time, during, in fact, the whole of the conquest period in Britain, the granaries were in existence long enough to undergo structural modification. Whether corn ships sailing from Richborough to Strathmore called in at a staging post and reservoir on the Tyne is not known. If they did, such a base, as has already been said, was on a different site from the Severan base. After South Shields itself, Richborough is the most fully known supply-base in Britain (cf. Cunliffe, 1968). At Fishbourne in west Sussex, the remains are even scantier, but parts of a timber supply-base, including at least one granary, are known below the remains of the Flavian palace. This, like Richborough, seems to have been constructed shortly after the Claudian invasion. It has been suggested that it may have formed a base for the campaigns of Vespasian in south-west England (cf. Cunliffe, 1971). It is possible to infer the existence of several other supply-bases in Britain, of various dates and in various locations. The two probable examples most closely connected with South Shields are Cramond, in Lothian, on the south side of the Firth of Forth, and Carpow, in Tayside, on the south side of the Firth of Tay. These were probably on the receiving end of supplies travelling north from South Shields. Carpow is much larger than South Shields; it has, in fact, the size and character of a vexillation fortress, and probably did not function exclusively as a supply-base, though it may have included this function alongside others. The closest functional parallel to South Shields is the site of Rödgen, in the Wetterau, in West Germany. The base, which is self-contained, is about half as large again as South Shields and is irregular in plan. Its interior buildings were entirely of timber. They consist, principally, of three enormous granaries, the total area of the three being greater than the total area of the twenty-two at South Shields. In addition there were barrack blocks for an estimated garrison of at least 500. The only other building appears to have been a small combined Headquarters building and commanding officer's house. Rödgen, like South Shields, seems to have had a short life as a base. Coin

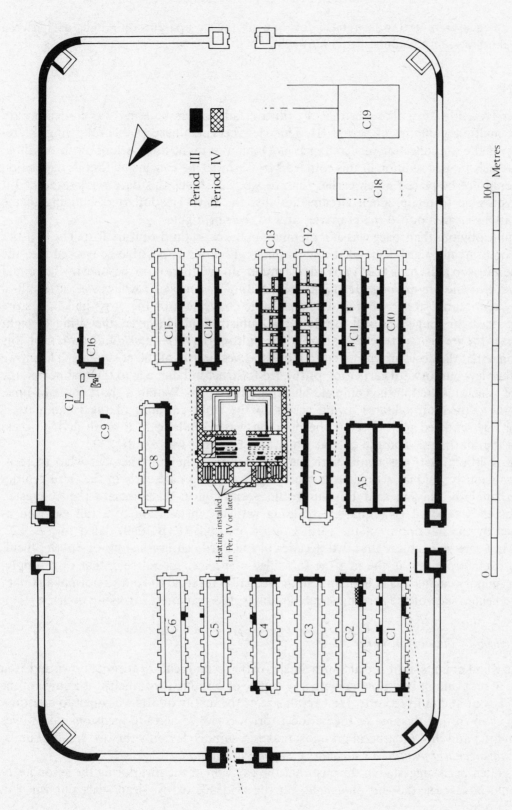

C19

C18

C13

C12

C15

C14

C11

C10

C16

C17

C9

C8

C7

A5

Heating installed
in Per. IV or later

C6

C5

C4

C3

C2

C1

0

100 Metres

Fig. 22. Periods III and IV.

evidence suggests that it was a base for one of the campaigns of Augustus between 10 B.C. and 8 B.C. (cf. Schönberger, 1976).

Period IV

Until very recently it was thought that the third Headquarters building was contemporary with the multiple granaries of period III. This view became unacceptable following the rediscovery in the site collection of a coin of Julia Domna from the foundations of the building. The extremely worn condition of this coin led Mr. Casey to the conclusion that its deposition date should not be placed much earlier than *c*. A.D. 220. Once this date was established it became possible to relate, albeit circumstantially, the third Headquarters building to the modifications carried out to the granaries and to the north gate.

It is quite obvious that space was at a premium in the early third-century fort. The logistics of the Scottish campaigns demanded that as many granaries as possible be packed into the fort. The garrison must have been reduced to a minimum and there is no reason why they could not have used the pre-existing Headquarters building of period II, which was, after all, a perfectly serviceable stone building. Even with the conversion of the cross-hall to a store building, the rear range was still usable for administration. However, the siting of eight granaries in the *praetentura* severely narrowed the width of the *via praetoria* and it was probably at this time that the decision was taken to block the west portal of the north gate. This, if we accept the view put forward earlier (cf. p. 16), led to structural damage to the east portal, the repair of which resulted in the complete blocking of the gate. Within a short space of time, one of the main thoroughfares giving access to the front entrance of the Headquarters building was rendered useless. Thus the building was re-built to face south giving access through the south gate, and the date at which this occurred was *c*. A.D. 220.

There is little pottery associated with the conversion of the granaries but what there is, though obviously residual, would seem more suggestive of a date early in the third century rather than late. Having said this, it would seem logical to associate the converted granaries and the third Headquarters building with the installation of a full garrison as evidenced by the inscription of the Fifth Cohort of Gauls (RIB 1060) dated to A.D. 222. Thus, what emerge from the first two decades of the third-century history of South Shields are two distinct periods: in the first the fort filled a specific, special role, that of a supply-base for military campaigns in Scotland; in the second it reverted to being a normal auxiliary fort, use being made of the existing stone buildings, the granaries, for living quarters.

The Garrison of the Fort in Periods I–IV

The actual unit or units stationed at South Shields in the second century are not known and even the type of unit cannot be estimated with any degree of certainty. Insufficient is known of the internal layout and until recently, the overall size of the first two forts was open to question. It is now known that the area of the period I fort was *c*. 3·75 acres (dimensions taken over the ramparts) and this, on general grounds, makes it suitable for only the two smallest units, a *cohors quingenaria peditata* or a *cohors quingenaria equitata*.

It has often been suggested in the past that the garrison of the fort during the second century could have been the *Ala Sabiniana*, on the evidence of two lead seals published in

Ephemeris Epigraphica (iii, 202 and iv, 706). In fact, it is highly likely that these two seals are the same seal reproduced twice with slightly different readings. Only one seal is recorded by Hooppell (1878, p. 79) and Bruce (1884, p. 233) and only one seal is now extant. The reverse reads ALSA, with ligatured AL. The obverse reading is difficult and the lead has deteriorated in modern times. Richmond was of the opinion that it read (C)VG (1934, p. 102, no. 19). The two readings given in *Ephemeris Epigraphica* are VRN and VBA. It could be either of these but is highly unlikely, in fact, to be CVG.

What is sometimes overlooked is that the seals could not have originated at South Shields. Lead sealings of this kind would have been used much as they are used today, by military, customs and other official state bodies for sealing crates, boxes, doors or lids. It is logical to assume that, as today, they would have been stamped with the insignia or initial of the unit or person despatching them as proof of their intact state at the time of despatch. Thus, the places where the seals turn up today, are the places where the articles which they sealed were sent to, but the seals themselves refer to the places where they were sent from. This was the case at Brough-under-Stainmore, where 133 seals, including stamps of an imperial nature, of the second and sixth legions, and of eight auxiliary units were found (Richmond, 1939). Thus, these seals came into South Shields from elsewhere, and the *Ala Sabiniana* cannot have formed the garrison of the fort.

Another unit loosely associated with the site is the *Ala I Asturum*, the unit of Numerianus patron of Victor whose tombstone was found on the site (RIB 1064). Whether Numerianus or his unit was ever at South Shields is again uncertain.

More is known of the early third century garrison. The unit in question is the *Cohors V Gallorum*, the epigraphic evidence for which is as follows:

1) RIB 1060 records the installation of a water supply for the use of the *Cohors V Gallorum* through the agency of the governor Marius Valerianus. The emperor is Severus Alexander and the attributes of singular tribunician power and consulship date the inscription precisely to A.D. 222/3.

2) Many *tegulae* were found bearing the stamp CVG, which can reasonably be restored as *Cohors V Gallorum*. These included several from the well which could have come from the roof of the third Headquarters building.

3) Of the many lead seals from the site a number (four are still extant, cf. p. 164, nos. 12–15) bear the stamp CVG.

4) RIB 2134, from Cramond, is an altar with the dedication IOM set up collectively by the *Cohors V Gallorum* under its prefect Lucius Minthonius Tertullus. The letters IOM are on the capital, not the die which, as Dr. Kewley has shown (cf. Kewley, 1973), is a third-century characteristic.

The evidence of RIB 1060 is unimpeachable, and means that the *Cohors V Gallorum* was at South Shields in A.D. 222/3. The stamped tiles could equally well belong to the same period. The function of lead sealings has already been discussed. The date of the CVG seals is not known but the inference is that at the time when they arrived at South Shields the unit was *not* stationed there. It is by no means impossible that the altar from Cramond dates to the time of Septimius Severus. The third-century occupation of Cramond seems to have been short and specifically linked with the Severan campaigns in Scotland. There are no coins later than Julia Domna and while the dating of third-century pottery is notoriously difficult there is very little, in fact, that is later than Antonine (leaving aside the pottery from the fourth-century occupation), (cf. Rae, 1974). The logical conclusion to be drawn from all this is that in the early years of the third century, during the campaigns in Scotland, the *Cohors V Gallorum* was stationed at Cramond, from whence came the CVG seals found at South Shields, and that by A.D. 222 it had moved, whether directly or not, to South Shields.

It has been necessary to state all this in somewhat categoric fashion because until recently it was thought possible that the *Cohors V Gallorum* was split between Cramond and South Shields and later re-united at Shields. The reason for this was that as long as the third Headquarters building was thought to date to the time of the Severan campaigns there was a possibility that the CVG tiles also dated to this time, and it is evident that only a small part of a normal auxiliary unit could have been accommodated while the fort functioned as a supply-base. That the unit was split between the two sites has not been ultimately disproved but what little supportive evidence there was, has, for the time being, vanished.

Post Period IV

The structures of the supply-base are the latest coherent structures anywhere on the site. While there is evidence of later occupation there does not seem to have been anything amounting to a coherent re-building. The modifications to the Headquarters building (the insertion of underfloor heating in the administrative offices on either side of the sunken strong-room of the rear range) cannot be dated, beyond saying that they occurred after A.D. 222. The fragmentary structures over the north gate can be dated on general grounds to the fourth century. The tile kilns in granary A5 are securely, though not precisely, dated by a small, but internally consistent group of pottery, to the turn of the third and fourth centuries. The patches of paving above building A3 seal pottery of a date no earlier than the middle of the fourth century. There is no evidence from the coins of a significant break in the occupation of the site though Mr. Casey does make the point that it is uncertain how much of the coinage relates to the site and how much, from the old collections, to the external settlement. Among the coarse pottery two points are worthy of note: the pottery from the supposed site of the civil settlement to the west of the fort contained almost no vessels from the fourth-century industry in east Yorkshire and only one vessel of a type which, on the evidence of Birdoswald and the Yorkshire Signal Sations, is usually considered to be post A.D. 367; among the pottery from both inside and outside the fort there is an absence of the latest types of Black Burnished Ware Category 1, those types which occur immediately before the flood of products from the east Yorkshire kilns (e.g. Gillam, 1976, nos. 12–14). Whether this can be regarded as evidence for a break in occupation of the site is uncertain for, as with BB2 and the dating of the Antonine fort, a word of warning is needed. Being an east coast site and thus possibly further from the centres of BB1 production than anywhere else in England, and bearing in mind that at the turn of the third and fourth centuries the area of BB1 distribution was probably shrinking anyway due to economic factors, South Shields could simply not have received the latest types rather than there not being anyone there to receive them.

From the evidence, or rather from the lack of it, there would not seem to have been a general re-building on the site at the time of Constantius Chlorus, as there certainly was at Birdoswald (cf. Richmond and Birley, 1930) and Housesteads (cf. Wilkes, 1961) and probably was at Great Chesters and Chesters. With regard to the pottery sequence in the vicus

the situation is exactly paralleled at Housesteads where "excavations in the vicus . . . .
have as yet produced not a single piece of pottery assignable to Wall period IV" (Wilkes,
1961, pp. 289, 290). Wilkes' hypothesis, following Bosanquet, was that "after 368 the
population lived entirely within the fort" (*op. cit.* p. 290) and such would also seem to have
been the case at South Shields except that the date when this commenced can be advanced,
on the pottery evidence from the tile kilns, to the late third or early fourth century.

Military occupation of the site at some time during the fourth century is attested by the
Notitia Dignitatum where a *Praefectus numeri barcariorum Tigrisiensium* is recorded at
Arbeia (cf. p. 1). The entry forms part of the command of the *Dux Britanniarum* which
included nine other *numeri*, three units of cavalry (*equites*) and a legion, and a collection of
cohorts and *alae* along the line of the wall (*item per lineam valli*). Leaving aside the
item per lineam valli section, whose date may be in dispute anyway, it would seem that the
higher grade troops, the *legio*, *equites* and *numeri*, of the main part of the Duke's command
together formed a mobile tactical group which was intended to reinforce the static troops on
the frontier and to repulse sea-borne attacks on the north-east coast. It has all the elements
of a coherent, localised, defensive group: legionary infantry supported by highly mobile
cavalry units with the more specialised *numeri*, (*barcarii*, *vigiles*, *exploratores*, *directores*,
defensores), placed at strategic intervals. The date at which the command was instituted
is likely to have been some time during the first quarter of the fourth century. The Birdoswald inscription (RIB 1912), which shows the Wall to have been under the command of a
praeses, makes it unlikely that it existed before A.D. 296/305 and the designation of the
equites at *Danum* as *Crispiani* (*Caesar Crispus*, A.D. 317–326) suggests that the units were
established before A.D. 326.

Units of *barcarii* are known in a number of places. In Britain a similar unit, though almost
certainly not the same one as at South Shields, as Dr. Shotter has pointed out (cf. Shotter,
1973), is attested on an inscription from Halton-on-Lune, three miles upstream from
Lancaster (RIB 601). Elsewhere they are known at Benian (*CIL* viii, 21568), Bregenz
(Not. Dig. Occ. XXXV, 32) and Ebrudunum Sapaudiae (*ibid.* XLII, 15). It is usually
assumed that the duties of this type of unit were those of lighterage and transportation of goods
from sea-going vessels up the river on which the unit was stationed. Dr. Shotter (*op. cit.*)
argues that the units in Britain, during the last stages of the Roman occupation, may have
been called upon to undertake a more combatant role in the defense of a river estuary
against sea-borne incursions but, if our view of the Duke's command as a coherent tactical
group is correct, then it would seem reasonable to suggest that the *barcarii Tigrisienses* were
intended to fulfill a combatant role from the first. How efficient and well trained a unit
they were is difficult to assess and raises questions concerning the general fighting efficiency
of the *limitanei*. Though they were obviously regarded as inferior to units of the field army
there is no reason to believe that, in general, within their localised spheres, limitanean units
did not represent a well disciplined and efficient fighting force.

To summarise, from the available evidence, the following hypothesis emerges. Some time
before the end of the third century the garrison of the fort, be it the fifth cohort of Gauls or
whoever, departed. There was no military occupation or re-building under Constantius
Chlorus. During the absence of the military the population of the *vicus* moved inside the
fort, where they were responsible for the building of the tile kilns inside granary A5, and
they continued to live there up to and throughout the last military occupation of the fort.

Some time during the first quarter of the fourth century the *numerus barcariorum Tigrisiensium* was installed in the fort from where it operated in defense of the Tyne estuary as part of the tactical force under the disposition of the *Dux Britanniarum*. From numismatic evidence, occupation on the site continued into the early years of the fifth century.

THE FINDS

A note is, perhaps, necessary here to explain the arrangement of the finds reports.

All the coins recovered from the site up to 1976 are included. All but the illegible fragments of stamped samian and all but the smallest fragments of decorated and plain samian recovered from the site up to 1973 are included. The stratified coarseware from the excavations of 1966 and 1967, a selection of the unstratified coarseware from the excavations of 1966, 1967 and 1973, and a selection of the coarseware from the collections of the Roman Fort Museum at South Shields and the Joint Museum of the Society of Antiquaries and the University of Newcastle upon Tyne are included. It was felt advisable to include as much of this primary dating evidence as possible although the report deals, in the main, only with the excavations of 1966 and 1967. Of the small finds from 1966 and 1967 only the glass has been included as the rest were in such small quantities and in such poor condition. A list of the extant lead seals has been included for reference purposes. A full catalogue of the small objects in the Roman Fort Museum at South Shields is forthcoming.

THE COINS FROM SOUTH SHIELDS (fig. 23)

John Casey

The coins from South Shields form one of the largest collections from a military site in Britain and are second only to Corbridge among collections associated with forts of the northern frontier. Unfortunately this important body of material, the result of a century of excavation and collection, has suffered a number of vicissitudes which makes the establishment of a site record difficult in the extreme.

The primary collection from the site consists of the material recovered in the excavations conducted by R. E. Hooppell between 1875 and 1877. These coins, listed simply by occurrence of emperors and members of the imperial family in Hooppell's account,[1]* were fully listed by J. Collingwood Bruce in his fuller report on the excavations.[2] Both lists were the work of Robert Blair, and the later list, which consists of obverse and reverse descriptions, supersedes the earlier. No attempt was made to define which coins were found during the course of the excavations since the catalogue includes all items from South Shields known to Blair; they are described as "... coins discovered within and near the Roman camp at South Shields (1874–1884) which have passed through the hands of R. Blair." Items contained in the list include material in Blair's own collection and in those of South Shields Museum and two local collectors, T. Wint and T. J. Bell. In the period following the excavations further items were recovered from the site by "... private speculators (who) have assiduously dug and sifted the ground, finding, as their reward, numberless articles. These they sell, for the highest prices they can obtain ...". Among those who appear to have purchased numismatic items from these "speculators" was W. Clapham whose collection was later recorded.

The Blair list includes a considerable number of coins that can be identified as part, or whole, of a hoard of *aurei* and *denarii* closing with issues of Commodus. The existence of this hoard was first made known in 1885,[3] and subsequent research by J. H. Corbitt has established that the hoard, consisting of twelve *aurei* and about two hundred *denarii*, was discovered in 1878 and that coins from the hoard were sold to the Duke of Northumberland.[4] Fifty-three *denarii* from the hoard are still to be found in the Alnwick Castle Collection and these items have been published by Corbitt. All of the coins so listed are to be found in Blair's site list, though one is given a specific find spot by Blair which precludes its inclusion in the hoard.[5] In the same list appear eleven *aurei* and a further sixty-two *denarii* which cover the period of the hoard. Evidently the hoard had been accessible to Blair who, for whatever reason, chose to list its components as individual items without allusion to their collective status. The coincidence between the recorded contents of the hoard, the established fact that items from it in Alnwick correspond with published items and the numbers of items in Blair's list make it almost certain that the contents of the hoard can be re-established from the published material. A further coin from the hoard may have escaped Blair's notice having been incorporated in another private collection, that of T. J. Bell.

* References indicated by superscript figures in the text of this chapter are to be found on page 96.
 References indicated by superscript figures in Lists of Coins appear at foot of relevant page.

The Bell Collection, first alluded to by Hooppell, was bequeathed to the Society of Antiquaries of Newcastle upon Tyne. Unfortunately, the coins and the envelopes in which they were stored had become disassociated so that individual provenances had been lost. An attempt to re-establish the South Shields element of the collection was made and sixteen were published, in summary detail, with mention of a further forty-five illegible specimens from South Shields from a collection total of three hundred and forty-seven coins.[6] A further listing of the Bell Collection was made by J. H. Corbitt who added twenty-eight provenanced coins to the site list. Among these new items was an *aureus* of Hadrian described as having been found in 1880 but which is probably an item from the 1878 hoard. Bell's enthusiasm for enhancing his collection extended to purchasing coins imported by seamen from overseas and at least four items regarded by Corbitt as site finds seem to be from such sources (p. 92).

A further important element in the site record consists of thirty-nine coins in the possession of W. Clapham, of Darlington. These had been purchased from the "prospectors" at South Shields; presumably these "prospectors" were Hooppell's "private speculators". The collection was listed by R. Blair in 1911 when it was recorded that they had been obtained "about 30 years ago".[7]

The largest extant collection of material associated with the fort is that in the Roman Fort Museum, South Shields. This collection comprises a number of elements of which coins from recent excavations by the South Shields Archaeological and Historical Society present few difficulties. However, the bulk of the collection of six hundred and seventy-four coins are without specific provenance. Further, it is clear that kind benefactions of non-local coins have been made to the Museum and that these have been incorporated in the collection. These items include a number of Arab coins, a Byzantine piece and eastern and Balkan mint Roman coins which are intruders into the well established supply pattern of currency in Roman Britain.

From time to time the *Proceedings* of the Society of Antiquaries of Newcastle upon Tyne reported the finding of Roman coins on the beaches in the vicinity of the South Shields fort after storms. These finds comprise three groups, those from the Trow Rocks, those from the Herd Sands and those from South Shields Beach. Some of the items in these records are known to have been incorporated in the Bell Collection.[8]

Because of the somewhat random nature of the recording of finds hitherto it is necessary to establish a set of procedures to be applied uniformly to the material. The Blair list, of seven hundred and seventy-six Roman coins, has been accepted as the basis for the catalogue. These coins, though frequently garbled in description, can be catalogued to modern references. In the event all but one or two coins have been assigned to references in the appropriate volumes of *The Roman Imperial Coinage* or, for the fourth-century coins to *Late Roman Bronze Coinage*. A similar recataloguing has been undertaken for the Bell Collection, as recorded by J. H. Corbitt, the Clapham Collection and the Roman Fort Museum Collection. In listing the coins from these collections in a single sequence it has been necessary to take cognisance of the possibility that coins owned by Bell, or which were then in South Shields Museum, had already been listed by Blair. In the event the assumption has been made that any coin duplicated in any of these three collections is the same coin and is listed once only. Whilst this prevents the duplication of the same specimen, and is thus useful in general terms, it must be recognised that cataloguing coins from century old descriptions leaves room for ambiguity and that coins which differ in significant minor details may have been catalogued as similar items. It is also more than possible that under this procedure very common coins, such as might be expected to occur in more than single specimens in site coin lists, may be under-represented. Nonetheless, the overall effect of such possible errors will not be of great statistical significance in as large a coin list as that of South Shields.

In the following listing of the coins from the old collections an attempt has been made to compress the references to as small a compass as is consonant with a full recording of the material:

1) Blair list coins are printed in *plain* type.
2) Bell Collection coins are indicated by an *asterisk* *.
3) Clapham Collection coins are indicated by a *diesis* ‡.
4) The Roman Fort Museum Collection coins are *italicised*.
5) When a Blair list coin is thought to be represented either in the Museum or the Bell Collections the appropriate extant coin bears a footnote reference to the Blair coin which has been excluded from the list. The item in the Blair list is noted in a footnote with reference to the appropriate page and item number in Collingwood Bruce's paper. When a Blair coin can be shewn *not* to be identical with a similar extant coin it is listed.

Hoards have been removed from the general listing of coins. Only one hoard is recorded from South Shields, the *aureus* and *denarius* hoard discussed above. However, a listing of the material and a collation of published lists with extant coins makes it clear that the contents of at least three other hoards are scattered among the recorded and surviving coins. The unprecedented proportion of coins of the period 317 to 330 is indicative of an early Constantinian hoard. This conclusion is reinforced by an examination of the coins of this period in the Fort Museum collection where most of the coins exhibit similar characteristics, being in virtually unworn condition and displaying a uniform patina. The incidence of hoards of this period is high and the incidence of individual site finds relatively small.[9] The anomalous position of the South Shields coins can be demonstrated by reference to other northern sites, themselves representative of the rest of the island. If we plot the proportions of earlier (317–330) to later (330–48) Constantinian coins we can see a reasonable degree of uniformity:[10]

	317–30		330–48	
	No.	%	*No.*	%
Binchester	38	= 21	143	= 79
Corbridge	249	= 12	1823	= 88
Housesteads	12	= 24	38	= 76
Malton	22	= 13·7	138	= 86.3
South Shields	97	= 44	123	= 56

If it is admitted that South Shields presents an anomaly and that this anomaly is the result of the records of site finds containing a hoard, in the same manner as the *aureus* and *denarius* hoard, how can the matter be rectified? The expedient adopted here is to assign to the status of hoard all items in the Fort Museum Collection which display the characteristics noted above i.e. unworn condition and similar patina. For the coins which are no longer available for inspection a rule of thumb device has been adopted, all coins in the Blair list which are described in full detail, that is in a condition in which all inscriptions, fieldmarks and mintmarks could be transcribed, are assumed to be in the unworn condition of the extant coins. The result of this treatment is to bring the South Shields coins, designated as site finds, into the proportion of 12·3 per cent early Constantinian to 87·7 per cent later Constantinian. These figures are within the range established for the other quoted sites with unambiguous evidence for the coins being individual items rather than components of a hoard. Even so the adoption of this expedient, the minimum of "hoard" coins and an over-representation of the coinage of this period almost certainly persists in the figures used to compute the histogram of the South Shields coins.

A similar situation exists in the coinage of another period normally ill-represented by site finds. The incidence of coins of Magnentius, and his brother Decentius, as individual finds is normally very small. The Roman Fort Museum Collection contains a number of Magnentian coins in uncirculated condition and of uniform patina. Further the published lists contain unprecedentedly high proportions of Magnentian issues; manifestly a hoard exists which has become integrated into the general list, once more. As with the earlier Constantinian "hoard", elimination of the Museum items and listed items which seem to claim hoard status has been undertaken. It is unlikely that the elimination of these items solves the problem of the over-representation of coins of the period 340–61 illustrated by the site histogram; numerous issues of Constans and Constantius II are present, again in uncirculated condition. However the criteria for withdrawing these items are not as clear cut as those for Magnentius. It is best in these circumstances to err on the side of caution. It is considered that the thirteen western mint, early tetrarchic coins purchased by Clapham constitutes whole, or part of a further hoard.

CATALOGUE

References

C.	Cohen, H. *Description historique des monnaies frappees sous l'empire romain.* 2nd ed. (1880–1).
CB.	Bruce, 1884
BMCRE.	*Catalogue of coins of the Roman Empire in the British Museum*
D.O.	*Byzantine coins in the Dumbarton Oaks and Whittemore Collections*
LRBC.1/2.	Carson, R. A., Hull, P. V. and Kent, J. P. C., *Late Roman bronze coinage.*
RIC.	Mattingly, H. and Sydenham, E. A. *Roman imperial coinage.*
S.	Sydenham, E. A. *The coinage of the Roman Republic.* 2nd ed. (1952).

Condition

The condition of the coins, from the recent excavation, at the moment of loss has been indicated by a notation of the wear displayed where this can be ascertained. This is a subjective assessment and has no absolute chronological significance.

UW/UW — unworn obverse, unworn reverse. A virtually uncirculated coin.
SW   — slightly worn. The highest relief slightly flattened by wear.
W   — worn. The relief abraded but all details of legends visible.
VW   — very worn. Considerable abrasion, legends indistinct.
EW   — extremely worn. Great erosion of details and legends.

REPUBLIC	*Den.* as S. 376
M. ANTONIUS	*Den.* as S. 1216
NERO	*As* RIC. *329/30*
VESPASIAN	*Den.* RIC. as 29‡, 101
	Dup. Illegible (1)
	Dup./As Illegible (1)[1]
	As RIC. 528‡
TITUS	*Den.* RIC. 11[2]
DOMITIAN	*Den.* RIC. *173*
	Sest. RIC. *342b, 344*
	Dup. RIC. as *331*
	Dup./As RIC. as 246[3], Illegible (3)[4]
TRAJAN	*Den.* RIC. *6, 104, 115, 120, 129*
	Sest. RIC. as 388, *390, 483*[5], 489 etc., *503*[6], ? 510, *519,* as 534, 547, Illegible (5)
	Dup. RIC. as *387, 605, 644, Illegible* (1)[7]
	Dup./As Illegible (3)
	As RIC. 434, 442, 459, *Illegible* (1)
HADRIAN	*Den.* RIC. *169, Illegible plated* copy (1)
	Sest. RIC. 562b, 563a, *563b*(3), *743,* 745d, *759/60, 770, 777,* 938c, *975* var.[8]
	As RIC. 673, Illegible (2). Illegible (3)
ANTONINUS PIUS	*Den.* RIC. *51,* 175[9]
	Sest. RIC. 612, 617, *619,*[10] 772, *967*(2), 1055b, Illegible (2)
	Dup. RIC. 551, 552, *554, 908,* as *920,* as *933*
	As RIC. *705a,* 934, *Illegible* (1)
FAUSTINA I	*Den.* RIC. *344, 377, 394a*
(Ant. Pius)	*Sest.* RIC. 1108, as 1126, Illegible (1)
	Dup./As RIC. 1155, *1162*(2), *1163*(2), *1171*

[1] CB. p. 56. "Found with two others on clay, about eight feet below present (? 1886) surface, near Thornton St., and a little east of road leading to Tyne Dock." See also 3.

[2] Listed as a hoard coin by Corbitt but in CB. p. 56 2 as "... found at back of Hedley Street."

[3] Found near Thornton St.

[4] CB. p. 57. Illegible *Dup./As* found in urn in Bath St.

[5] CB. p. 59 2(4)

[6] CB. p. 59 2(6)

[7] CB. p. 60 3

[8] Listed only as *As* in RIC.

[9] Found Baring St., 1976

[10] CB. p. 63 1(6)

FAUSTINA II (Ant. Pius)	*Den.* RIC. *502a* *Sest.* RIC. 1371* *Dup./As* RIC. *1405a*[11]
MARCUS AURELIUS, Caes. (Ant. Pius)	*Sest.* RIC. *1314/21* *Dup./As* RIC. as 1354 etc. *Aureus* RIC. 474(a)
MARCUS AURELIUS	*Sest.* RIC. *797, 911/23*, 929, *1005*,[12] 1230, Illegible (1) *Dup.* RIC. 965 var.[13]
LUCIUS VERUS	*Sest.* RIC. *1308/10*
LUCILLA (Marcus Aurelius)	*Den.* RIC. *781*[14] *Sest.* RIC. *1755, 1765*
FAUSTINA II (Marcus Aurelius)	*Sest.* RIC. *1668*[15]
COMMODUS (Marcus Aurelius)	*Sest.* RIC. ? 1524
COMMODUS	*Den.* RIC. *122a* *Sest.* RIC. *371(2)*, 441A, *495*, Illegible (1), *Illegible (1)* *As* RIC. 393
CRISPINA (Commodus)	*Sest.* RIC. *655*

SEPTIMIUS SEVERUS	*Den.* RIC. as 56, 57, *61*, 85, 87, 99, *111a*, as 113, 122c,
	  166, 168a, *176*,[16] *196*,[17] *198/208*,[18] 211, *265*,[19] as
	  266
	Dup. RIC. *802*

JULIA DOMNA	*Den.* RIC. 551, 557, 564, 574
GETA	*Den.* RIC. *2*,[20] 3, *13*,[21] 18, 30, 34
CARACALLA	*Den.* RIC. 2 var.,[22] 11, 33, 196, *214*, 232 *Ant.* RIC. 280
PLAUTILLA	*Den.* RIC. 363

SEVERAN COPIES
  SEVERUS
	Den. RIC. *1/PIETAS AVG … COS 11*,[23] *IMP SEV
	  PIVS AVG/150*,[24] *122/Geta 15a, 1/Geta 13a, 258*

GETA	*Den.* RIC. *1/Severus 196, Illegible (2)*
CARACALLA	*Den.* RIC. as *239/Domna 377*,[25] *Illegible (1)*
MACRINUS	*Den.* RIC. 80
ELAGABALUS	*Den.* RIC. 28/40, 42a, 87/8, 141, 146, 162, *220* var.[26]

---

[11] CB. p. 66
[12] CB. p. 65 1(1)
[13] RIC. quotes *As* only
[14] CB. p. 66 1(2)
[15] CB. p. 65
[16] CB. p. 67 5(2)
[17] CB. p. 67 5(3)
[18] CB. p. 68 (5)

[19] CB. p. 67 5(1)
[20] CB. p. 69 2(1)
[21] CB. p. 69 1(1)
[22] Obverse variant, as RIC. 6(b)
[23] CB. p. 68 9
[24] CB. p. 68 7
[25] CB. p. 64 4
[26] No star on rev.

AQUILIA SEVERA   *Den*. RIC. 225/7
JULIA SOEMIAS   *Den*. RIC. 237(2), 243
SEVERUS ALEXANDER   *Den*. RIC. 5, as 7, 23, 27(2), 45, 73*, 89, 110, *133*,[27]
                               168,[28] 173, 205(2), 219a, 236, 285, *Illegible* (1)
                               Plated copy *110*
                               As RIC. 624

JULIA MAMAEA   *Den*. RIC. 335, 338, 341, *343*,[29] (2), 360
MAXIMINUS   *Den*. RIC. 13, 14
GORDIAN III   *Ant*. RIC. 54, 55, 64, 88, 93, 95, 241*, *Illegible* (1)
                               Plated copy *1/95*

PHILIP I   *Ant*. RIC. *28c*, *94*[30]
TRAJAN DECIUS   *Ant*. RIC. 28, Plated copy *10b/Philip 63b*[31]
HERENNIA ETRUSCILLA   *Ant*. Copy RIC. 55b/Gordian III 88
VOLUSIAN   *Ant*. RIC. *141*, 193
                               Sest. RIC. 251

VALERIAN   *Ant*. RIC. 71, *72*, 89*[32] *117*,[33] 126/7, 293
GALLIENUS   *Ant*. RIC. *159*,[34] *163*,[35] 164, 166, *176/181*, 179(4),
(sole reign)   *181(2)*, 181‡, *207*,[36]*(2)*, 207*, 208(2), 230, 244, 245,
                               249, *256*,[37] 280, *283*, *287*,[38] (2), 297, *299*,[39] *325*,
                               465a, 468a, 488, *572*, 585, *Illegible* (3), Illegible (3)

SALONINA   *Ant*. RIC. *13*, 13(2), *24*, *25*, *67*
(sole reign)
SALONINUS   *Ant*. RIC. 7
POSTUMUS   *Ant*. RIC. 58, *60*, *67*,[40] 73, *89*,[41] 90, 93, 93‡, 309, 311,
                               316, *318*,[42] (3), 337, *Illegible* (1)
                               Sest. RIC. 123

VICTORINUS   *Ant*. RIC. 40, 41*, *55*, *57* (3), *61*,[43] (2), *67*,[44] (4) as
                               67, *71*,[45] (4), *78*,[46] (4), *105*, *114*,[47] 114*, *118*,[48] (6),
                               118*

TETRICUS I   *Ant*. RIC. 56*[49], *56/9*, 68, *70*, *76/81*(3), 79, 87, 88,
                               89, *89/90*, *90*(4)[50] *100*(4),[51] ? 100, *100/101*, *100/2*(2),
                               100/4, *101/2*, *106*, 123, *127*, 130 etc.‡, *130/2*, *136*,[52]
                               141, 145, 148, *Illegible* (5)

[27] CB. p. 71 3(1)   [40] CB. p. 74 (3)
[28] CB. p. 71 3(7)   [41] CB. p. 75 (10)
[29] CB. p. 71 1(4)   [42] CB. p. 75 (8)
[30] CB. p. 72 (1)   [43] CB. p. 75 (4)
[31] CB. p. 72 2   [44] CB. p. 75 (7)
[32] CB. p. 73 1(2)   [45] CB. p. 75 (5)
[33] CB. p. 73 2(1)   [46] CB. p. 75 (8)
[34] CB. p. 73 1(1)   [47] CB. p. 75 (2)
[35] CB. p. 74 (15)   [48] CB. p. 75 (3)
[36] CB. p. 73 (9), (10)   [49] CB. p. 75 1(1)
[37] CB. p. 74 (18)   [50] CB. p. 75 1(5)
[38] CB. p. 74 (21)   [51] CB. p. 76 (6)
[39] CB. p. 74 (22)   [52] CB. p. 76 (7)

TETRICUS II   *Ant.* RIC. 224, 234, 235, 238*, 238/9*,[53] 248,[54] (2), 255, 258, *258/9*, 260, *270*,[55] *270/2*(2), *270/4*, 272,[56] (6), *Illegible* (1)

CLAUDIUS II   *Ant.* RIC. 14, 18, *32*,[57] ? *33*, 34/8, *36*, 39, *40/3*, 46, 48, 49*, 56, 60, 66(2), *72*, 91, 98, 104, *109*, *109/10*, 111, 113(2), 151, *157*, 159, 172, Illegible (2), *Illegible* (2), Illegible (1)‡

CLAUDIUS II, Posthumous   *Ant.* RIC. *261/2*(8), 261, 261‡, *266*,[58] (3)

QUINTILLUS   *Ant.* RIC. 6, *20*,[59] Illegible (1)

GALLIC EMPIRE   *Ant.* RIC. Illegible (8)

RADIATE COPIES (Reference is given to the orthodox prototype)

GALLIENUS   RIC. *256*,[60] Illegible (1)

VICTORINUS   RIC. 71, *114*, 114(2), *116*(2), Illegible (1)

TETRICUS   RIC. *76/81*, *100*(5), *100/4*, *101*(2), *102*, *110/12*, *130/6* (5), *Illegible* (5)

TETRICUS II   RIC. *254*, *258*, *270*, *270/2*(3), *248*(2), Illegible (4)

CLAUDIUS II   RIC. *261/2*(2), *Illegible* (2)

QUINTILLUS   RIC. *37*

Non-specific   *Illegible* (16)[61]

AURELIAN   *Ant.* RIC. *38* var.[62]

     Post-reform. RIC. as *59*

SEVERINA   RIC. 4

PROBUS   RIC. *38*, 84, 121, 430, Illegible (1)

TACITUS   RIC. 45, 65

CARAUSIUS   RIC. *101*(3) $\dfrac{\text{B/E}}{\text{ML}}$, $\dfrac{\text{B/E}}{\text{ML}}$, $\dfrac{\text{B/E}^{63}}{\text{MLXXI}}$, 101(3) $\dfrac{1}{\text{ML}}$, $\dfrac{\text{F/O}}{\text{ML}}$,

$\dfrac{\text{B/A}}{\text{MLXXI}}$, *118* $\dfrac{\text{S/P}}{\text{ML}}$, *121*[64] $\dfrac{\text{F/O}}{\text{ML}}$, *235* var.,[65] *258*, *295*, *300*, *302*, 303, 340, 398, 471, 478, *481* var.,[66] *484*, 796, *807* var.,[67] 810, 823, 855, *881*(2), *855*, *878*, as *878*, *880*, as *899*, 903, *983*[68] (2), 1000, as *1040*, 1038, *Illegible* (1)

[53] CB. p. 76 (5)
[54] CB. p. 76 (6)
[55] CB. p. 76 (10)
[56] CB. p. 76 (9)
[57] CB. p. 76 1(3)
[58] CB. p. 77 3(2)
[59] CB. p. 78 (1)
[60] CB. p. 74 (19)
[61] Three coins with the reverse type "Fortuna" are obverse and reverse die duplicates

[62] Obv. IMP C L DOM AVRELIANVS AVG.
[63] CB. p. 80 (8)
[64] CB. p. 80 (10)
[65] RIC. quotes only for "C" mint, this unmarked
[66] *S/P* for *S/C*
[67] Rev. INVICTVS for INVICTVS AVG.
[68] CB. p. 80 (14)

Irregular. Obv. IMP CARAVSIVS PF AVG
Rev. PIETAS AVG Pietas standing to right[69]
Obv. IMP CARAVSIVS (PF AVG)

Rev. SPES ... $\dfrac{1}{RSR}$ (all retrograde)

ALLECTUS   RIC. *22,*[70] 24, *28*(2) $\dfrac{S/A}{ML}$, $\dfrac{S/P}{ML}$, *33*(2) $\dfrac{S/A}{ML}$[71] $\dfrac{S/P}{ML}$,

as 55, *69* var.,[72] 69, 91, 128, brockage (1)

DIOCLETIAN   RIC. VI (TRIER) 581
MAXIMIAN   RIC. *VI (LONDON)* 6b, VI (TRIER) 766, *Illegible* (1)
CONSTANTIUS I   RIC. *VI (LONDON)* 22, as VI (LUGDUNUM) 150,
    VI (ROME) 95a, VI (TICINUM) 32a, as VII
    (ROME) 105

SEVERUS II   RIC. VI (LONDON) 46 var.[73]
GALERIUS   RIC. VI (LONDON) 15*, VI (LONDON) 36
MAXIMINUS DAZA   RIC. VI (TRIER) 717a/720a

CONSTANTINIAN 317–30
CONSTANTINE I   RIC. VI (LONDON) 245/6, VII (LONDON) 106/7,
    as 203, *VII (TRIER) 303*(2), as 303*, 304, *368,* 449‡
    Illegible (1), *Illegible* (1)

CRISPUS   RIC. VII (LONDON) as 186, 231/2‡, as *291,* 295‡,
    VII (TRIER) as 308, 561, Copy as 440/39

CONSTANTINE II   RIC. VII (LONDON) as 181, 293, as 298, VII
    (TRIER) 463, *479,* VII (LUGDUNUM) as 217‡,
    VII (ARLES) 322/33, VII (SISCIA) 133‡, 183

CRISPUS/CONSTANTINE II   *Illegible* (2)
FAUSTA   RIC. VII (LONDON) as 26/7‡
LICINIUS I   RIC. VII (ARLES) 59,[74] 196, VII (*HERACLEA*) *as*
    13, VII (NICOMEDIA) 69a*, VII (CYZICUS) as
    4.

LICINIUS II   RIC. *VII (SISCIA) 143*

CONSTANTINIAN 330–37
CONSTANTINE I   LRBC.1. 60/2(2), 67, *92,* 650 87, *197, 1428.*
CONSTANTINE II, Caes.   LRBC.1. as 49, 49, *56*(2), *68,*[75] *73,* as 73, 88*[76],
    181(2), *187*(2), 193, *198,* 363‡, *374, 379,* as *385*‡,
    88, as *88, 93*(2), 226 etc., as *226,* 241, as *411*

[69] CB. p. 80. 13
[70] CB. p. 80 (2)
[71] CB. p. 81 (5)
[72] var. MILIT for MILITVM.
[73] var. FEL for FELIX

[74] CB. p. 81 1
[75] CB. p. 85 1(4)
[76] CB. p. 85 1
[76] CB. p. 85 4

CONSTANTIUS II? Caes.   LRBC.1. as *50*(2), *64*,[77] 64, *74*, 75, 89, *182*(2), *218*, as 352, *744*, 89, *94*, 182(2), 400/12, *401*, *413*, as *413*, 756

CONSTANS   LRBC.1. as *90*, 131‡

DELMATIUS   LRBC.1. *402a*, 402/402a

URBS ROMA   LRBC.1. as *51*,[78] 58‡, 65, 65‡, 70, *85*, *184*, 184, *190*(2), *195*, *360*,[79] 365(2)

CONSTANTINOPOLIS   LRBC.1. *52*(5), 52‡, as *52*,[80] 59, 59‡, *66*[81](2), *77*[82] (2), 86, *88*, 185, *191*, *536*

CONSTANTINIAN COPIES

CONSTANTINE I   LRBC.1. *48*(4)

CONSTANTINE II   LRBC.1. as *49*(3), as *56*, 88

CONSTANTIUS II   LRBC.1. 50/132, *50*, 64

CONSTANS   LRBC.1. *127*, *138*, as *138*, 227, *243/4*

URBS ROMA   LRBC.1. *51*(5), 51/2(2), *184*(2)

CONSTANTINOPOLIS   LRBC.1. *52*(6), 52/51, 190*

CONSTANTINIAN 337–48

CONSTANTINE I,
Posthumous.   LRBC.1. as 78, as 106

CONSTANTINE II   LRBC.1. *241*. as 247, *854*

CONSTANTIUS II   LRBC.1. as 100, as *102*,[83] *108*, *126*(3), 132, as *248*, as 248‡, *250*, *426*(2), *1391*, 1066, 1067, *137*, *145/7*, *259*, *Illegible* (1)

CONSTANS   LRBC.1. *126*, *127*, *131*, 131, *133*[84] (2), 133, 152, *243/4*, *351*, *775*, as *137*, 138(3), *140*(2), as 140, 145/7(2), *148*(3), *148/50*, *149*(2), *150*(2), 158/60[85], 158/60, *163*, *176*, as *258*(2)

CONSTANTIUS II/CONSTANS   LRBC.1. as *256*(3)

HELENA   LRBC.1. 104, as 104*(2), *112*, as *112*[86](5), *119*,[87] 128

THEODORA   LRBC.1. 105, *113*(2), *as 113*(4), *120*[88] (2), *129*

CONSTANTINIAN 348–364

CONSTANS   LRBC.2. 29/30a(2), *35*, *39*, *43*[89], 43, 199, Illegible (1)

CONSTANTIUS II   LRBC.2. as 28/30, *31*, *40*, 44, *70* var.,[90] 76, 249/50, *253*, *254*, 409/10, *455*[91] (2) 457(4), 689/90*(3), as *1687*

---

[77] CB. p. 87 5(3)
[78] CB. p. 83 (1)
[79] CB. p. 84 (5)
[80] CB. p. 83 1(1)
[81] CB. p. 83 1(4)
[82] CB. p. 83 1(2)
[83] CB. p. 87 7(2)
[84] CB. p. 86 2(4)

[85] CB. p. 86 3(4)
[86] CB. p. 79 (1)
[87] CB. p. 79 (3)
[88] CB. p. 79 (1)
[89] CB. p. 86 1(2)
[90] var. no star in field
[91] CB. p. 88 9(3)

CONSTANTIUS GALLUS	LRBC.2. as *456*
COPIES	LRBC.2. *26*, as 26*, as *72*(11), as *76*(4), *256*, *455*, as 457*
MAGNENTIUS	LRBC.2. as *1*, as 1*, *2*, as *19*(2), 49, as *64*, 212, as 238, 415/9*
DECENTIUS	LRBC.2. as 9
MAGNENTIUS/DECENTIUS	LRBC.2. as *19*

COPIES

MAGNENTIUS	LRBC.2. as 58, *72, 238*(2)
DECENTIUS	LRBC.2. as *9*
JULIAN	*Siliqua* C *146* (Plated copy) C. *158* LRBC.2. 268
VALENTINIAN	LRBC.2. as *275, 300, 307*, 506, *518, 521, 525*(2), 527, *986*, 1014*, *1035*, 1327, 1408/18
VALENS	LRBC.2. as 93, as 94*, *as 97*[92], 282, as *282*,[93] as 282, *303, 316*, as 477‡, *480, 483*, as 483, as 513, 516, *526*, as 526‡, 705, *1428*
GRATIAN	LRBC.2. *371*,[94] as 503, *517*, 517*, *523a*(3), *529*[95] (4), as 531, 533, *545* 545, 552
VALENTINIAN II	LRBC.2. 738
VALENTINIANIC	LRBC.2. as 82*, as *96*(2)
MAGNUS MAXIMUS	*Solidus* RIC. IX (LONDON 26[96]
THEODOSIUS I	LRBC.2. 140‡
VALENTINIAN II	LRBC.2. as 796[97]
HONORIUS	LRBC.2. 2573[98]*
ARCADIUS	LRBC.2. as 566*, *571*,[99] 793, as 798*
THEODOSIAN	LRBC.2. as *798*(2)

---

[92] CB. p. 60 (6)
[93] CB. p. 89 (2)
[94] CB. p. 90 2(2)
[95] CB. p. 90 1(2)

[96] Found 1976
[97] CB. p. 90(9) where listed as Valens
[98] CB. p. 90
[99] CB. p. 90

EXCAVATIONS 1966-7

	Issuer	Denom.	Type	Ref.	Date	Condition
1.	TRAJAN	Sestertius	Obv. [IMP CAES NERVAE TRAIANO AVG] GER DA [C PM TRP COS V PP] Rev. [S.P.Q.R. OPTIMO PRINCIPI—S.C.]	RIC. 543	103–11	VW/VW
2.	TRAJAN	Dupondius	Obv. IMP CAES NERVAE TRAIANO GER DAC … Rev. Illegible	RIC.—	103–17	VW/VW
3.	HADRIAN	Sestertius	Obv. IMP CAESAR TRAIANVS HADRIANVS AVG Rev. PONT MA [X TR POT COS III] SC	RIC. 561 (a)	119	W/W
4.	HADRIAN	Dupondius	Obv. Illegible Rev. Illegible	RIC.—	117–38	EW/EW
5.	SABINA	Denarius	Obv. SABINA AVGVSTA Rev. CONCORDIA AVG	RIC. 391	117–38	W/SW
6.	M. AURELIUS	Sestertius	Obv. M ANTONINVS AVG [TPP …] Rev. [SALVTI AVG COS III—SC]	RIC. 965/79	168–70	W/VW
7.	LUCIUS VERUS	As	Obv. L VERVS AVG ARMENIACVS Rev. LIBERAL AVG TR P V IMP II COS II—SC	RIC. 1418	164–5	W/W
8.	COMMODUS	Dupondius	Obv. M COMMODVS ANTONINVS AVG … Rev. Illegible	RIC.—	181–3	SW/Corroded

				RIC./BMCRE	Date	Condition
9.	PERTINAX	*Denarius*	Obv. IMP CAES P HELV PERTIN AVG Rev. [VOT DECEN TR P COS II]	RIC. 13a	193	W/Corroded
10.	SEVERUS	*Denarius* —plated copy	Obv. L SEPT SEV PERT AVG IMP X Rev. [VICT AV] GG [COS II PP]	BMCRE 258	(197–8)	UW/Corroded
11.		*Denarius*	Obv. SEVERVS PIVS AGV Rev. AFRICA	RIC. 254	207	W/W
12.	CARACALLA	*Denarius* —plated copy	Obv. ANTONINVS PIVS AVG GERM Rev. [PM TR P XVII COS IIII P] P	BMCRE 99	(214)	UW/UW
13.	ELAGABALUS	*Denarius* —plated copy	Obv. IMP CAES M AVR ANTONINVS AVG Rev. SALVS ANTONINI AVG	RIC. 140	(218–22)	W/UW
14.	Illegible	Plated "*Antoninianus*"	Obv. Illegible Rev. Illegible	RIC. —	(214–58)	Corroded
15.	GALLIENUS	"*Antoninianus*"	Obv. GALLIENVS AVG Rev. DIANAE CONS AVG	RIC. 179	259–68	SW/UW
16.	VICTORINUS	"*Antoninianus*"	Obv. IMP C VICTOR [INVS PF AVG] Rev. [INVICTVS]	RIC. 114	269–71	SW/SW
17.	TETRICUS II	"*Antoninianus*"	Obv. ... TETRICVS CA [ES] Rev. [PIETAS AVGG]	RIC. 254/5	271–3	UW/UW
18.		"*Antoninianus*"	Obv. [... TETRI] CVS CAES Rev. SPES [...]	as RIC. 270/1	271–3	UW/UW
19.		"*Antoninianus*" —copy	Obv. C PIV ESV TETRICVS CAES Rev. SPES [PVBLI] CA	RIC. 272	(271–3)	UW/UW

Issuer	Denom.	Type		Ref.	Date	Condition
20. CLAUDIUS II, Posthumous	"Antoninianus"	Obv.	DIVO CLAVDIO	RIC. 261	269+	W/W
		Rev.	CONSECRATIO			
21.	"Antoninianus"	Obv.	DIVO CLAVDIO	RIC. 266	269+	VW/W
		Rev.	CONSECRATIO			
22. RADIATE COPY	"Antoninianus"	Obv.	Illegible	—	(270–80)	
		Rev.	Illegible			
23. CARAUSIUS		Obv.	IMP CARAVSIVS PF AVG	RIC. 990	287–93	SW/SW
		Rev.	SALVS AVG			
24. DIOCLETIAN	"Follis"	Obv.	IMP DIO [CLETIANVS PF AVG]	RIC. VI (LON) 12	300	W/SW
		Rev.	GENIO POPV-LI [ROM] ANI			
25. CONSTANTINE I	—	Obv.	CONSTAN-TINVS AVG	RIC. VII (TRIER) 303	321	UW/UW
		Rev.	BEATA TRAN-QVILLITAS VOT/IS/XX			
26. CONSTANTINE II, Caesar	—	Obv.	[CONSTANTI] NVS IVN NC	LRBC.1. 49	330–35	UW/SW
		Rev.	[GLOR IA EXER-C] ITVS			
27. URBS ROMA	—	Obv.	VRBS ROMA	LRBC.1. 200	330–35	UW/UW
		Rev.	Lupa Romana			
28.	—	Obv.	VRBS ROMA	LRBC.1. 365/71	330–35	W/UW
		Rev.	Lupa Romana			
29. HELENA	—	Obv.	[FL IVL HELE-NAE AVG]	LRBC.1. as 104	337–41	Corroded
		Rev.	[PA-XPV-BLICA]			
30.	copy	Obv.	FL IVL HELE-NAE AVG	as LRBC.1. 104	(337–41)	UW/SW
		Rev.	PA-XPV-BLICA			

| 31. | MAGNENTIUS | — | Obv. DN MAGNEN-TIVS PF AVG
Rev. VICTORIAE DD NN AVG ET CAE | LRBC.2. 8 | 351–3 | UW/UW |

I. A. RICHMOND EXCAVATION, 1949

The following three coins appear to be from the early post-war excavations; the locations are transcribed from the data on the coin envelopes.

	Issuer	Denom.	Type	Ref.	Date	Condition
1.	IULIA DOMNA	Denarius	Obv. IVLIA AVGVSTA Rev. FORTVNAE FELICI	RIC. 554	207–11	W/W

"Found in the cobble foundation of Principia III, 2'0" south of early foundation crossing west wall."

| 2. | TETRICUS I | "Antoninianus" | Obv. . . . ESV TETRICVS [PF AVG]
Rev. Illegible | RIC.— | 270–3 | UW/Corroded |

"Found between Principia III and small drain on *via principalis* to west of building."

| 3. | URBS ROMA | — | Obv. VRBS ROMA
Rev. Lupa Romana | LRBC.1. 76 | 330–5 | UW/UW |

"Found on the surface of the roadway near the Principia, 14.10.49."

BEACON STREET, 1959

The following coins, with one exception, were published by J. H. Corbitt as an adjunct to the excavation report. (Thornborrow, 1959) Re-examination of the coins has allowed for further attributions to be made. The figure in parenthesis is that borne by the coin in the original listing.

	Issuer	Denom.	Type	Ref.	Date	Condition
1(1)	DOMITIAN, Caesar	As	Obv. Illegible Rev. Illegible	RIC.—		EW/EW
2(2)	VESPASIAN	Dupondius	Obv. Illegible Rev. Illegible	RIC.—	68–78	EW/EW
3(8)	HADRIAN	As	Obv. [HADRIANVS AVGVSTVS] Rev. [COS III—SC]	RIC. 669c	125–8	Corroded
4(5)		As	Obv. HADRIANVS AVGVSTVS Rev. COS III—[SC]	RIC. 669c	125–8	SW/SW
5(6)		As	Obv. HADRIANVS AVGVSTVS Rev. COS III—SC	RIC. 669c	125–8	W/SW
6(3)		Sestertius	Obv. HADRIANVS AVGVSTVS Rev. FELICITATI AVG COS III PP SC	RIC. 719	132–4	SW/SW
7(4)		Sestertius	Obv. HADRIANUS AUG COS III PP Rev. [RESTITVTORI NICOMEDIAE—SC]	RIC. 961	134–8	SW/SW
8(7)		As	Obv. Illegible Rev. Illegible	RIC.—	117–38	Corroded
9(16)		As	Obv. Illegible Rev. Illegible	RIC.—	117–38	Corroded

10(13) ANTONINUS PIUS	*As*	Obv. [ANTONINVS AVG PIVS PP TR P] COS [III . . .] Rev. S. C.—Apollo	RIC. 685/824	140–61	SW/Corroded
11(11)	*As*	Obv. [ANTONINVS AVG PIVS PP TR P . . .] Rev. [LIBERTAS COS IIII]—SC	RIC. 908[1] etc.	152–4	SW/UW
12(—)	*As*	Obv. [ANTONINVS AVG PIVS PP TR P XVIII] Rev. [BRITANNIA COS IIII—SC]	RIC. 934	154–5	Corroded
13(15)	*As*	Obv. [ANTONINVS AVG PIVS PP TR P XVIII] Rev. [BRITANNIA COS IIII—SC]	RIC. 934	154–5	Corroded
14(9)	*As*	Obv. [ANTONINVS AVG PIVS PP TR P XVIII] Rev. [BRITANNIA COS IIII—SC]	RIC. 934	154–5	Corroded
15(12)	*As*	Obv. [ANTONINVS AVG PIVS PP TR P XVIII] Rev. [BRITANNIA COS IIII—SC]	RIC. 934	154–5	SW/SW
16(10)	*Dupondius*	Obv. ANTONINVS AVG PIVS [PP TR P] XVIII Rev. [LIBERTAS COS IIII—SC]	RIC. 933	154–5	SW/SW
17(14) Illegible	*As*			2nd century	Corroded
18(17) Illegible[2]	—			4th century	

[1] Recorded as *dupondius* only
[2] Coin now missing

PEARSON STREET, 1962

This coin was published by J. H. Corbitt but without standard reference, an illegible *sestertius* mentioned in the text is now missing.

Issuer	Denom.	Type	Ref.	Date.	Condition
Severus	Denarius	Obv. L. SEPT SEV AVG IMP XI P [ART MAX] Rev. ANNONA—EAVGG	RIC. 123	198–200	SW/W

"HOARD" I

NERO	*Aureus*	RIC. 45
	Den.	RIC. 45, 52, as *53*
GALBA	*Den.*	RIC. 4(4), 20 var.[1]
VESPASIAN	*Den.*	RIC. 10, 37, 50, 65, 65 var.,[2] 66, 91, 109, Illegible (3)
TITUS, Caesar	*Den.*	RIC. (Vesp.) 218, *220*
TITUS	*Den.*	RIC. 9, *17/17a*
DOMITIAN, Caesar	*Aureus*	RIC. (Vesp.) 240
DOMITIAN	*Aureus*	RIC. 19
	Den.	RIC. 26, *148*,[3] 154, 158, 177
NERVA	*Den.*	RIC. 14, *16*[4]
TRAJAN	*Aureus*	RIC. 49, 142, 823
	Den.	RIC. *6*,[5] as 32, 58/9, as 60, 67, 80, 118, 122(2), *128*,[6] 142, 147, 183/4, 219, 241, 271, 294, 303, 318, as 343, 347, Illegible (1)
HADRIAN	*Aureus*	RIC. 72(a), 253(c)*,[7] 254(a), 283(a)
	Den.	RIC. 13(a), *39(b)*,[8] 40(a), 71(b), 80(b), as 82, 85(a), 85(b), 102(b)(2), 116(b), 127(a), 128(a), 137(a), 137(b), 173(c), 178(c), 202(c), 226(a), 242(a), Illegible (2)
SABRINA	*Den.*	RIC. 390
ANTONINUS PIUS	*Aureus*	RIC. 141(c), 147(d)
	Den.	RIC. 42, 46 var.,[9] 48(b), as 61, 63B(c), 64(c), 111(c), 127(c), 175, as 178, 179, 200(c), 203, 231, 240
FAUSTINA I	*Den.*	RIC. (Pius) 394(a), 351(b), 377, 382(a), ? 356, Illegible (1)
MARCUS AURELIUS, Caesar	*Den.*	RIC. (Pius) 468, 475(a), 482, 649
MARCUS AURELIUS	*Den.*	RIC. 34, 212, 233, 248, 349, 418, 436, Illegible (1)
FAUSTINA II	*Den.*	RIC. (Marcus) Illegible (1)
LUCILLA	*Den.*	RIC. (Marcus) 781, 786, 788
COMMODUS	*Den.*	RIC. 10(a), 26B, 61, 102, 122(a), 241, 267
CRISPINA	*Den.*	RIC. (Commodus) 286(a)

The closure date of this hoard, as reconstructed, is A.D. 192. However the penultimate coin is an issue of 185 and a seven year gap between the terminal issues is unusual. In the event the hoard is listed as closing with RIC. 241, with the caveat that the last coin may be a site find rather than a hoard item.

[1] Head *bare* for *laureate*
[2] Figure seated *left*
[3] CB. p. 57 3
[4] CB. p. 58 (1)
[5] CB. p. 58 1(1)
[6] CB. p. 58 4(2)
[7] "Found 1880" Bell Collection
[8] CB. p. 60 1(1)
[9] Head *laureate* for *bare*

"HOARD" II
(Bell Collection)

DIOCLETIAN   RIC. VI (LUGDUNUM) 14a, 73, 200a, VI (ROME) 94a
MAXIMIANUS   RIC. VI (LUGDUNUM) 372
MAXIMINUS DAZA   RIC. VI (LONDON) 117a
ILLEGIBLE TETRARCHIC
(6)

"HOARD" III

CONSTANTINE   RIC. VI (LONDON) 121a, VII (LONDON) *163*, 168, *191*, 192, 222, 223, 293
                      VII (TRIER) *209*,[1] 209(2), 303*, 304, *342*, *369*, 371, *372*, as 429, 435
                      VII (ARLES) 252
                      VII (ROME) 318
                      VII (SISCIA) 183
CRISPUS   RIC. VII (LONDON) *115*,[2] *188*, *250*,[3] 251, 273*, *275*, 281, 291
                      VII (TRIER) 307, *308*(2),[4] *372*, 395, *431*(2),[5] *432*, 432, *452*
                      VII (SISCIA) *147*
                      VII (HERACLEA) 76
CONSTANTINE II,   RIC. VII (LONDON) *237*, 292*, 292, *296*[6]
Caesar
                      VII (TRIER) 143, *173*, 312, 435, 441, 454, 455, *489*, *512*
CONSTANTIUS II,   RIC. VII (TRIER) 322/3, 463
Caesar
                      VII (NICOMEDIA) 124
FAUSTA   RIC. VII (TRIER) 459

"HOARD" IV

MAGNENTIUS   LRBC.2. 3/4(2), as *4*, as *5*, 8(2) *35*, *50*, 50/52, *55*, *58*, as *58*, 60, as *66*, *209*, 214, 227, 423
DECENTIUS   LRBC.2. 226

---

[1] CB. p. 82 6(2)   [4] CB. p. 84 5(2)
[2] CB. p. 84 7   [5] CB. p. 84 9(2)
[3] CB. p. 84 1   [6] CB. p. 85 1(2)

REJECTED COINS

Allusion has already been made to the unfortunate practice of mixing the kind benefactions of the residents of South Shields with the site collection. Coin lists from sea port sites are always prone to contain elements imported in recent times and the practice of T. J. Bell of purchasing Roman coins from overseas has already been mentioned. In rejecting the following coins cognisance has been taken of their non-occurrence on other sites in Britain and their profusion among the possessions of collectors. Some coins, such as the small hoard of *"folles"* of manifestly eastern provenance, are clear examples of recent imports, as too are specimens of Arab (unlisted) and Byzantine coins. Others are less readily proven as imports; the criterion for rejection ultimately rests upon the writer's experience of British site finds and the absence of these coins from Blair's listing. All of the coins are in the Roman Fort Museum Collection.

TIBERIUS	*Denarius*	RIC. 3
	—plated copy	
	As	RIC. 32
CLAUDIUS	*As*	RIC. 66, copy of 66
SEVERUS		
ALEXANDER	*Sestertius*	RIC. 635
JULIA MAMMAEA	*Sestertius*	RIC. 701
MAXIMINUS I	*Sestertius*	RIC. 64
GORDIAN III	*Sestertius*	RIC. 331a
PHILIP I	*Sestertius*	RIC. 175(a)
CARINUS		RIC. 253
NUMERIAN		RIC. 338
DIOCLETIAN		RIC. VI (CARTHAGE) 37a
		RIC. VI (ALEXANDRIA) 32a
MAXIMIAN		RIC. V 515
		RIC. VI (ALEXANDRIA) 16b
CONSTANTIUS I, Caesar		RIC. VI (ALEXANDRIA) 31a (2)
		RIC. VI (CARTHAGE) 32a
GALERIUS		RIC. VI (CYZICUS) 68
MAXIMINUS DAZA		RIC. VI (ANTIOCH) 103
LICINIUS		RIC. VII (ROME) 38[1]
		RIC. VII (ALEXANDRIA) 28, 144a var.[2]
		RIC. VII (CYZICUS) 15, as 15
CONSTANS		LRBC. I. 1476
HERACLIUS		D.O. 196

[1] Donated with "Phoenicean oil lamps"
[2] var. IMP C VAL for IMP C VALER

Reference has already been made to the finding of coins on the beaches in the vicinity of the fort in the early years of the present century. These finds comprising both Roman coins and mediaeval and early modern issues appear to derive from Newcastle where, in the years during which the coins appeared, dredging took place in the area of the Swing Bridge. The detritus from these operations was dumped at the mouth of the river and specifically on the Trow Rocks.[11] In consequence of this evidence of the movement of material from Newcastle all coins from South Shields beach, the Herd Sands and the Trow Rocks have been excluded from the catalogue.

DISCUSSION

The problems experienced in achieving a representative collection of genuine site finds from South Shields have already been discussed and some validation of the methods used is offered when the results are expressed in graphic form. A histogram of the coinage presents a distribution characteristic of Roman sites in Britain. In constructing the histogram (fig. 23) uniformity of presentation with other sites has been achieved by representing the site coin totals as 1000 coins using the formula:

$$\frac{\text{COINS PER REIGN}}{\text{LENGTH OF REIGN}} \times \frac{1000}{\text{TOTAL FOR SITE}}$$

In this computation all copies and counterfeits are excluded, though their significance is discussed, hoards are treated as single coins. The periods into which the coins are divided are generally regnal years though after the mid-third century regnal periods have little significance and the issue periods of specific coins are more important.

The coin issue period divisions used in this study are as follows:

1.	Claudian	A.D. 43–54
2.	Neronian	A.D. 54–68
3.	Flavian I	A.D. 68–81
4.	Flavian II	A.D. 81–96
5.	Trajanic	A.D. 96–117
6.	Hadrianic	A.D. 117–138
7.	Antonine I	A.D. 138–161
8.	Antonine II	A.D. 161–180
9.	Antonine III	A.D. 180–192
10.	Severan I	A.D. 193–217
11–17.	Severan II	A.D. 217–260
18.	Gallic Empire	A.D. 260–273
19.	Aurelianic	A.D. 273–286
20.	Carausian	A.D. 286–296
21.	Diocletianic	A.D. 296–317
22.	Constantinian I	A.D. 317–330

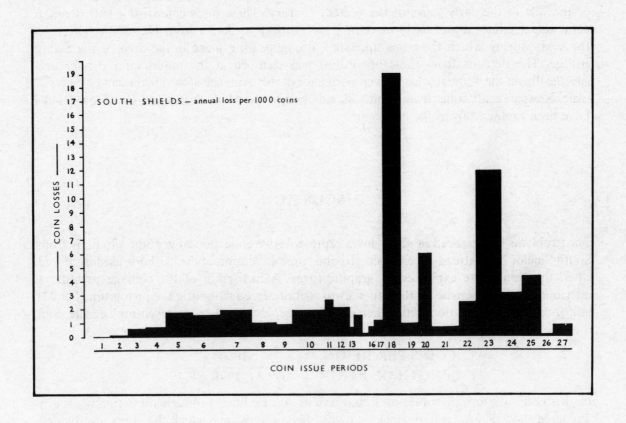

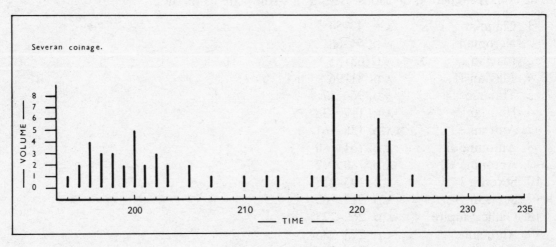

Fig. 23. Coins.

23. Constantinian II   A.D. 330–348
24. Constantinian III   A.D. 348–364
25. Valentinianic   A.D. 364–378
26. Theodosian I   A.D. 378–388
27. Theodosian II   A.D. 388–402

The resulting coin distribution diagram shows a pattern already familiar from sites of the Roman period in Britain. The major fluctuations in the graph largely reflect economic and political factors which influenced coin supply in general rather than unique events which impinged on individual sites.[12]

These fluctuations are largely alternating high and low deposits which can be correlated, in many instances, with imperial monetary problems. Falls in coin deposits coincide with the reigns of Marcus and Commodus (periods 8, 9) when a change from a largely *aes* coinage to a largely silver coinage took place. Deposits of this period are high in monetary value but low in individual coins. The mid-third century (periods 13–16) is characteristically poorly represented and in the Aurelianic and Diocletianic periods (periods 19, 21) conform to a pattern imposed by major currency reforms. It has already been noted that the reformed coinage of Constantius II (period 25) is over-represented at South Shields perhaps because of the distribution of a coin hoard among the individual site-finds. The usual abrupt decline in representation of coins in the period coinciding with the revolt of Magnus Maximus (period 26) occurs, though the presence of a recently discovered *solidus* of Maximus demonstrates activity in the area of the fort at this time. Theodosian coinage takes site activity into the fifth century.

The abrupt peaks in the graph are again largely reflections of monetary events coinciding with the collapse of the silver currency in the reign of Gallienus and his Gallic rivals (period 18). The volume of losses in this period are an accurate reflection of the intrinsic worthlessness of the coins themselves. The reign of Carausius (period 20) saw an injection of coins into the island economy whilst further currency collapses and/or inflations are detectable in the peaks of the Constantinian and Valentinianic periods (periods 23, 25).

If these fluctuations in coin deposits are mostly determined by external factors, the provision of copies of the official coinage shows a response to shortages of currency at a local level. These copies occur in the later third century and in the fourth. Considerable numbers of crude copies of the coins of the Gallic Empire are present at South Shields with evidence, in the form of three die linked specimens, of their having been produced locally. These copies have convincingly been shewn to have been produced to make good a deficiency of small change created by Aurelian's reform in 273, this shortage was not alleviated until the Carausian period. A similar situation pertains in the years between the coin reform of 348 and the advent of bulk supplies of Valentinianic currency, though for different reasons. The twenty-five copies of this period include a number of straight counterfeits, in the case of the Magnentian element in this total. But the copies are overwhelmingly crude attempts to produce a currency which, whilst wholly unofficial, did not contravene the severe edict of Constantius II apparently designed to suppress the coinage of the usurper Magnentius which dominated the coinage of the western provinces in the middle of the fourth century.[13]

There is no evidence from numismatic sources of any significant break in the occupation of the site, though caution should be exercised in using the evidence from sources of such mixed value as have been used in compiling the South Shields site record. It is for instance uncertain as to how much of the coinage relates to the fort itself and how much, from old collections, derives from the *vicus* and port which we may assume flourished in the vicinity of the fort. However, the coins from the 1966–7 excavations accurately reflect the pattern of the older finds and it seems unlikely that interpretation based on the composite coin list would lead to serious systematic error. Changes in the composition of the garrison do not seem to be reflected in the coins. The weight of Severan coinage, which is virtually all silver, when compared with that of earlier periods, which is largely *aes*, reflects the increases in military pay initiated by Severus and Caracalla. An analysis of the distribution of dated Severan coins (i.e. omitting the issues of Julia Domna and Julia Mamaea which are not closely dated) seems to indicate a decline in the circulation of new coinage in a period coinciding with the Severan campaigns in the north (fig. 23). It is in this period that the fort fulfilled the function of a supply base and the diminution in coin activity may reflect a diminution of the garrison strength at this time.

The presence of a worn late issue *denarius* of Julia Domna in the foundations of the latest *principia* suggests that the third-century garrison *Cohors V Gallorum* was established at a post-Severan I date. This may, on the statistically heavy representation of his coinage, occur in the reign of Elagabalus (period 11) as easily as in the reign of Severus Alexander (period 12).

The overall proportions in coins between earlier and later periods tends to reflect the effect of the operation of the *annona militaris* in the fourth century with a consequent diminution of coin representation on military sites. At South Shields this trend is not as strongly marked as in the relatively isolated economic communities of the forts *per lineam valli* no doubt reflecting the mixed nature of the occupation and commercial activity to be expected at a port. The lack of attention to earlier levels on the site before the post-war excavations may well have resulted in under representation of second-century coinage, a fact which is highlighted by the incidence of such issues in the material recovered in the Beacon Street excavations as much as by the composition of the gold and silver hoard.

The coin series does not point to any specific period for the change of garrison from *Cohors V Gallorum* to the unit attested in the *Notitia Dignitatum*, the *Numerus Barcariorum Tigrisiensium*. A move by a garrison from the east might have resulted in the presence of an eastern element in the coinage, unfortunately the history of the collection with its known additions from non-site sources precludes the acceptance of such eastern mint coins as exist as genuine site evidence. In any event such a unit may have experienced several postings before reaching Arbeia.

References

1. *Natural History Trans.* of Northumberland and Durham, VII, 1878, 126–67—cited hereafter as CB.
2. *Archaeologia Aeliana*, X, 1884, 223 ff.
3. *Archaeologia Aeliana* N.S. X, 1895, 271.
4. *South Shields Arch. & Hist. Soc. Papers* 1–3, Jan.–Dec., 1955.
5. CB. p. 56 2.
6. *Archaeologia Aeliana*, 4th ser., IX, 1932, 89–95.

7. *Proc*. Soc. Ants. Newcastle upon Tyne, 3rd ser., V, 1911–12, 66–7.

8. *Proc*. Soc. Ants. Newcastle upon Tyne, 3rd ser., III, 1907–8, 193; IV, 1909–10, 124, 288; V, 1911–12, 3, 103, 161, 188; VII, 1915–16, 6.

9. Robertson, A., Romano-British coin hoards *in* Casey, P. J. and Reece, R. *eds*., *Coins and the Archaeologist* (1974).

10. Author's site records.

11. *Proc*. Soc. Ants. Newcastle upon Tyne, 3rd ser., IV, 1909–10, 222.

12. Casey, P. J., The interpretation of Romano-British site finds *in* Casey, P. J. *and* Reece, R. *eds*., *Coins and the Archaeologist* (1974).

13. Codex Theodosianus 9.23.1.

THE SAMIAN

This report, besides dealing with material from the excavations of 1966, 1967 and 1973, also includes most of the samian recovered in the excavations of 1875, which now forms part of the collections of the Joint Museum of Antiquities of the Society and of the University of Newcastle upon Tyne, and the Roman Fort Museum in South Shields. The catalogue of stamps represents all the identifiable stamps which are known from the site at this time. Although these will shortly be appearing in Mr. Hartley's major catalogue, it was felt that a full and up to date list should be included here. The section on the decorated ware includes all but the smallest pieces from the recent excavations and both museum collections. It must be pointed out, however, that there is some doubt as to South Shields being the provenance of pieces from box no. 578 in the Joint Museum of Antiquities collection. The samian in this collection came mainly from the collection of Thomas Bell, one of the original excavators, and this particular box, which is marked "South Shields chiefly" may contain material from other sites.

The samian from the site ranges in date from the late first century to about the middle of the third. The foundation of the fort is dated to between A.D. 120 and 130 by the presence of coarse ware of BB1 type beneath the mason's chippings of the north guard chamber of the west gate, and by fragments of a Dr.27 and a Dr.18/31, both of Hadrianic date, securely stratified in the lower levels of the rampart backing. The six pieces of South Gaulish decorated ware (Nos. 1–5) must therefore be regarded as imported survivals. The two pieces of Trajanic date (Nos. 6 and 7) could still have been on the market at the time of the fort's foundation.

The chronological distribution of the stamps would seem to indicate that the fort was not occupied in the period *c.* A.D. 140–160. Study of the decorated ware would seem to bear this out. There is, admittedly, a higher proportion of Hadrianic-early Antonine material among the decorated pieces than among the stamps, and a not insignificant number of pieces from the earlier East Gaulish factories of La Madeleine and Lavoye. Mr. Hartley has remarked, however, that by no means all these sherds might have been on the market before A.D. 140. Some of the pieces from La Madeleine will probably be Hadrianic but those from Lavoye are much more likely to be fully Antonine.

Thereafter, as far as can be ascertained, occupation continued uninterrupted into the third century. Here the samian ceases to have great value as an accurate chronological indicator owing to the difficulty of dating material from the factories at Rheinzabern or Trier.

The amount of plain ware from the site is represented graphically in fig. 34. With a reasonably large sample such as this only rim sherds were used, except in cases where wall sherds only were present and the vessel would not otherwise appear. In such a case a vessel's presence is recorded as an open circle. Each line represents a total percentage rim length for a particular type of vessel, which was obtained by taking the circumferential length of each rim and expressing it as a percentage of a theoretical, complete vessel. The subdivision in each line shows the relationship between material from inside the fort, and from the *vicus* outside. At the right the actual numbers of rims are given.

Abbreviations used

Ch. and G.	=	Chenet and Gaudron, 1955
D.	=	Déchelette, 1904
Fölzer	=	Fölzer, 1913
JMN	=	The Joint Museum of Antiquities of the University and the Society of Antiquaries of Newcastle upon Tyne. Following numbers are the museum store box number and accession number.
Oelmann	=	Oelmann, 1914
O.	=	Oswald 1936/7
O. and P.	=	Oswald and Pryce, 1920.
RFM	=	The Roman Fort Museum, South Shields. Following letters and numbers are the museum catalogue numbers.
R. and F.	=	Ricken and Fischer, 1963.
Ricken	=	Ricken, 1934
R./Lud. VI	=	Ricken/Ludowici, 1948
Rogers	=	Rogers 1974
S. and S.	=	Stanfield and Simpson, 1958.

Full references will be found in the bibliography on p. 168.

THE POTTER'S STAMPS

B. R. Hartley and Miss B. Dickinson

1. Advocisus 2a Dr.38 ADV[OCISI·O] Vicus 1973 Lezoux[1]. Bainbridge, Catterick (2), Malton. *c.* A.D. 160–195.
2. Advocisus Dr.33 ADVOCISI·O[RFM BA 276 Lezoux. This stamp appears to be missing from the Museum. Probably 2a again.
3. Albusa 1a Dr.33 (2) [A]-Ƙ-BV·SΛ and]BV·SΛ RFM BA 279 and 297 (or 314) Lezoux[1]. At Lezoux many examples of the stamp were in a kiln of *c.* A.D. 165–185.
4. Aprilis ii 3a Dr.31 [APRIL]IS·F RFM BA 322 Lezoux[1]. There are no dated contexts. Other stamps are on forms 18/31R, 27 and 80(?), and there is one from a pit at Alcester with many whole pots, presumably from a shop, datable to *c.* A.D. 150–160. *c.* A.D. 140–170.
5. Attius ii 5a Dr.18/31 [ATTI]VƧFI Vicus 1973 Lezoux[2]. An example of another stamp of Attius ii was in the Erdkastell at the Saalburg. His production was mainly forms 18/31 and 27. *c.* A.D. 120–145.
6. Austrus 1a Dr.37 AVSTRI·OF Vicus 1973 Lezoux[1]. As on *S. and S.* pl. 95, no. 20.
7. Banuus 1a Dr.37 BANVI retr. *Bruce*, 1884, p. 274. Now missing. Lezoux[1]. Brougham cemetery, Carrawburgh, Chesterholm. *c.* A.D. 160–185.
8. Beliniccus i 9a Dr.33 BELINICCI·M RFM BA 120 Les Martres-de-Veyre,[2] and Lezoux[2]. Corbridge, Hadrian's Wall? (Chesters—2), Neckarburken-West. This stamp was probably used at both the centres noted. *c.* A.D. 120–150.
9. Belsa Arve(rnicus?) 1a Dr.31R BEL[SA·ARVEF] RFM BA 356 Lezoux[1]. There were many examples from the kiln noted under Albusa. Catterick, Halton-chesters, Pudding Pan Rock. *c.* A.D. 165–195.
10. Cambus 2a Dr.31 [C]AMBVS F 1966 Drain Lezoux[1]. Benwell (2) Carrawburgh, Chesters. *c.* A.D. 155–185.
11. Camulinus 2a Dr.31 CAMVLINVS 1949, now lost Lezoux[1]. Chesters, with the use of Dr.15/31, suggests, *c.* A.D. 150–180.
12. Capitolinus 1a Concave dish CAPITOLINVS RFM BA 280 Rheinzabern[1]. Hadrian's Wall (Chesters) and the use of forms 32 and 32R point to the late second or early third century.
13. Caratillus 2a Dr.18/31 CARATILLI JMN now lost Lezoux[1]. Birrens (Antonine I), Camelon, Newstead. *c.* A.D. 145–165.
14. Carus ii 1a Dr.31R ·C·A·[RI·MA·] RFM BA 7 Lezoux[1]. Ilkley and the use of forms 27 and 31R combine to suggest a date *c.* A.D. 150–175.
15. Carussa 3a Dr.31 CARVS[SÆ] RFM BA 281 Lezoux[1]. Catterick, Halton-chesters, Piercebridge, with forms 31R and 79. *c.* A.D. 155–185.
16. Casurius ii 5a Dr.37 CASV[RIVSF] retr. RFM BA 73 Lezoux[1]. Bainbridge, Cappuck and many decorated bowls in mid- or late-Antonine contexts. *c* A.D. 155–185.
17. Catussa Dr.37 [C]ᴀTV[SSᴀ] retro. Vicus 1973 Lezoux[1].

18. Celsianius 8a Dr.38? [CEL]SIANIF RFM BA 318 Lezoux[1]. Chester-le-Street, Piercebridge. Forms 31R, 79 and 80. At Lezoux his work appears in contexts suggestive of a date late in the second century. *c.* A.D. 170–200.

19. Celsus ii 1a Dr.33 CELSI·MΛ RFM BA 283 Lezoux[2]. This is the only example of the stamp, but the general record for Celsus ii suggests activity *c.* A.D. 150–190.

20. Cinnamus ii 5b Dr.37 CINNAMI retr. RFM BA 3 Lezoux[1].

21. Cinnamus ii 5b Dr.30? CINNAMI retr. Bruce, 1884, p. 274 now lost. The standard decorated ware stamp of Cinnamus, used within the period A.D. 150–180.

22. Cintugenus 3a Dr.31 [CIИT·V]GENI Vicus 1973 Lezoux[3]. Newstead, Hadrian's Wall? (Chesters) and f.79. *c.* A.D. 150–190.

23. Cintusmus i 2c Dr.33 CINTVS[MIM] Vicus 1973 Lezoux[2]. No dated sites are recorded for this, but it is not an early stamp of Cintusmus, as it was used on forms 31R and 79R. *c.* A.D. 155–180.

24. Cintusmus i 56 Dr.33 CINTVS[M] JMN 1956. 128. 26A Lezoux[2]. An occurrence on Hadrian's Wall and the use of form 79 with this stamp again suggests Cintusmus's later work. *c.* A.D. 155–180.

25. Clemens ii 2a Dr.31R CLEMENTI JMN 1956. 128. 26A Lezoux[1]. Wasters with this stamp were in the kiln noted under Albusa. *c.* A.D. 165–190.

26. Comus iii 4a Dr.38 ƧVMOϽ RFM BA 285 Argonne[2] and Trier[2]. As often with East Gaulish ware, there are no closely dated sites in the record, but since the stamp was used on form 27, a date in the mid-second century is likely.

27. Conatius 3a Dr.31R CONATIVSF 1966 Rheinzabern[1]. The record of forms, including 31R, 32, 40, 79 and Ludowici Tb, suggests late second- or early third-century date.

28. Craca 1a Dr.33 CRACA·F RFM BA 286 Trier[2]. Neither the distribution nor the forms help much with dating. Probably Antonine.

29. Cracuna i 2a Dr.18/31 CRACVNA·F RFM BA 381 From the well Lezoux[1]. Balmuildy, Castlecary, Inveresk, the Castleford pottery shop, Verulamium Per. IIB, *c.* A.D. 130–155.

30. Cunissa ii 2b Dr.31 CVNISSA RFM BA 287 Rheinzabern[2]. No closely dated sites. The use of forms 31R and 32 points to the late-second or early-third century.

31. Dagomarus 11a Dr.18/31 DAGOMRI RFM BA 288 Les Martres-de-Veyre,[2] Lezoux[2]. This stamp probably belongs to Dagomarus's period at Lezoux. It occurs in the Castleford pottery shop, where it may, however, be residual. *c.* A.D. 120–140.

32. Dester 1a Dr.31 DESTERF Now lost Lezoux[1]. Dester's work is not common, but a record at Catterick, taken with the use of forms 31R and 79 suggests a date *c.* A.D. 155–195.

33. Divixtus i 9d Dr.37? [DI]VIXF *Bruce*, 1884, p. 274, now lost Lezoux[1]. The common large decorated ware stamp, frequent in Antonine Scotland. *c.* A.D. 150–175.

34. Divixtus iii 1b Dr.31 DIV[IXTVƧ] RFM BA 289 Rheinzabern[1]. The forms, including 31R and 32, suggest a late second- or third-century date.

35. Do(v)eccus i 11f. Dr.38? DOECCVS (circular) JMN 1956.128.106A Lezoux[2]. This uncommon stamp was used on form 79 and presumably is of the same date as the decorated bowls of Doveccus, *c.* A.D. 160–190.

36. Do(v)eccus i 13a Dr.37 [D]OIICCVS retr. *Bruce*, 1884, p. 274, now lost. Lezoux[1]. This stamp appears at Benwell and in the Brougham cemetery. *c.* A.D. 160–190.

37. Euritus 1a Dr.31 EVRITVSF RFM BA 290 Rheinzabern[1]. As usual, for Rheinzabern only the record of forms hints at the date. Late second- or third-century.

38. Gemenus 1a Dr.33 GEMENI.M RFM BA 291 Lezoux[1]. The potter's decorated ware and his use of forms 31R, 79/80 and 79R all suggest mid- or late-Antonine production. *c.* A.D. 160–195.

39. Genitor ii 5b Dr.31R GENITORF RFM BA 116 Lezoux[1]. Catterick, Chesterholm, Ebchester, Hadrian's Wall (2, Chesters). Used on 31R and 79. *c.* A.D. 160–195.

40. Genitor iii 2a Dr.31 [GENI]TOR RFM BA 317 La Madeleine[2]. The use of forms 18/31, 18/31R and 27 is typical of La Madeleine in the period A.D. 130–160.

41. Habilis 5c Dr.31 and Walters 79 HABILIS[F] and HABILISF both Vicus 1973 Lezoux[2]. At Lezoux, Habilis's work has been recorded in mid-Antonine contexts. Other stamps are known from Chesters and Chester-le-Street. That and the forms used, including 15/31, 18/31R, 27, 79 and 80 suggests a range *c.* A.D. 150–180.

42. Ianuarius vi 3a Dr.31R IANVARI[VSF] RFM BA 292 Rheinzabern[1]. Also used with form 32. This potter's other records include the Brougham cemetery, Chesterholm and Malton. Probably late-Antonine.

43. Illianus 1a Dr.33 IKKIANI·M RFM BA 293 Lezoux[1]. There are no closely dated sites for this stamp. Its use on forms 31, 31R and 38 points to the Antonine period, however.

44. Iulianus iii 3e Dr.37 IVLIANVS retr. RFM BA 96 Rheinzabern[1]. A record at Niederbieber, the decoration of his bowls, and the use of forms 31R and 32 all suggest dating to *c.* A.D. 180–220.

45. Iulius viii Cursive signature Dr.37 RFM BA 4 Rheinzabern[1]. If it is permissible to judge by the nastiness of his decoration, Iulius viii will have worked in the third century.

46. Iullinus ii 3a Dr.37 IVLLINIM retr. Bruce, 1884, p. 274, now lost Lezoux[1]. This stamp was also used on plainware. It was in the Pudding Pan Rock cargo and occurs at Chesterholm. *c.* A.D. 165–195.

47. Iustus ii 3a Dr.37 IVS+[M] RFM BA 67 Lezoux[1]. Used only on decorated ware, this appears at Great Chesters, Malton and Piercebridge. *c.* A.D. 160–190.

48. Lugetus i 10c Dr.33 KVGETVS JMN 1956.128.106A Argonne[3]. Presumably Antonine, but neither the forms nor the sites allow precision.

49. Macrianus 1a Dr.31R MAC·RIA·NI RFM BA 296 Lezoux[2]. Records from Bainbridge, Pudding Pan Rock and on forms 31R and 79R show this to be a late stamp of the potter. *c.* A.D. 150–185.

50. Macrianus 4a Dr.18/31 [M]CRIANI 1967 U/S. Lezoux[3]. If the same man as the last, then his early stamp in view of its use on forms 18/31 and 27. *c.* A.D. 140–160?

51. Macrinus iii 5b Dr.33 MACRINI RFM BA 298 Lezoux[1]. Chesters, Newstead, the Wroxeter Gutter group, but also on f.27. *c.* A.D. 150–180.

52. Macrinus III 5d Dr.31 MACRINI RFM BA 297 Lezoux[1]. Bainbridge, Hadrian's Wall (Chesters) and forms 31R and 79 suggest a slightly later range than 5b. *c.* A.D. 155–185.

53. Mainacuus 2a Dr.31 M·AINCNI RFM BA 300 Lezoux[1]. Pudding Pan Rock, Rudchester, with forms 31R and 79/80. *c.* A.D. 160–195.

54. Maior i 6b Dr.33 M⅄IORIS JMN 1956.128.106A Lezoux[1]. Piercebridge and f.80. *c.* A.D. 160–190.

55. Maior i 11a Dr.31R [MAIO]R·I RFM BA 361 Lezoux[1]. Haltonchesters, Malton and forms 31R and 79R. *c.* A.D. 160–190.

56. Mammius 1a Dr.31R ⋋AMMI· JMN 1956.128.106A now lost Lezoux[1]. Benwell, Chester-le-Street, Ilkley and f.80. *c.* A.D. 160–190. (A broken die, originally giving M⅄MMI oF.)

57. Mammius 2a Dr.33 MAMM·OΓ JMN 1956.128.106A Lezoux[2]. Bainbridge, Chesterholm, Great Chesters, Haltonchesters, Ilkley. *c.* A.D. 160–190.

58. Marcellinus ii 2a Dr.33 MARCELLIИII RFM BA 299 Lezoux[1]. Chesters, Ebchester, Greta Bridge, Pudding Pan Rock. This stamp is also on many wasters in the Lezoux kiln noted under Albusa. *c.* A.D. 165–195.

59. Marcus v 5a Dr.33 and Walters 79R MARCIM retr. Both JMN 1956.128.106A Lezoux[1]. Chesters, Piercebridge with forms 31R, 79, 79R. *c.* A.D. 160–195.

60. Marcus v 8a Dr.33 MARCII JMN 1956.128.106A Lezoux[1]. Chesterholm, Chesters, Haltonchesters. *c.* A.D, 160–195.

61. Martinus v 4a Dr.31R [MⅠꓤTI]Ɲ retr. RFM BA 321 Rheinzabern[1]. Martinus probably moved to Pfaffenhofen from Rheinzabern, but as he made forms like 32 at the latter, he is probably to be dated *c.* A.D. 180–200, there.

62. Martio 3a Walters 79 MARTIOM RFM BA 115 Lezoux[1]. The stamp was used on moulds for f.37 of Antonine date and on forms 79 and 80. *c.* A.D. 150–180.

63. Martio 4a Dr.33 MARTIIO JMN 1956.128.106A Lezoux[1]. Bainbridge, Catterick (2), Haltonchesters, Hadrian's Wall (Chesters). *c.* A.D. 155–185.

64. Mascellio i 4b Dr.31R MASCEⱢⱢIO JMN 195.128.106A now lost Lezoux[1]. Catterick, Haltonchesters, Wallsend, with stamps from other dies at Bainbridge, Brougham cemetery. Catterick, Piercebridge, Pudding Pan Rock. *c.* A.D. 165–195.

65. Martius iv 1b Dr.33 (2) MARTIM RFM BA 302 and JMN 1956.128.26A Lezoux[1]. Brougham cemetery, Chesters, Malton with form 80. *c.* A.D. 160–190.

66. Matina 3a Dr.31R MATINA JMN 1956.128.26A Rheinzabern[1]. Niederbieber (2) with 32 and Ludowici Tl′. *c.* A.D. 180–220.

67. Max(i)minus i 9a Dr.31 and Dr.33 M⅄XMIИ 1967 U/S and RFM BA 301 Lezoux[1]. Bainbridge, Chesterholm, Cramond and two examples in the Sompting grave with a coin of Geta as Caesar in fresh condition (Britannia V (1974), p. 312, where the stamp is given incorrectly). *c.* A.D. 170–200.

68. Mercator iv 3a Dr.37 MERCATORM retr. *Bruce*, 1884, p. 274, now lost Lezoux[1]. Binchester, Chesters, Catterick. The decorated ware is common in contexts of A.D. 160–190 or so.

69. Mercator iv 39 Dr.30 [ME]RCATOR retro RFM BA 8 Lezoux[1] as for no. 68.

70. Mossius ii 1a Dr.33 [MOSSI]MA/ RFM BA 320 Lezoux[1]. Verulamium Per. IID and form 80. Other stamps at Benwell and Malton, but also on form 27. *c.* A.D. 150–180.

71. Mox(s)ius v 1a Dr.31R [M]oXIMⱯ RFM BA 324 Lezoux[2]. Bainbridge, Chesters and used on the rims of bowls in the style of Paternus v and Do(v)eccus i *c.* A.D. 160–190.

72. Muxtullus 1a Dr.31 ·M[VXTVLLI·M] Lezoux[2]. One of Muxtullus's later stamps, this is known from Catterick, Chester-le-Street, Hadrian's Wall and the Wroxeter Gutter. His early work appears *c.* A.D. 140–155, so this stamp will have been current *c. A.D.* 155–175.

73. Namilianus 1a Dr.31 NΛMILIANI·M RFM BA 357 Lezoux[2]. Chesterholm, Malton, Wallsend and forms 31R and 79. *c.* A.D. 160–195.

74. Namilianus 3b Dr.31R [NAMILIⱵNI RFM BA 326 Lezoux[1]. Benwell (2), Catterick, Cesterholm, Forden Gaer, Pudding Pan Rock. *c.* A.D. 160–195.

75. Parentinus Incomplete Dr.31R PAREN.TIΛV[RFM BA 354. Trier[2]. This stamp is unique, but others of the same man are from the Brougham cemetery and Niederbieber. *c.* A.D. 180–220.

76. Paterclinus 4a Dr.33 PATERCLINI RFM BA 304 Lezoux[1]. Bainbridge, Benwell, Chesterholm, Chesters, Ilkley, Malton, Wroxeter Gutter. *c.* A.D. 155–185.

77. Paternus iii 2c Dr.31 PATE[RNI·] RFM BA 305 Lezoux[1]. This is the man who stamped moulds in common with Ianuaris ii and used this stamp on forms 18/31, 18/31R and 27. *c.* A.D. 130–155.

78. Paternus v ?a Dr.37 PΛΞ RNIΞ retr. RFM BA 97 Lezoux[1]. The contracted stamp of the well-known mid- and late-Antonine maker of decorated ware. His work is characteristic of Hadrian's Wall, the reoccupied hinterland forts and the Wroxeter Gutter. *c.* A.D. 160–195.

79. Pottacus 2a Dr.33 (2) POTTACI RFM BA 306–7 Lezoux[1]. Chesterholm, Malton, forms 31R, 79 and the Lezoux kiln noted for Albusa. *c.* A.D. 165–195.

80. Quadratus iii 1a Dr.79 QVADRATI RFM BA 308 Lezoux[1]. Brougham Cemetery, Malton, Wallsend and forms 31R, 79, 79R. *c.* A.D. 160–190.

81. Quintilianus i 1b Dr.31 QVINTILI[ANIM] Vicus 1973 now lost Lezoux[1]. Castleford Pottery shop, Catterick, Inveresk. His decorated bowls are from moulds with this stamp. *c.* A.D. 125–150.

82. Quintus v 5b Dr.31R QVIN[TI.M] RFM BA 309 now lost Lezoux[1]. Malton and forms 31R, 79. Other stamps are better attested with: Benwell, Birdoswald, Catterick, Chester, Haltonchesters and Pudding Pan Rock. *c.* A.D. 160–195.

83. Quintus v 5b Dr.31R QVIN[TI M] JMN 1956.128.26A Lezoux[1], as for no. 83.

84. Reginus vi 7k Dr.31 REG[IN]VSF RFM BA 319 Rheinzabern[1]. No closely dated sites, but Reginus was one of the early potters of Rheinzabern, having moved there from Heiligenberg. *c.* A.D. 160–190.

85. Remicus 1b Dr.33 EMIC RFM Ba 294 East Gaul 1b or b f.33]EMI ₋₋₋ RFM BA 295. Remicus's stamps are always poorly impressed and often illegible. He is not a late potter, as he made forms 18/31 and 27 (perhaps at La Madeleine?) and his stamp is in period II of Zwammerdam (before *c.* A.D. 130–160). Probably *c.* A.D. 130–160.

86. Sabellus 6a Dr.18/31 (3) ƧΔBEⱢⱢVƧ RFM BA 277, 355 and 122 La Madeleine. Cardurnock, Stanwix. *c.* A.D. 130–160.

87. Sacrillus 5a Dr.33 SACRILLI RFM BA 310 Lezoux[1]. Bainbridge, Catterick, Haltonchesters with form 31R. Other stamps appear at Pudding Pan Rock and on the rim of a bowl from a mould of Do(v)eccus. *c.* A.D. 160–190.

88. Sadiodus 1a Dr. 33 SADIOꟼ RFM BA 284 Trier? An uncommon stamp with

the only other records in the Landesmuseum, Trier (from Trier?), Arentsburg and the Valkenberg ZH Woerd. Probably late-Antonine.

89. Sanciro 1a Dr.33 SA/CIRO 1973 Vicus Lezoux[1]. Chesters and the use of form 79–80. Mid- to late-Antonine.

90. Scoplus 1a Dr.31 and Dr.33 SCOPL[and SCOPLIM JMN 1956.128.106A and 1973 Vicus Lezoux[1]. Bainbridge, Carrawburgh, Catterick, Chesterholm (4), Forden Gaer, Haltonchesters, Ilkley. c. A.D. 160–195.

91. Secundinus v 4a Dr.33 (2) SECVNDINI and SECVN[JMN 1956.128.106A BA 311 Lezoux[1]. This stamp has no sound dating evidence, but another of this man's was used on moulds of mid- or late-Antonine date and on forms 31R, 79 and 80. Probably c. A.D. 155–190.

92. Severianus ii 3e Dr.31 SIIVIIRIANV[2F] RFM BA 312 Rheinzabern[1]. Only the forms (32 etc., 36) may be used as evidence of date. Probably late second- or third-century.

93. Severus iv 3e Dr.31R SEΛERIM JMN 1956.128.106A Lezoux[1]. Bainbridge, Chesters, Chesterholm, Malton and the Lezoux kiln noted under Albusa. c. A.D. 165–195.

94. Sollemnis iii 1a Dr.31 SOLLEMNISF Rheinzabern[1]. Except for one record from Dragonby, all the other examples of this stamp are from Germany. Its use on forms 32, Ludowici Tb and Tr suggests a late second- or third-century date.

95. Tittus 5a′ Dr.27 TITTV RFM BA 314. From a broken die originally giving TITTVSF. Lezoux? No closely dated sites, but consistent use of form 27 and the precise form suggest Hadrianic date.

96. Tituro 1a Dr.31 TITVRONISƆ 1966 U/S. Benwell, Chesterholm, Malton, Wallsend, Wroxeter Gutter. c. A.D. 160–190.

97. Venerandus 5a Walters 79 VENERΛND RFM BA 316 Lezoux[1], Toulon sur Allier[2]. The only dating is derived from the forms (31R, 79, 79R and 80). Probably c. A.D. 150–180.

98. Verecundus iii 1a Dr.31 ·VERE[CVNDI] RFM BA 359 Lezoux[2]. Chesters, Malton. Other stamps Birdoswald, Chester-le-Street, Housesteads. c. A.D. 155–195.

99. Vnas? 1a Dr.33 RFM BA 313 Lezoux? Perhaps an illiterate stamp. Antonine.

100. Vnicus 1a Dr.33 (2) VNICVSF RFM BA 358, 315 Lezoux[1]. A rare stamp with hints of dating only from the Brougham cemetery. Mid- or late-Antonine.

Stamps possibly from South Shields include:

101. Asiaticus 6a Dr.31 Blair Coll. South Shields? Lezoux[1]. Catterick. Antonine.

102. Aticus i 2a Dr.18/31 OFA.T.ICI South Shields? (JMN in a box with Corbridge samian but the sherd is marked L(awe) 18.4.81. Cf. AA[2]X—the only recorded example anywhere other than La Graufesenque. Flavian-Trajanic.

103. Firmo ii 3a Dr.18R ·FIRMONS "Blair Coll., South Shields?" Perhaps unlikely, as the stamp was used on f.29 and should be Flavian rather than Flavian-Trajanic.

We have not listed unidentified fragments.

Each entry reads as follows: Name of potter; Form; Reading; Date of finding or museum collection in which the piece now resides or publication from which it is taken; Pottery; Parallels; Date.

The superscript numbers attached to the names of potteries mean:

1. An example, or examples, of the same stamp are known from the pottery.
2. That other stamps of the same man are known from the pottery or potteries in question.
3. That the stamp is assigned to the pottery named on grounds of fabric and, or, distribution.

In quoting parallels for the stamps the sites and forms named refer to examples from the same die, unless otherwise stated. What we have done is to note occurrences at all military sites in Scotland and the north of England and any other finds significant for dating.

Comments

It will be seen that there are no potters' stamps certainly from South Shields from the South Gaulish potteries. It is possible that the single stamp of At(t)icus i could be from South Shields, especially as South Gaulish decorated ware has been recorded there, but its presence need not imply any pre-Hadrianic occupation.

The numbers of central Gaulish stamps definitely of pre-Antonine date are small, but not exceptionally so for forts associated with the Hadrian's Wall system. What is very noticeable, and will be clear from examination of the parallels, is that the distribution of stamps chronologically fits remarkably well with the general record for Hadrian's Wall. This certainly seems to imply that the fort at South Shields was either not occupied in the period around A.D. 140–160, or that there was a much lower density of activity then.

Having checked such records as we have for the decorated ware from South Shields, and it probably includes almost everything down to the recent excavations, this seems to tell the same story.

The only other matter calling for comment is the source of the samian ware. As usual, a little of the pre-Antonine material is from Les Martres-de-Veyre, but both at that period, and more so in the Antonine period, it is clear that South Shields was supplied basically from Lezoux. The only other central Gaulish pottery which might be in question is Toulon-sur-Allier (Venerandus), but that particular stamp was used at Lezoux and the probability is that this particular piece is from the latter. The East Gaulish ware falls into a pattern which is familiar for sites in north-east England, namely that the bulk of it is from Rheinzabern, with Trier and the Argonne potteries having a marginal representation. Of the earlier East Gaulish factories only La Madeleine has any significant contribution.

THE DECORATED WARE (figs. 24–33)

John Dore, Kevin Greene and Catherine Johns
Drawings by Miriam Daniels

South Gaulish

1. 1967, from the lower levels of the rampart backing, to the west of the north gate. Dr.37. Thin ware, high gloss, high relief, clear moulding. For festoons and style of lower frieze see *Knorr*, 1919, taf. 36a and c, (Germanus). Without definitely being able to assign this piece to Germanus, the style belongs to him, or a potter of similar date. Not later than A.D. 90.

2. RFM/BA 13 and 41. Dr.37. A.D. 90–110. For similar style on a Dr.29 using the same leaf see *Knorr*, 1919, taf. 74e (from Rottweil).

3. RFM/BA 17. Dr.37. A.D. 90–110. For similar use of small panels see *Knorr*, 1919, taf. 26b. Bird is probably *O*.2237, *Knorr*, 1919, taf. 27 no. 6.

4. RFM/BA 71. Dr.37. A.D. 90–110. For similar style see *Knorr*, 1919, taf. 84f (of Vitalis).

5. RFM/BA 7. Dr.37. A.D. 90–110. The ovolo, large leaf spray and rosette tipped spiral occur together on *Knorr*, 1919, taf. 57h, from Rottweil. The lion and the large and small leaf sprays occur on *ibid*. taf. 68 also from Rottweil.

Central Gaulish

6. RFM/BA 61. Dr.37. IOENALIS or DONNAUCUS *c*. A.D. 100–120. The acanthus leaves were used by both Ioenalis and Donnaucus, (*S. and S.* fig. 10, no. 45 and fig. 11, no. 15). *Ibid*. pl. 45, no. 517 shows a similar use in the upper frieze. For exact parallel cf. *Bushe–Fox, 1913*, pl. XV, no. 14, found in a pit with late South Gaulish ware. Illustrated.

7. JMN/455/1956.128.25A. Dr.37. MEDETUS–RANTO style. *c*. A.D. 100–125. Les Martres-de-Veyre fabric. Ithyphallic Pan: *O*.717, *D*.419. For fine wavy lines with column in between cf. *S. and S.* pl. 30, nos. 355, 356, 357. Illustrated.

8. 1967. Found over the floor of the extension to the West Guardchamber of the north gate. The sherd had been burnt and is obviously a survival in this context. Dr.37. Possibly COCATUS *c*. A.D. 100–120. The ovolo is very close to that of Cocatus (*S. and S.* fig. 6, no. 1) but the possibility remains that it could be any one of a number of Hadrianic ovolos with wavy line borders.

9. RFM/BA 9. Dr.37. Probably X–5 or X–6. *c*. A.D. 125–150. The ovolo is probably that of X–5 (*S. and S.* fig. 16, no. 1, *Rogers* B31). Coquerel: *O*.2361, *D*.1025b, Two figures: *O*.155 and 96, *D*.100 and 338. The chevrons are similar to those used by X–6 (*S. and S.* pl. 75, no. 15). For the wavy lines with rudimentary astragalus terminals, cf. *ibid*. pl. 67, nos. 2 and 3. Illustrated.

10. RMF/BA 66. Dr.37. Probably X–6. *c*. A.D. 125–150. Man holding scyphos: *O*.571,

D.534a. X–6 uses wavy lines with trifid terminals, cf. *Rogers* G32 and *S. and S.* fig. 18, no. 2, and also the triple bordered festoon, cf. *S. and S.* pl. 75, no. 16. Illustrated.

11. 1973. Dr.37. Probably X–6. *c.* A.D. 125–150. Fragment of foot-ring and bottom of decoration, including a basal wreath of chevron motifs as on *S. and S.* pl. 75, no. 15.

12. 1973. Dr.37. Possibly X–6. Fragment including large double-bordered ovolo with central projection and rosette-tipped tongue, and wavy line border. Probably *Rogers* B32, *S. and S.* fig. 18, no. 2.

13. 1973. Dr.37. Probably BUTRIO. *c.* A.D. 120–140. Although no close parallels can be cited, the tiered cups are very close to *S. and S.* fig. 13, no. 7, and the ovolo could be that of Butrio (*ibid.* fig. 13, no. 2). The rosette, however, resembles that of Acaunissa. For its use in a double-bordered festoon, cf. *ibid.* pl. 80, no. 20. Illustrated.

14. 1973. Dr.37. BUTRIO. Dog: *O*.1915a, no exact parallels for other animals. Ovolo: *S. and S.* fig. 13, no. 2, with bead row. Freestyle decoration with feathered leaves is typical of Butrio, though the particular leaf used here is not usually found on his bowls. The style is very close to *S. and S.* pl. 57, no. 653. Illustrated.

15. 1973. Dr.37. BUTRIO. Ovolo: possibly *S. and S.* fig. 13, no. 2. Latticed column beneath festoon: *ibid.* fig. 13, no. 16. Details and fabric suggest Butrio. Illustrated.

16. 1966. Dr.37. Possibly the QUINTILIANUS group. *c.* A.D. 120–150. Fragment showing a single-bordered ovolo with central projection, and beaded tongue with rosette tip (possibly *S. and S.* fig. 15, no. 2 or fig. 43, no. 1). Such ovolos were used by Quintilianus and the fabric would suggest a Hadrianic or early-Antonine date.

17. 1967. Dr.37. Possibly the QUINTILIANUS group. Fragment showing double ring and wavy line border with eight-lobed rosette terminal. All these details were used by Quintilianus or associates, as on *S. and S.* pl. 70, no. 19.

18. 1966. Dr.37. ACAUNISSA or SACER. *c.* A.D. 120–150. The ovolo could be that of Sacer (*Rogers* B14, *S. and S.* fig. 22, no. 1) though too little remains for certain attribution. Hercules with serpents: *O*.783, *D*.464. Charyatid: *O*.1203, *D*.658. Sphinx: *O*.857, *D*.497. The rosette seems to be that used by Acaunissa (*Rogers* C249, *S. and S.* fig. 21, no. 5). Illustrated.

19. 1966. Dr.37. SACER. *c.* A.D. 120–150. The ovolo is that of Sacer (*Rogers* B12, *S. and S.* fig. 22, no. 2). *Birds: O*.2270d, 2239d. Female figure with cornucopia: *O*.802. The large leaves are used by Attianus and Cinnamus (*Rogers* H72). Illustrated.

20. 1967. Dr.37. SACER. The ovolo is used by Sacer (*Rogers* B14, *S. and S.* fig. 22, no. 1) as is the spear-shaped leaf between the festoons (*S. and S.* fig. 22, no. 3) and the triple plume motif (*Rogers* G56). Dog: *O*.1979. Hare: *O*.2129a. For style cf. *S. and S.* pl. 82, nos. 2, 3, 6 and 7. Illustrated.

21. RFM/BA 14. Dr.37. Probably SACER. Ovolo: *Rogers* B14, *S. and S.* fig. 22, no. 1. Male figure: *O*.698 (used by Sacer) Amor: *O*.378 (?). Illustrated.

22. JMN/113/1956.128.99A. From vent 4 of granary C8. Probably SACER. The row of circles is used by Donnaucus (*S. and S.* pl. 45, no. 522). The stag is used by Sacer. Illustrated.

23. RFM/BA 1, 20, 21 and 22. DONNAUCUS–SACER (*Rogers* potter X–14). *c.* A.D. 120–150. The ovolo is *Rogers* B18, used by Austrus, Sacer, Attianus and Donnaucus–Sacer. Gryphon: *O*.864, *D*.501. Apollo: *O*.91b, *D*.54. Lion: *O*.1379, *D*.737. Medallion is *Rogers* E2. Trifid motif is *Rogers* G73, for its use with the St. Andrew's Cross motif

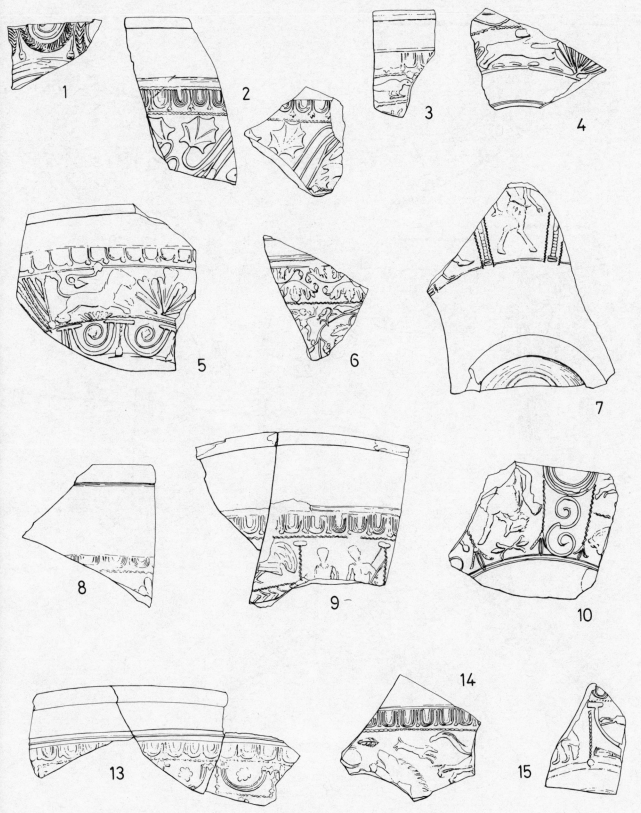

Fig. 24. 1:2.

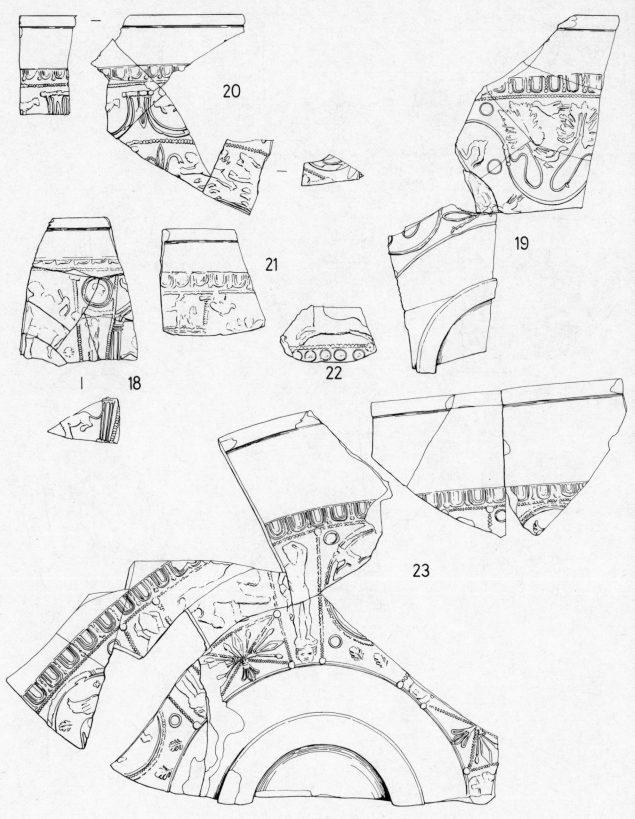

Fig. 25. 1:2.

cf. *S. and S.* pl. 84, no. 5 (Donnaucus–Sacer style). Leaves in field are *Rogers* J122. The examples of the ovolo, trifid and leaves which Rogers quotes from South Shields are from this piece. Illustrated.

24. JMN/578/1956.128.100A. Dr.37. DONNAUCUS–SACER. Ovolo: *Rogers* B14. Tree: *Rogers* N1, *S. and S.* pl. 83, no. 10 (Sacer), pl. 85, no. 9 (Attianus). Style similar to *S. and S.* pl. 42, no. 555, pl. 49, no. 584. Illustrated.

25. 1975. From the upper clay floor inside the east guardchamber of the north gate. Dr.37. DONNAUCUS–SACER. The ovolo is used by Sacer (*Rogers* B12, *S. and S.* fig. 22, no. 2). Both the lion (*O.*1422, *D.*574) and the "rock" ornament (*Rogers* U.141) occur on Donnaucus-style bowls, cf. *S. and S.* pls. 43–9. Illustrated.

26. RFM/BA 70. Dr.37. Possibly DRUSUS. *c.* A.D. 125–150. Victory: *O.*826, *D.*484. Hercules: *O.*784, *D.*469. *O.*784 occurs on the signed work of Drusus, who also uses fine bead rows, cf. *S. and S.* pl. 89, nos. 12, 14, 15 and 16. Illustrated.

27. JMN/455/1956.128.25A. Dr.37. Possibly DRUSUS. Lioness: *O.*1559. Leaves in field: tips of *Rogers* K2. For style, and use of tip of K2 and wavy line borders cf. *S. and S.* pls. 88 and 89. Illustrated.

28. 1973. Dr.37. Possibly ARCANUS or DRUSUS. Fragment of bottom of decoration, showing part of a beaded border and two trifid leaves placed end to end. Trifid leaves appear to be *Rogers* G89 used by Donnaucus–Sacer and Drusus. Fabric indicates an early-Antonine date.

29. JMN/455/1956.128.25A. Dr.37. Possibly DRUSUS or the LARGE S. POTTER. Clumsily applied foot-ring, thick patchy slip. The leaf tips could be *Rogers* K23, used by Drusus, who also uses fine beaded borders and the rings in field (*S. and S.* pl. 89). The Large S potter also uses fine borders and the rings, and the slightly larger version of the two gladiators (*O.*1001 and 1002), cf. *S. and S.* pl. 76, nos. 31–3. Illustrated.

30. 1967. From above the floor of the extension to the west guardchamber of the north gate. Dr.37. DOCILIS. *c.* A.D. 130–150. Ovolo: *Rogers* B24, *S. and S.* pl. 24, no. 1. Bird is probably *O.*2252. Festoon: *Rogers* F71, *S. and S.* pl. 24, no. 3. Illustrated.

31. 1973. Dr.37. AUSTRUS. Signed AVSTRI.OF. Stamp no. 6. For exact parallel cf. *S. and S.* pl. 95, no. 20 (formerly in the Black Gate Museum, Newcastle upon Tyne). Illustrated.

32. 1967. Dr.37. AUSTRUS. *c.* A.D. 125–150. Ovolo: *Rogers* B18, *S. and S.* fig. 25, no. 2, though the border of squarish, elongated beads is not normally used by Austrus. Tiered cups: *Rogers* Q53, *S. and S.* fig. 25, no. 9 Acanthus leaf: *Rogers* K5, *S. and S.* fig. 25, no. 11. Tiny spotted vase: *Rogers* T37, *S. and S.* fig. 25, no. 6. Illustrated. Since cataloguing this piece it has been realised that the fabric and finish of the vessel is very similar to that of ware from La Madeleine. The ovolo is similar to Ricken's ovolo C (1934, taf. VII C) and the bead row also occurs on work from La Madeleine (*op. cit.* taf. X).

33. 1973. Dr.37. Probably AUSTRUS. Fragment of lower part of decoration, including parts of three panels separated by bead rows with eleven-point rosette terminals. In l.h. panel Venus drying herself (*O.*290). In centre panel crouching animal to left. The rosette is probably that of Austrus (*S. and S.* fig. 25, no. 4) on whose signed work *O.*290 appears.

Fig. 26. 1 : 2.

34. JMN/578/1956.128.100A. Dr.30. LAXTUCISSA. *c.* A.D. 150–180. Ovolo: *Rogers* B106, *S. and S.* fig. 27, no. 1. Apollo: *O.*91a, *D.*54a. The large leaf is used by the Quintilianus group (*Rogers* H117), the smaller by Laxtucissa (*Rogers* J162, *S. and S.* fig. 27, no. 1). For style cf. *S. and S.* pl. 98, no. 15. Illustrated.

35. 1973. Dr.37. Possibly LAXTUCISSA. The bead rows and coarseness indicate a relatively advanced date. *S. and S.* pl. 97, nos. 3 and 4 show similar vertical rows of rather rectangular beads. The ring is the same size as that used by Laxtucissa (*S. and S.* fig. 27, no. 7). The fabric has a deceptively early appearance. Illustrated.

36. 1973. Dr.37. Possibly LAXTUCISSA. Fragment of large winding scroll with corded "cigar" in field. The size of the "cigar" and its cording is close to that used by Laxtucissa (*S. and S.* fig. 27, no. 4).

37. JMN/578/1956.128.100A. Dr.37. LAXTUCISSA or PATERNUS. The ovolo is used by both Paternus and Laxtucissa (*Rogers* B105, *S. and S.* fig. 27, no. 2 and fig. 30, no. 1). Both these potters use corded borders but only Paternus is recorded as having signed figure type *D.*261. Illustrated.

38. RFM/BA 97. Dr.37. PATERNUS. *c.* A.D. 160–190. Signed PATERN(——. Stamp no. 78. Illustrated.

39. JMN/578/1956.128.100A. Dr.37. PATERNUS. Ovolo: *Rogers* B106, *S. and S.* fig. 30, no. 4. The figure of Amor holding rods (*O.*450, *D.*265), occurs on the signed work of Paternus, as does the corded circle (*Rogers* E71, *S. and S.* fig. 30, no. 15). Illustrated.

40. RFM/BA 16 and 24. Dr.37. PATERNUS. Ovolo: *Rogers* B106, *S. and S.* fig. 30, no. 4. The sphinx (*O.*857, *D.*497) occurs on the signed work of Paternus. Illustrated.

41. RFM/BA 26. Dr.37. PATERNUS. Small fragment showing ovolo used by Paternus (*Rogers* B106, *S. and S.* fig. 30, no. 4).

42. RFM/BA 60. Dr.37. Possibly PATERNUS. Paternus uses the tripod (*Rogers* Q16, *S. and S.* pl. 105, no. 16), the double medallion, small circles and corded bead rows (cf. *S. and S.* pls. 104 and 105). Illustrated.

43. RFM/BA 67. Dr.37. IUSTUS. Signed IVST(——. Stamp no. 47. Illustrated on *S. and S.* pl. 111, no. 16.

44. RFM/BA 45 and 47. Dr.37. IUSTUS. *c.* A.D. 170–190. Ovolo: *Rogers* B234, *S. and S.* fig. 32, no. 2. Dolphin: *O.*2382, *D.*1050. Lozenge motif: *Rogers* U32, *S. and S.* fig. 31, no. 11. Illustrated.

45. RFM/BA 64. Dr.37. ADVOCISUS. *c.* A.D. 160–180. Female draped figure: *O.*926, *D.*540. Pan on mask: *O.*709, *D.*411. Male draped figure: *O.*907, *D.*524. The small rosette (*Rogers* C122, *S. and S.* fig. 33, no. 3) and fine-beaded borders are used by Advocisus who also signed *O.*709. For style cf. *S. and S.* pl. 112, no. 8 and pl. 114, nos. 34 and 36. Illustrated.

46. 1973. Dr.37. ADVOCISUS or DIVIXTUS. The ovolo could be that of Advocisus (*Rogers* B102, *S. and S.* fig. 33, no. 2) or Đivixtus (*Rogers* B12, *S. and S.* fig. 33, no. 4). The bead row terminals appear to be small rosettes as used by Advocisus (*S. and S.* pls. 112–14) within rings, as used by Divixtus (*S. and S.* pls. 115 and 116). The cornucopia, however, is closest to that used by Iullinus (*Rogers* U.260). Illustrated.

47. 1967. Dr.37. Probably CRICIRO. Poorly moulded, details unclear. Ovolo: probably *Rogers* B12, *S. and S.* pl. 33, no. 4. Snake and rock motif: *S. and S.* fig. 33, no. 5. For style cf. *S. and S.* pl. 117, no. 1. Illustrated.

Fig. 27. 1 : 2.

48. JMN/455/1956.128.25A. Dr.37. ALBUCIUS. *c.* A.D. 150–190. Ovolo: *Rogers* B107, *S. and S.* pl. 121, no. 13. Bear: *O.*1620. Lion attacking boar: *O.*1491, *D.*778 (but smaller). Leaf: *Rogers* J160, *S. and S.* pl. 120, no. 4. For style cf. *S. and S.* pl. 123. Illustrated.

49. 1973. Dr.37. ALBUCIUS. Ovolo: *S. and S.* fig. 35, no. 1. Rosette: *S. and S.* fig. 35, no. 1. For terminal on bead row cf. *S. and S.* pl. 120, no. 4. Illustrated.

50. 1973. Dr.37. ALBUCIUS. Small fragment showing double-bordered ovolo with central projection, and tongue with ring tip, bead row and vertical border with knobbed terminal. Cf. *S. and S.* pl. 122, no. 19.

51. RFM/BA 31. Dr.37. IULLINUS. *c.* A.D. 170–190. Ovolo: *Rogers* B156, *S. and S.* fig. 36, no. 2. Pillar with acanthus capital: *Rogers* P21, *S. and S.* fig. 36, no. 5. Large leaf: *Rogers* H70, *S. and S.* pl. 126, no. 18. Illustrated.

52. JMN/578/1956.128.100A. Dr.37. IULLINUS. Ovolo: *Rogers* B164, *S. and S.* fig. 36, no. 1. Illustrated.

53. 1973. Dr.37. IULLINUS. Ovolo: *Rogers* B164, *S. and S.* fig. 36, no. 1. Illustrated.

54. 1973. Dr.37. IULLINUS or CALETUS and SEVERUS. Conical basket: *Rogers* T29. Cantharus: *Rogers* T16. Latticed pillars can be found on the work of Albucius (*S. and S.* pl. 120, no. 1, which also has the cantharoi). Iullinus uses many arches, the large basket, the loose astragalus and the small cantharus (*S. and S.* pl. 127, nos. 24 and 25, and fig. 36, no. 11). All occur together with the latticed pillar on *S. and S.* pl. 128, no. 9, assigned to Caletus and Severus. Illustrated.

55. RFM/BA 73. Dr.37. CASURIUS. *c.* A.D. 160–195. Signed CASV(—— retro. Stamp no. 16. Illustrated.

56. JMN/578/1956.128.100A. Dr.37. CASURIUS. Ovolo: *Rogers* B176, *S. and S.* fig. 40, no. 2. Bird: *O.*2239, *D.*1037. Festoon: *Rogers* F38, *S. and S.* p. 137, no. 57. Acanthus leaf: *Rogers* K16, *S. and S.* pl. 133, no. 17. Illustrated.

57. JMN/455/1956.128.25A. Dr.37. Probably CASURIUS. Mask: *O.*1275. The dolphin and basket motif is similar to but smaller than *Rogers* Q58, used by Cinnamus. The undulating godroon is probably *Rogers* U151, *S. and S.* pl. 136, no. 46. For wavy line borders with small rosette terminals cf. *S. and S.* pl. 132, nos. 1–7. Illustrated.

58. 1973. Dr.37. Possibly CASURIUS or SERVUS ii. The ovolo is possibly that of Tetturo (*S. and S.* pl. 131, nos. 1 and 2). Stag: *O.*1784. Pan: *O.*717, *D.*419. For details of the corded pillar with astragalus capital cf. *S. and S.* pl. 131, no. 6 (Servus ii). The design has much in common with the bowls of Servis ii and possibly the wavy line bowls of Casurius, although the ovolo appears on neither of these. Illustrated.

59. 1973. Dr.37. Possibly CASURIUS. Fragment of lower part of decoration including part of two panels, one containing large leaf and tendril (*Rogers* H98) and the other the figure type *O.*638, *D.*344, both of which are used by Casurius.

60. JMN/578/1956.128.100A. Dr.37. Probably CASURIUS. Small fragment showing ovolo (*Rogers* B223, *S. and S.* fig. 40, no. 1), and part of a large leaf used by Casurius and Doeccus (*Rogers* H59).

61. JMN/455/1956.128.25A. Dr.37. BANUUS. *c.* A.D. 170–200. Ovolo: *Rogers* B153, *S. and S.* fig. 41, no. 2. Kneeling man: *O.*204, *D.*394. Female captive: *O.*1142a, *D.*642. Both signed by Banuus. Trifid leaf: *Rogers* G57, *S. and S.* fig. 41, no. 13. Rosette: *Rogers* C165, *S. and S.* fig. 41, no. 3. Illustrated.

62. JMN/578/1956.128.100A. Dr.37. BANUUS. Ovolo: *Rogers* B159, *S. and S.* fig. 41,

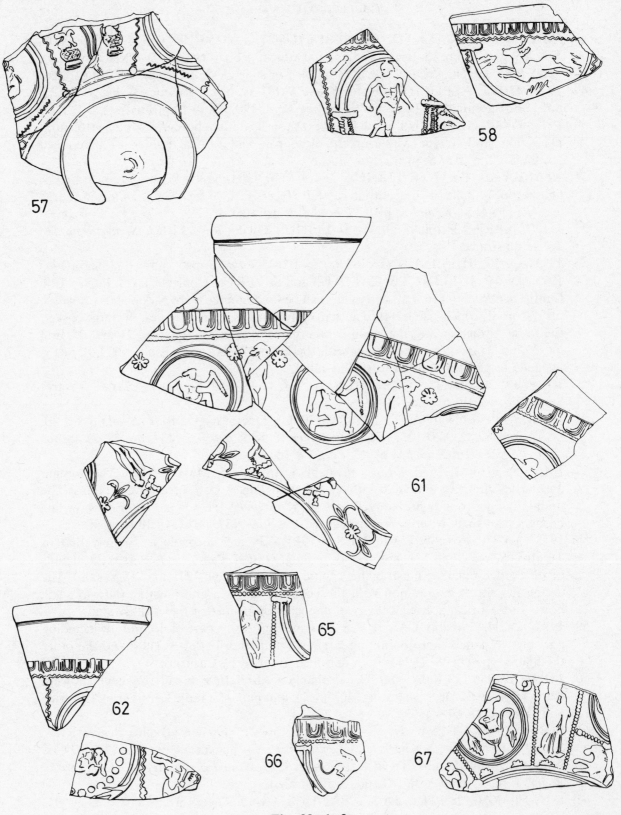

57

58

61

62

65

66

67

Fig. 28. 1:2.

no. 3. For an example of wavy lines on the work of Banuus cf. *S. and S.* pl. 140, no. 11. Illustrated.

63. 1973. Dr.30. DOECCUS. *c.* A.D. 170–190. Ovolo: *Rogers* B161, *S. and S.* fig. 44, no. 1. Kneeling man: *O.*204, *D.*394. Cupid: *O.*395, *D.*238. Dolphins in festoons: *O.*2382, 2392, *D.*1050, 1051. Sea horse: *O.*33, *D.*33. Large dolphin: *O.*2393/4, *D.*1052. Triton with double tail and club: *O.*19, *D.*16. Cornucopia: *Rogers* U246, *S. and S.* fig. 44, no. 8. For style cf. *S. and S.* pl. 148. Illustrated.

64. JMN/578/1956.128.100A. Dr.30. DOECCUS. Fragment in exactly the same style as no 189 but definitely not from the same vessel. Includes parts of three panels containing the Triton in double medallion, dolphin to R. in double-bordered festoon and kneeling man.

65. RFM/BA 44. Dr.37. DOECCUS. Ovolo: *Rogers* B160, *S. and S.* fig. 44, no. 2. The size of the beads is suggestive of Doeccus cf. *S. and S.* pl. 150, no. 41. Illustrated.

66. 1973. Dr.30. Probably DOECCUS. Ovolo is probably *Rogers* B160, *S. and S.* fig. 44, no. 2. The sphinx (*O.*853, *D.*496) appears on the signed work of both Doeccus and Banuus. For style see *S. and S.* pl. 151, no. 59. Illustrated.

67. RFM/BA 65. Dr.37. DOECCUS. Draped female: *O.*926, *D.*540. Sea horse: *O.*33, *D.*33. Both are signed by Doeccus. Vase: *Rogers* T27, used by Doeccus. Rosette: *S. and S.* fig. 44, no. 5. The large squarish bead rows are typical of Doeccus. Illustrated.

68. JMN/455/1956.128.25A. Dr.27. Probably DOECCUS. Ovolo is probably *Rogers* B161, *S. and S.* fig. 44, no. 1. Figure: *O.*687, *D.*402, signed by Doeccus. Small leaves below: *Rogers* J149, *S. and S.* fig. 44, no. 27. Large leaf: *Rogers* H15, *S. and S.* fig. 44, no. 37. Small leaves: *Rogers* H117, *S. and S.* fig. 44, no. 24 and *Rogers* H152, *S. and S.* fig. 44, no. 26. Illustrated.

69. 1973. Dr.37. Possibly DOECCUS. Only a medallion survives, containing a marine lion (*O.*46, *D.*38) and beneath it a fish (*O.*2417, *D.*1062). Both figure types are used by a number of Antonine potters. For a close parallel cf. *S. and S.* pl. 147, no. 1 (Doeccus).

70. 1973. Dr.30. Possibly DOECCUS. Double medallion containing a cornucopia (*S. and S.* fig. 43, no. 4). Below is a dolphin (*O.*2394a). Both occur on the signed work of Doeccus.

71. JMN/455/1956.128.25A. Dr.37. Possibly DOECCUS. Medallion containing a dancing maenad and large leaf (*S. and S.* fig. 44, no. 6).

72. RFM/BA 8. Dr.30. MERCATOR iv. *c.* A.D. 170–190. Signed within medallion ——)RCATOR// retro. Stamp no. 69. Ovolo: *Rogers* B180, *S. and S.* fig. 43, no. 3. Gladiators in combat: *O.*1001 and 2, *D.*582 and 3. Illustrated.

73. RFM/BA 35. Dr.37. MERCATOR iv or DOECCUS. Ovolo: *Rogers* B180, *S. and S.* fig. 43, no. 3. Figure: *O.*638, *D.*344 used by Doeccus (*S. and S.* pl. 148, no. 25). Astragalus used by Mercator iv (*S. and S.* pl. 146, no. 10). Illustrated.

74. RFM/BA 56. Dr.37. MERCATOR iv or DOECCUS. Ovolo could be that of either potter (*S. and S.* fig. 43, no. 3, fig. 44, no. 2). The bird (*O.*2250a) appears on the signed work of Mercator iv but the festoon and the large squarish beads would be more appropriate for Doeccus. Illustrated.

75. 1973. Dr.37. Possibly MERCATOR iv. Fragment showing only ovolo which is poorly moulded but similar to *S. and S.* fig. 43, no. 3.

63

68

72

73

74

76

77

78

80

83

Fig. 29. 1 : 2.

76. RFM/BA 99. Dr.37. Possibly TITTIUS. *c.* A.D. 160–195. Goats: *O*.1836, *D*.889. Large eight-lobed rosette: *Rogers* C53. For its use as a repetitive motif cf. *S. and S.* pl. 146, no. 1. Illustrated.

77. 1973. Dr.37. CATUSSA ii. After A.D. 150. Signed ——)ATV(—— retro. Stamp no. 17. Cf. *S. and S.* p. 257 and pl. 152. Illustrated.

78. RFM/BA 32. Dr.37. PUGNUS. *c.* A.D. 150–195. Ovolo: *Rogers* B143, *S. and S.* fig. 45, no. 4. Rosette: *Rogers* C2, *S. and S.* pl. 155, no. 26. Crouching hare: *O*.2117. Panther: *O*.1518, *D*.799, signed by Pugnus. Maenad: *O*.819a. Spotted vase: *Rogers* U60. Illustrated.

79. 1973 and RFM/BA 22. Two fragments, not conjoined but almost certainly from the same vessel. Poor underfired orange fabric. Dr.37. Probably PUGNUS. Ovolo: *Rogers* B233, *S. and S.* fig. 45, no. 1.

80. RFM/BA 52. Dr.37. Probably PUGNUS. Ovolo: *Rogers* B233, *S. and S.* fig. 45, no. 1. Female captive: *O*.1142, *D*.642. Illustrated.

81. 1973. Dr.37. Probably PUGNUS. Fragment showing only ovolo (probably *Rogers* B233, *S. and S.* fig. 45, no. 1) and wavy line border.

82. RFM/BA 3 and 6. Dr.37. CINNAMUS. Signed CINNAMI retro. Stamp no. 20. Ovolo: *S. and S.* pl. 47, no. 1. Hercules with cantharos: *O*.774, *D*.449. Caduceus: *Rogers* Q27, *S. and S.* fig. 47, no. 27. Seated figure: *O*.156, *D*.93. Horseman: *O*.245, *D*.156. Cornucopia: *Rogers*: U254. Illustrated.

83. JMN/455/1956.128.25A. Dr.37. CINNAMUS. Ovolo: *Rogers* B223, *S. and S.* fig. 47, no. 1. Tree *Rogers* N7, used by Attianus and Sacer. Coquerel: *O*.2344a. Illustrated.

84. RFM/BA 11. Dr.37. CINNAMUS. Ovolo: *Rogers* B233, *S. and S.* fig. 47, no. 1. Stag: *O*.1791. Lion: *D*.795. Triton: *O*.25, *D*.20. Illustrated.

85. 1967. Dr.37. CINNAMUS. Ovolo: *Rogers* B143/4, *S. and S.* pl. 47, no. 3. For style cf. *S. and S.* pl. 163, no. 71. Illustrated.

86. 1973. Dr.37. CINNAMUS. Ovolo: *Rogers* B143/4, *S. and S.* pl. 47, no. 3. Figure: *O*.840. Hare: *O*.2116. Festoon: *Rogers* F41. For close parallel cf. *S. and S.* pl. 157, no. 7. Illustrated.

87. RFM/BA 36. Dr.37. CINNAMUS. Ovolo: *Rogers* B144, *S. and S.* pl. 47, no. 3. Sea horse: *O*.48a, *D*.34. Cornucopia: *Rogers* U.248, *S. and S.* fig. 47, no. 19. Large and small trifid leaves: *Rogers* G67, *S. and S.* fig. 47, no. 24, and *Rogers* G100, used by various Trajanic potters. For style cr. *S. and S.* pl. 159, no. 33. Illustrated.

88. RFM/BA 19. Dr.37. CINNAMUS. Ovolo: *Rogers* B231, *S. and S.* fig. 47, no. 2. Illustrated.

89. JMN/578/1956.128.100A. Dr.37. CINNAMUS. Ovolo: *Rogers* B143. *S. and S.* fig. 47, no. 3. Figure on right: *O*.143, *D*.88. Illustrated.

90. 1973. Dr.37. CINNAMUS. Ovolo: *Rogers* B231, *S. and S.* fig. 47, no. 2. Winged victory: *O*.809, *D*.474. Illustrated.

91. JMN/113/1956.128.9A. From vent 4, granary C8. Dr.37. CINNAMUS. Horseman: *O*.254, *D*.156, signed by Cinnamus. Horse: *O*.1904, *D*.905, signed by Cinnamus. Bear/boar: *O*.1618. Leaves: possibly *Rogers* N15, *S. and S.* fig. 47, no. 5. Illustrated.

92. 1973. Dr.37. CINNAMUS. Small fragment showing ovolo (*Rogers* B223, *S. and S.* fig. 47, no. 1).

93. 1973. Dr.37. CINNAMUS. As no. 92.

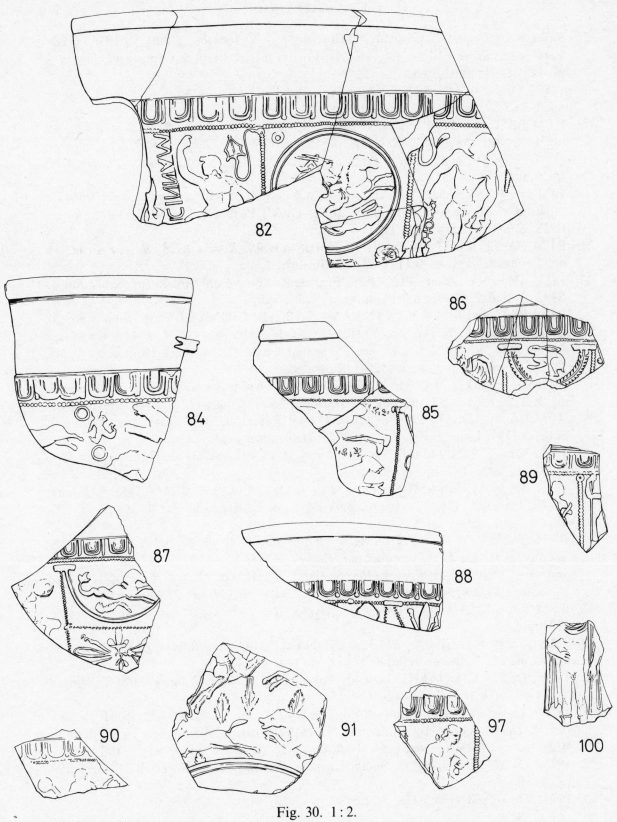

Fig. 30. 1 : 2.

94. JMN/578/1956.128.100A. Dr.37. CINNAMUS. Small fragment showing ovolo (*Rogers* B223, *S. and S.* fig. 47, no. 1) and part of a double-bordered medallion.

95. 1973. Dr.37. Probably CINNAMUS. Small fragment showing ovolo (*Rogers* B223, *S. and S.* fig. 47, no. 1).

96. 1967. Dr.37. Probably CINNAMUS. Small fragment showing ovolo (*Rogers* B143, *S. and S.* fig. 47, no. 3) and the head of a lion (*O*.1491, *D*.778).

97. 1967. Dr.37. CINNAMUS. Ovolo: *S. and S.* fig. 47, no. 3. Figure: *O*.78, *D*.46, signed by Caletus and Doeccus. Good quality, thin fabric. Probably early-Antonine.

98. RFM/BA 57. Dr.37. Small fragment showing ovolo: *Rogers* B153, used by a number of Antonine potters.

99. 1973. Dr.37. Small fragment showing part of a double-bordered medallion containing a Victory (*O*.812, *D*.475), used by Paternus and Catussa 1. Good, clear moulding.

100. RFM/BA 79. Déchelette 72. Appliqué figure, as on *O. and P.* pl. LXXXIV, no. 1.

East Gaulish

La Madeleine

101. RFM/BA 62. Dr.37. Spirals: *Fölzer*, taf. XXV, no. 98. Six-lobed rosette terminals to bead rows: *ibid*. no. 107. Acanthus leaf below festoon: *ibid*. no. 74. Figure of Apollo: *O*.77a, *Fölzer*, taf. XXV, no. 40. For example showing same scheme of decoration but using ovolos instead of spirals cf. *Fölzer*, taf. II, no. 34. Illustrated.

102. RFM/BA 5. Dr.37. Ovolo: *Fölzer*, taf. XXV, no. 119. Notched festoon: *ibid*. no. 111. Acanthus leaf: *ibid*. no. 74. Festoon with small gladiator (*O*.1056a): *ibid*. no. 50 and taf. II, no. 38. Illustrated.

103. RFM/BA 68. Dr.37. Six-lobed rosette and figure of Apollo as no. 101. Illustrated.

104. RFM/BA 53. Dr.37. Spiral in centre panel as no. 101. Illustrated.

105. JMN/578/1956.128.100A. Dr.37. Small fragment showing spirals (*Fölzer*, taf. XXV, no. 98) between bead row and raised line.

106. 1973. Dr.37. Small fragment showing running spirals in place of ovolo (*Ricken*, taf. VII, no. 33 and taf. IX, nos. 1 and 2).

107. Small fragment showing a frieze of small double medallions containing large eight-petalled rosettes. The latter could be Rheinzabern (*R. and F.* 0.64) but cf. also a La Madeleine type (*Ricken*, taf. 7, no. 37).

Lavoye

108. RFM/BA 2. Dr.37. Soft fabric, very abraded. Ovolo: *Ch. and G.* T6 or 7. Large leaves: *Fölzer*, taf. XXVIII, no. 406. The goat is found in panels on *Ch. and G.* fig. 57G, the stag on *ibid*. fig. 59, no. 2. Male figure: *Fölzer*, taf. XXVIII, no. 350. Illustrated.

109. RFM/BA 25, 75 and 85. Dr.37. Ovolo: *Ch. and G.* T7. Male figure in arch: *O*.144, *Fölzer*, taf. XXVIII, no. 350. Large fern leaves: possibly *ibid*. no. 389. Large leaf in field: *ibid*. no. 406. For example showing figure in arch cf. *Ch. and G.* fig. 62, no. 11. Illustrated.

110. RFM/BA 29. Dr.37. Ovolo not closely matched by any in *Ch. and G.* Horses: *Ch. and G.* fig. 59B. Running hares: *Ch. and G.* fig. 59C. Illustrated.

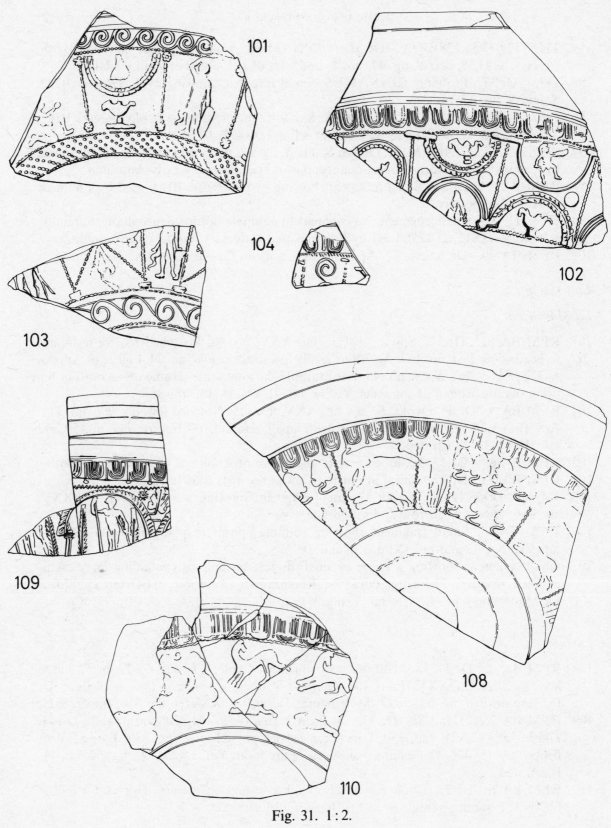

Fig. 31. 1 : 2.

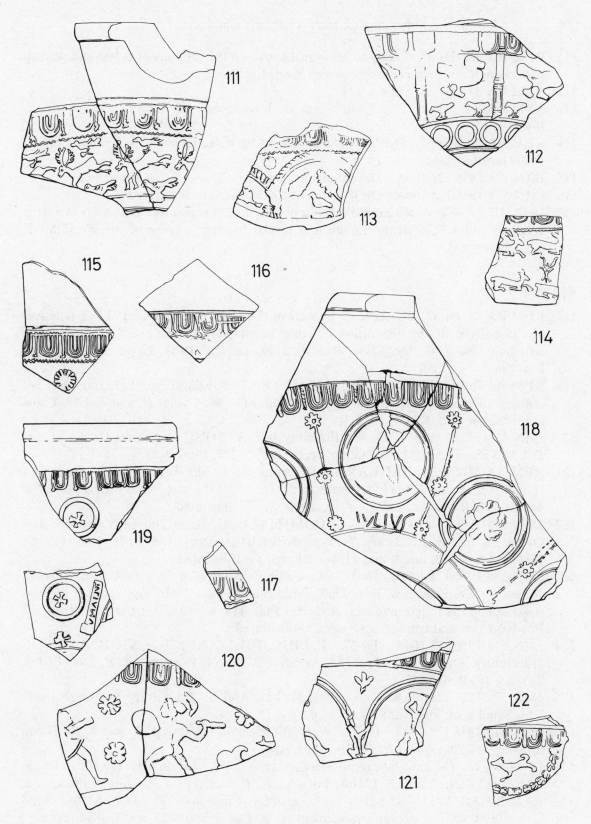

Fig. 32. 1 : 2.

111. RFM/BA 10. Dr.37. Likely to be from Lavoye on the grounds of fabric and general style though no exact parallels can be found. Illustrated.

112. RFM/BA 33. Dr.37. As no. 111.

113. RFM/BA 51. Dr.37. Ovolo: *Ch. and G.* U1. Arches: *Ch. and G.* fig. 59, no. 2. Illustrated.

114. RFM/BA 50. Dr.37. Ovolo would appear to be Ricken's ovolo B. Kneeling fawns: *O.*1703a. Illustrated.

115. JMN/578/1956.128.100A. Dr.37. Ovolo: possibly *Ch. and G.* S2. Illustrated.

116. JMN/578/1956.128.100A. Dr.37. Ovolo: *Ch. and G.* X6. Illustrated.

117. 1967. Dr.37. The ovolo cannot be closely matched. It is possibly *Ch. and G.* Y5. It is definitely not a Trier ovolo though it is similar in type to some of the Werkstatt II ones. Illustrated.

Rheinzabern

118. RFM/BA 4. Dr.37. JULIUS I. 1st half of third century. Signed IVLIVS (cursive) at the bottom of the decoration. Stamp no. 45. Ovolo: *R. and F.* E42. Rosette terminals: *ibid.* O48. Medallion: *ibid.* K20. Acorn: *ibid.* P161. Large leaf: *ibid.* P71. Illustrated.

119. RFM/BA 96 and JMN/578/1956.128.100A. Dr.37. JULIANUS I. Late 2nd–early 3rd century. Signed IVLIANV(——, retro. Stamp no. 44. Ovolo: *R. and F.* E17. Cross in medallion: *ibid.* K14.

120. JMN/455/1956.128.25A. Dr.37. Probably B.F. ATTONI. Antonine. Ovolo: *R. and F.* E3. Warrior: *ibid.* M176a. Other figure: *ibid.* M207. Illustrated.

121. RFM/BA 37. Dr.37. IANUARIUS II. Antonine. Ovolo: *R. and F.* E70. Amor with fruit basket: *R. and F.* M115a. Figure: *ibid.* M167. For the two arches with trifid leaf in between cf. *R./Lud. VI* taf. 19, particularly no. 7. Illustrated.

122. JMN/578/1956.128.100A. Dr.37. COMITIALIS II. Late 2nd–early 3rd century. Ovolo: *R. and F.* E2. Leafy festoon: *ibid.* KB123. Dog: *ibid.* T141. For style cf. *R./Lud. VI* taf. 80, nos. 9 and 11, taf. 81, no. 1a. Illustrated.

123. JMN/578/1956.128.100A. Dr.37. Ware mit Eierstab E25, 26. 3rd century. Ovolo: *R. and F.* E26. Bead row: *ibid.* 0206. Trifid motif: *ibid.* P116b. For example of bead row running right up to ovolo cf. *R./Lud. VI* taf, 114, no. 13. For trifid cf. *ibid.* no. 24. For bead row and trifid cf. *ibid.* no. 25. Illustrated.

124. JMN/578/1956.128.100A. Dr.37. JULIUS II/JULIANUS I or VICTORINUS II. 3rd century. Ovolo: *R. and F.* E45. Archer *ibid.* M174. For style cf. *R./Lud. VI* taf. 215, no. 10. Illustrated.

125. JMN/578/1956.128.100A. Dr.37. Possibly LUCANUS. 3rd century. Ovolo: *R. and F.* E53. Small bird: *ibid.* T258. Illustrated.

126. JMN/578/1956.128.100A. Dr.37. Ware mit Eierstab E8. Ovolo: *R. and F.* E8. Small dolphin: *O.*2396, *R. and F.* T192B. Illustrated.

127. RFM/BA 18. Dr.30. Ware B mit Zierglied *O.*382, 383. 3rd century. Ovolo: *R. and F.* E44. Small deer: *R. and F.* T110A. For style cf. *R./Lud. VI* taf. 228, no. 8. Illustrated.

128. RFM/BA 88. Dr.37. JULIUS I. 3rd century. Charioteer: *R. and F.* M164a. Bifid leaf: *ibid.* P149. For similar arrangement cf. *R./Lud. VI* taf. 153, no. 4. Illustrated.

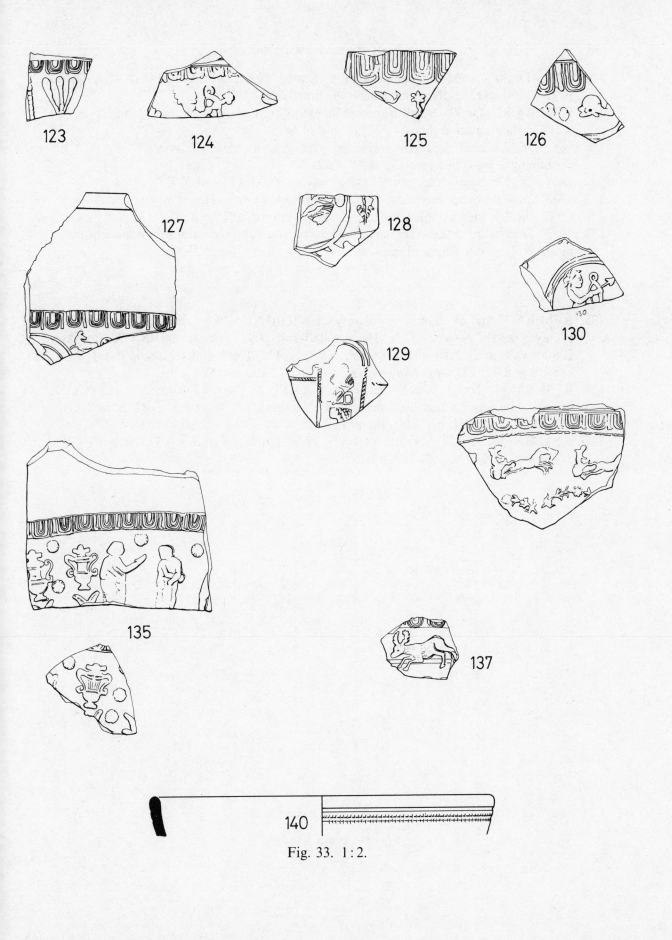

123   124   125   126

127

128

129

130

135

137

140

Fig. 33. 1 : 2.

129. 1973. Dr.30. Arch: *R. and F.* KB138. Seated figure: M258. Pedestal: *ibid.* O176. Borders: *ibid.* O242. Rosettes: *ibid.* R48. Illustrated.

130. RFM/BA 82. Dr.37. Small fragment including part of a double medallion (*R. and F.* K19) containing an archer (*O.272, R. and F.* M174).

13. 1966. Dr.37. Small fragment including part of a double medallion (*R. and F.* K19) containing a praying figure (*R. and F.* M213).

132. 1967. Dr.37. Small fragment showing only an ovolo (*R. and F.* E8).

133. 1973. Small fragment including dolphins and basket motif. This is apparently *R. and F.* O177, though the example illustrated seems cruder than that on no. 133.

134. 1973. Dr.37. Small fragment including part of a medallion containing an unidentifiable motif. Apparently Rheinzabern ware.

Trier

135. RFM/BA 30 and 58. Dr.37. Probably CENSORINUS. Late 2nd–early 3rd century. Figures: *O.988, Fölzer*, taf. XXIX, no. 480 and *O.990, Fölzer*, taf. XXIX, no. 482. Ovolo, vase and rosettes: *Fölzer*, taf. XV, no. 44. Ovolo and figures *ibid.* taf. XVI, nos. 19 and 32. Cf. also *Oelmann*, taf. VI, no. 10. Illustrated.

136. RFM/BA 34. Dr.37. Ovolo: *Fölzer*, taf. XXXI, no. 945. Chariot: *ibid.* taf. XXIX, no 504. The festoon was used both at Rheinzabern (cf. *R. and F.* KB125) and Trier (cf. *Fölzer*, taf. XXI, no. 728). Illustrated.

137. RFM/BA 54. Dr.37. Ovolo: possibly *Fölzer*, taf. XXII, no. 933. Stag: *O.1795, Fölzer*, taf. XXX, no. 624. Illustrated.

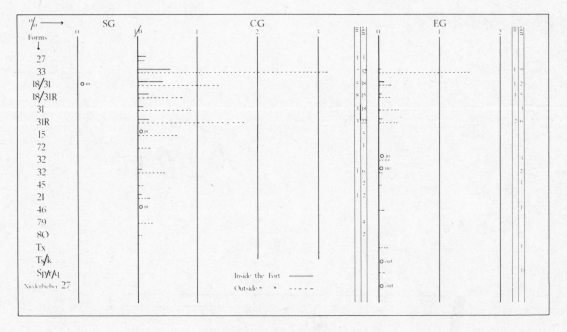

Fig. 34. Plain Samian.

138. 1973. Dr.37. Small fragment including a double leaf wreath, apparently used vertically in the design. The type is used both at Rheinzabern and Trier. This is almost certainly the latter. Fölzer's type 906 is very close.

139. 1973. Dr.37. Small fragment including small double rings in place of ovolo with part of a corded arch or medallion below. This is certainly not a Rheinzabern type. There are similar small rings at Trier, but nothing closely matching.

Other Fabric

140. 1967, from over the floor of the extension of the west guardchamber of the north gate. Small fragment of a bowl in African Red Slip Ware. Hayes form 9. A.D. 100–160. cf. Hayes, 1972, fig. 4, no. 2 and Dore and Greene, 1976, pp. 186–9.

THE COARSE POTTERY (figs. 35–46)

From the lower levels of the earth backing of the fort wall, to the west of the north gate. Included in this group were the following fragments of plain samian: 1 wall sherd Dr.27, 1 wall sherd Dr.18/31, both in a late South Gaulish fabric. 1 rim sherd Dr.27, 1 rim sherd Dr.18/31R, both in Hadrianic, Central Gaulish fabric.

1. Neck of flagon in light buff fabric. Trajanic–early Hadrianic.
2. Small jar or c-p. (cooking-pot) in light grey fabric with darker grey core. Trajanic–early Hadrianic.
3. Small jar or c-p. in brown fabric with dark grey surface. Trajanic–early Hadrianic.
4. Small jar or c-p. in light grey fabric with darker grey surface. Trajanic–early Hadrianic.
5. Small jar or c-p. in grey fabric with darker surface. Trajanic–early Hadrianic.
6. C-p. in grey fabric with rustic decoration. Trajanic–early Hadrianic.
7. C-p. in greyish brown fabric. Impressed decoration. The left hand edge of each impression has been pushed up to give the effect of rustication. Trajanic–early Hadrianic.

Nos. 1 to 7 are all of types which came on the northern market before the building of Hadrian's Wall, but continued in use afterwards. As pre-Hadrianic or early Hadrianic pottery was still in use, the defences are to be assigned to the earlier rather than the later part of Hadrian's reign.

From the drain cut into the lower end of the earth backing, to the west of the north gate

8. C-p. in light grey fabric with darker grey surface. Trajanic–early Hadrianic.
9. C-p. in BB2 fabric. Mid-Antonine.
10. C-p. in light grey fabric with darker grey surface. Trajanic–early Hadrianic.

Nos. 8 and 10 had doubtless survived as rubbish from the period of initial construction, while no. 9 is the significant fragment; the drain was still open late in the century.

From the foundation trench of the storehouse (*Building A1*)

11. C-p. in hard light grey fabric with darker grey surface. A.D. 110–130.
12. C-p. in BB1 fabric. Hadrianic–early Antonine.
13. C-p. in BB1 fabric. Hadrianic–early Antonine.
14. C-p. in BB1 fabric. Hadrianic–early Antonine.
15. C-p. in BB1 fabric. Hadrianic–early Antonine.
16. C-p. with rustic decoration in hard light grey fabric with darker grey surface. Trajanic–early Hadrianic.
17. C-p. in hard, fine, light grey, burnished fabric.

While nos. 11 and 16, like nos. 1 to 7, are of types which lasted into Hadrian's reign from earlier, nos. 12 to 15, with which no. 17 may be contemporary, are of a ware which made its first appearance in the north in *c*. A.D. 120. This has been disputed, but the evidence, both negative and positive, is overwhelming. An internal building of the fort, the earliest on its site, is thus shown to be no earlier than the early years of Hadrian.

From a pit cut by the foundations of the storehouse

18. Small carinated bowl in hard coarse grey fabric. Trajanic–early Hadrianic.
19. Beaker or crucible in grey fabric, burnt white. Intense heat has fused material on to the bottom of the vessel.

No. 18, like nos. 1 to 7, 11 and 16, is of a type found both before and after the building of the Wall, while no. 19 is undatable.

From the foundations of one of the storehouse partitions

20. Bowl or dish in hard dark grey fabric with black surface. The drooping rim has a fortuitous resemblance to a BB2 form. The fabric is quite other. Hadrianic–early Antonine.

No. 20, related to BB1 rather than BB2, provides yet another Hadrianic *terminus post quem.*

Sealed by the mason's chippings inside the north guardchamber of the west gate

21. C-p. in BB1 fabric. Hadrianic. Two examples.
22. C-p. in BB1 fabric. Hadrianic–early Antonine.

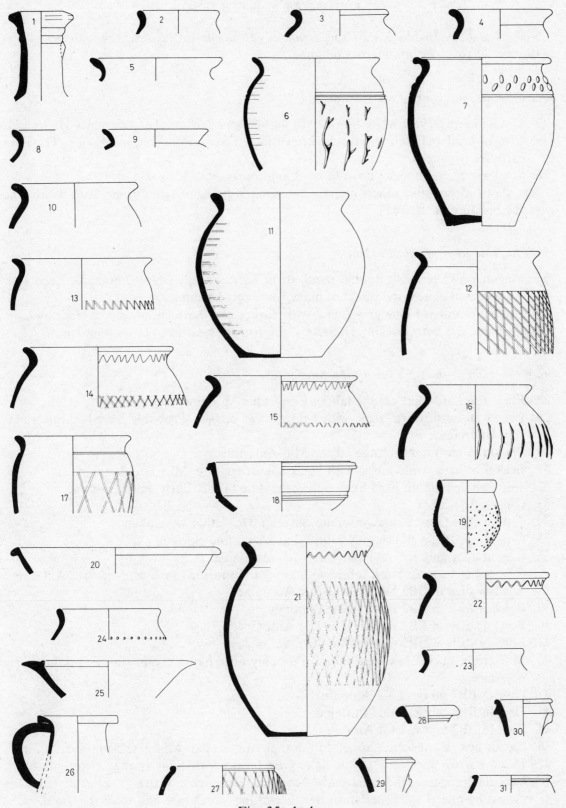

Fig. 35. 1:4.

Nos. 21 and 22 provide a Hadrianic *terminus post quem* for the defences in the same way as do nos. 12 to 15 for an internal building.

Sealed by the clay floor of the storehouse

23. C-p. in hard greyish white fabric with darker grey surface. Trajanic–early Hadrianic.
24. C-p. in hard buff fabric with darker surface. Decoration of small knobs. Trajanic–early Hadrianic.
26. Small segmental flanged bowl in hard light orange fabric. A.D. 120–150.

Nos. 23 to 25 resemble others already discussed in being of types in use both before and after the building of the Wall.

From the clay floor of the storehouse

26. Flagon neck, possibly double handled, in hard greyish white fabric with lead grey surface. Not closely datable, but likely to be pre-Antonine.
27. Small c-p. in hard blue grey fabric with darker grey burnished surface. Hadrianic.

Nos. 26 and 27, both possibly Hadrianic, are from the earliest occupation deposit.

From the drain at the west side of the *praetentura*

28. Flagon in hard light orange fabric. Early–mid Antonine.
29. Flagon in hard white fabric with light orange surface. Probably once had an orange slip. Hadrianic.
30. Flagon in hard light orange fabric. Mid-Antonine.
31. Beaker in hard white fabric with black colour coating. Mid–late Antonine.
32. Two-handled *olla* in hard light yellowish white fabric. Early–mid Antonine.
33. C-p. in BB1 fabric.
34. C-p. in BB2 fabric. Late Antonine–Severan. One other example.
35. C-p. in hard light bluish grey fabric. Late Antonine–Severan.
36. C-p. in light grey fabric. Hadrianic–early Antonine.
37. C-p. in hard coarse black fabric with gritty unburnished surface. Mid–late Antonine.
38. Bowl or dish in BB2 fabric. Mid–late Antonine.
39. Bowl or dish in BB2 fabric. Late-Antonine.
40. Bowl or dish in BB2 fabric. Mid–late Antonine.
41. Bowl or dish in BB2 fabric. Mid–late Antonine.
42. Mortarium in soft brick-red fabric. Probably once had a cream slip. Hadrianic–early Antonine.
43. Dish in BB2 fabric. Late-Antonine.
44. Dish in BB2 fabric. Mid-Antonine.
45. Dish in BB2 fabric. Mid-Antonine.
46. Castor box. Hard white fabric, dull orange colour coat. Mid–late Antonine.
47. Large narrow mouthed jar in light grey fabric with light orange core and black burnished surface. Hadrianic–early Antonine. Fragments of this vessel came from the pit cut by one of the foundation trenches of the storehouse and from the drain.

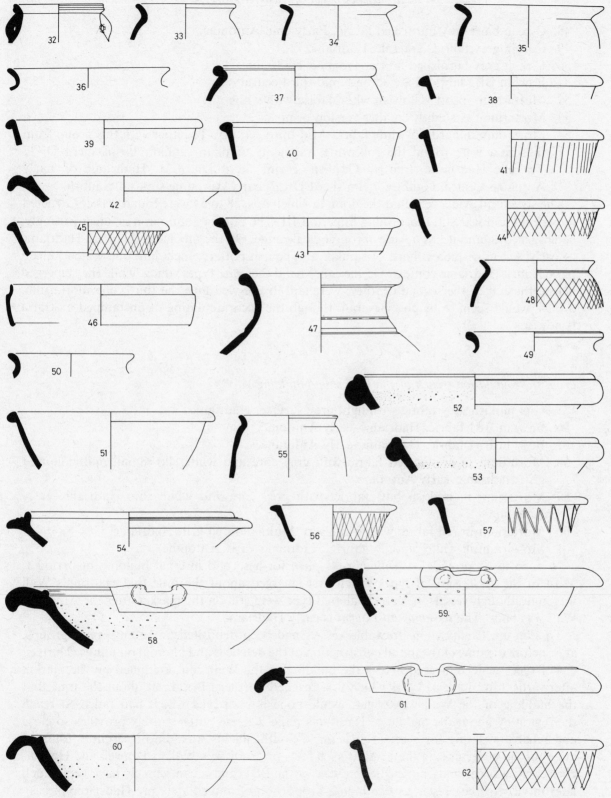

Fig. 36. 1:4.

48. C-p. in hard grey burnished fabric. Early–mid Antonine.
49. C-p. in grey fabric. Trajanic–Hadrianic.
50. C-p. in grey burnished fabric. Trajanic–Hadrianic.
51. Bowl in BB2 fabric. Late second–mid-third century.
52. Mortarium in soft yellowish white fabric with white grit.
53. Mortarium. A slightly smaller version of no. 52.
54. Mortarium in hard off-white fabric. Mid-third century. Together with this group from the drain were found the following fragments of plain samian: 1 rim sherd Dr.27 Trajanic–Hadrianic, Central Gaulish. 1 rim sherd Dr.18/31, Hadrianic or Early Antonine Central Gaulish. 1 rim sherd Dr.33, early Antonine Central Gaulish.

The structural evidence is that the drain in which nos. 28 to 54 were found was constructed in period I and was still functioning in period III. The pottery found in it is, unsurprisingly, heterogeneous, and it has a wide chronological range. On the one hand there are Hadrianic to early Antonine pieces, both of samian and coarse pottery, including one which joins a piece from a Hadrianic context. On the other hand there are types which, while they emerged before the end of the second century, were still in use well into the third; one mortarium, no. 54, would seem to be post-Severan, though the accurate dating of unstamped mortaria is not easy.

From the foundation trench of the workshop (*Building A6*)

55. C-p. pinkish grey fabric with light grey surface. Hadrianic.
56. Bowl in BB1 fabric. Hadrianic–early Antonine.
57. Bowl in BB1 fabric. Hadrianic–early Antonine.
58. Mortarium in orange red fabric with grey core and white slip. Small multicoloured grit. Hadrianic–early Antonine.
59. Mortarium in pinkish buff fabric, with grey core and white slip. Hadrianic–early Antonine.
60. Mortarium in red fabric with white slip. Multicoloured grit. Hadrianic.
61. Mortarium in white pipeclay fabric. Hadrianic–early Antonine.

Nos. 55 to 61 provide a *terminus post quem* for a second internal building of period I. Most of the vessels are of types which first emerged about the time that Hadrian's Wall was built, though vessels of scarcely altered type were still on the market after the Antonine Wall was built. The *terminus post quem* is early Hadrianic.

To sum up; twenty-eight drawable vessels had been deposited, in seven several groups, at or before the time of the initial construction of the defences and internal buildings. Thirteen are of types which emerged before the building of the Wall, but continued on the market afterwards, fifteen are of types which first reached northern Britain at about the time that the building of the Wall was begun, while none is of a type which had failed to reach the region by about the middle of Hadrian's reign. Coarse pottery rarely provides so close and reliable a dating for a set of structures. South Shields was almost certainly founded at about the same time, in the 120s, as such forts on Hadrian's Wall as Benwell and Halton-chesters; it was certainly not earlier, in view of the BB1, and it can scarcely have been much later in view of the presence of so high a proportion of immediately pre-Hadrianic pieces.

Period II

From the upper clay floor inside the east guardchamber of the north gate

62. Bowl in BB2 fabric. Mid-Antonine.
63. Bowl in BB2 fabric. Mid-Antonine.
64. Bowl in light grey fabric.
65. C-p. in grey fabric. Trajanic–Hadrianic.
66. C-p. in hard medium grey fabric with black burnished surface. Trajanic–Hadrianic.
67. C-p. in grey burnished fabric. Trajanic–Hadrianic.
68. Bowl or dish in BB2 fabric. Late Antonine–Severan.
69. Bowl or dish in BB2 fabric. Late Antonine–Severan.

Nos. 62 to 69 are an occupation from a floor of period II. Of the datable pieces three are residual, having survived as rubbish from the earlier occupation, two are mid- and two are late-Antonine; none is of a type which first emerged after the probable date of construction of the granaries.

From the amphora in the floor of the extension to the north guardchamber of the west gate

70. C-p. in hard light grey fabric with dark grey surface. Hadrianic–early Antonine.
71. C-p. in hard coarse greyish brown fabric containing shell grit. Early–mid Antonine.
72. Dish in BB2 fabric. Late second–early third century.

Of nos. 70 to 72 one is a survival while the others are vessels in use during period II.

Sealed by the first gravel surface over the storehouse. Together with this group were the following fragments of plain samian: 1 rim and 1 wall sherd Dr.33, Hadrianic or early Antonine central Gaulish. 1 wall sherd Dr.35. 1 rim sherd Dr.18/31, east Gaulish. 1 wall sherd Curle 15, Antonine central Gaulish. 1 rim sherd Ludowici SMb/SMc, Antonine, east Gaulish.

73. C-p. in BB1 fabric. Hadrianic.
74. Bowl in BB1 fabric. Burnt. Early–Antonine.
75. Bowl in medium grey fabric, burnished inside and out. Early-Antonine.
76. Small bowl in greyish white fabric with dark grey surface. Early–mid Antonine.
77. Large bowl or dish in hard coarse brick red, brick textured fabric.

Nos. 73 to 77 were deposited after the dismantling of a period I building and before a period II re-surfacing. Some vessels seem to be from the first occupation, while others may have been newly broken. The *terminus post quem* is *c.* A.D. 160.

From the foundation trench of building B1

78. Lid in hard dirty white fabric. Early–mid Antonine.

From a construction trench of building B2

79. Bowl or dish in BB2 fabric. Mid-Antonine.

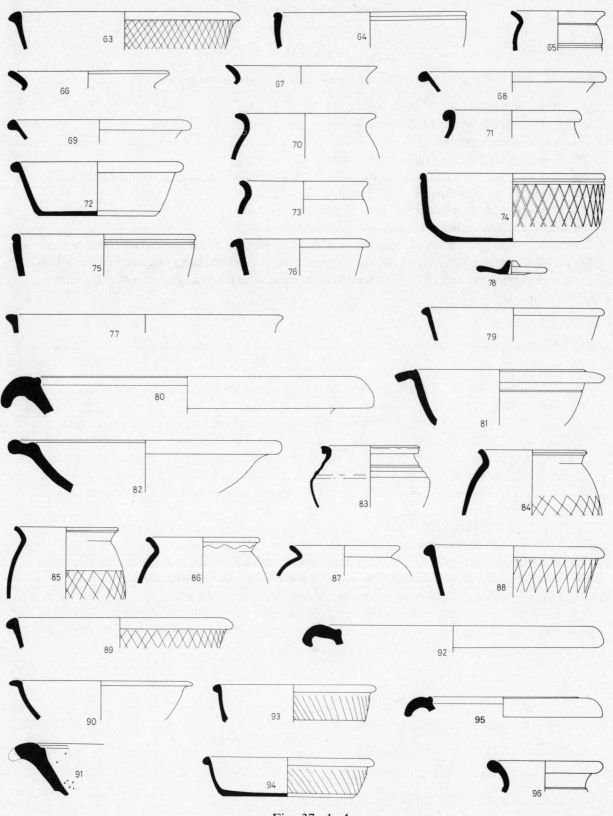

Fig. 37. 1:4.

From the wall core of building B5

80. Mortarium in sandy whitish buff fabric. Sparse grey grit. Probably Hadrianic–early Antonine.

From the floor of building B6

81. Bowl in hard smooth greyish buff fabric. Trajanic–Hadrianic.

From the core of the settling tank wall

82. Mortarium in pinkish buff fabric. Large white grit. Second century, but not closely datable.

Nos. 78 to 80, and probably no. 82, sealed by structures of period II, seem to be residual, as does also no. 81.

From the fill of the settling tank

83. Unusual small jar or beaker in fine hard sandy buff fabric.
84. C-p. in BB1 fabric. Hadrianic–early Antonine.
85. C-p. in BB1 fabric. Hadrianic–early Antonine.
86. C-p. in BB2 fabric. Late Antonine–Severan.
88. Bowl in BB2 fabric. Mid-Antonine.
89. Bowl or dish in BB2 fabric. Mid-Antonine.
90. Segmental bowl in orange-red burnished fabric. Hadrianic–mid Antonine.
91. Mortarium in sandy buff fabric. Sparse, worn, small sparkling grey grit. Possibly mid to late second century.
92. Mortarium in hard pinkish white fabric.
93. Dish in BB2 fabric. Mid-Antonine.
94. Dish in BB2 fabric. Mid-Antonine.

Among nos. 83 to 94 there seem to be residual fragments, fragments from vessels broken while the tank was in use, and fragments from vessels broken shortly before the erection of a granary partly over the tank. The *terminus post quem* for the overlying structure is late second century.

From the broken drain leading from the settling tank

95. Mortarium in hard buff fabric with orange slip. Hadrianic–mid Antonine.

From the drain at the east ends of buildings B2 and B3

96. Narrow-mouthed jar in grey fabric. Early–mid Antonine.

Nos. 95 and 96 are probably both residual.

To sum up; of the seven drawable and datable coarse-pottery vessels sealed by structures of period II, two could already have been on the market before *c.* A.D. 140, four are of

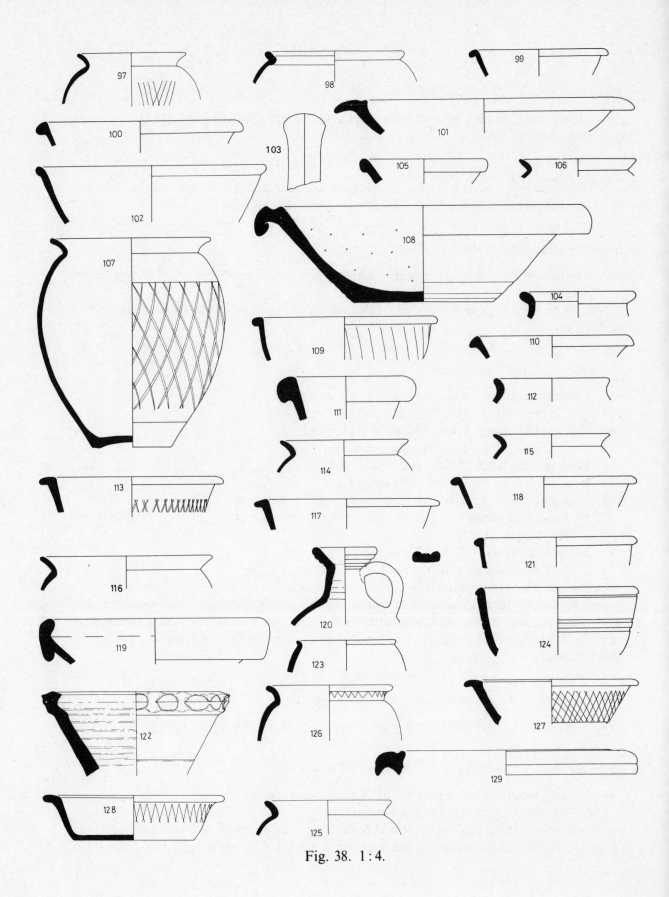

Fig. 38. 1 : 4.

types which had emerged before *c*. A.D. 160 but continued on the market at least until then, and one is of a type which only began to be imported into north-eastern England at the time of the withdrawal from Scotland. This provides a firm *terminus post quem* for the structures of period II.

Period III

Sealed by the flags of the extension to the west guardchamber of the north gate

97. C-p. in BB2 fabric. Mid–late Antonine.
98. C-p. in grey slightly gritty fabric. Mid–late Antonine.
99. Bowl or dish in BB2 fabric. Mid-Antonine.
100. Bowl in BB2 fabric. Late second–mid-third century.

Nos. 97 to 100 form a consistent group of the late second century and provide a *terminus post quem* for the extension.

On the flags of the extension to the west guardchamber. Found with this group were the following fragments of plain samian: 1 rim sherd Dr.33, late Antonine central Gaulish. 3 wall sherds Dr.33, Antonine central Gaulish. 1 rim sherd Dr.31, late Antonine central Gaulish. 1 rim sherd Dr.31R, late Antonine central Gaulish. 1 rim sherd Dr.31R, east Gaulish. 1 rim sherd Dr.38, east Gaulish.

101. Mortarium in light buff fabric. Hadrianic.
No. 101 is residual.

Sealed by the flags at the south end of the west portal of the north gate

102. Bowl in BB2 fabric. Mid-Antonine.
The flags may be measurably later than the single vessel, no. 102, which they seal.

From the build-up sealed by the flagged surface to the south of the east guardchamber

103. Stopper in brick-red fabric. End abraded indicating that it could have been used as a pounder.
104. Narrow-mouthed jar in light grey fabric with darker surface.
105. C-p. in brown fabric with grey core and dark grey surface.
106. C-p. in BB2 fabric. Mid–late Antonine.
107. C-p. in BB2 fabric with kiln distorted base. Late second–mid-third century.
108. Mortarium in light buff fabric. Grey/brown grit. Raetian, Antonine.
109. Bowl in BB2 fabric. Late second–mid-third century.
110. Bowl or dish in BB2 fabric. Mid-Antonine.

Nos. 103 to 110 are not all datable; those which are form a consistent group with, once again, a *terminus post quem* in the late second century.

Sealed by the period III road surface to the north of granary C1

111. Amphora in hard gritty yellowish-white fabric.

112. C-p. in hard fine light grey fabric.
113. Bowl or dish in BB1 fabric. Hadrianic–early Antonine.
   Nos. 111 to 113 are either residual or not closely datable.

Lying on the cobbled roadway to the west of the north end of granary C1

114–16. C-p.s in highly-burnished BB2 fabric. Late Antonine–Severan.
117. Bowl or dish in BB1 fabric. Early–mid Antonine.
118. Bowl or dish in BB2 fabric. Late Antonine–Severan.
119. Mortarium in hard gritty pale yellow fabric. Pale orange-yellow surface. Mid second–early third century.
120. Flagon in soft pale yellowy-white fabric. Early–mid Antonine.
121. Bowl or dish in BB2 fabric. Mid-Antonine.

Lying on the road between granaries C4 and C5

122. Tazza in hard orange-red fabric with dark blue-grey core. Possibly Antonine.
   Nos. 114 to 122, deposited after the construction of the granaries, form a group, with the usual proportion of survivals, mainly of the turn of the second and third centuries; mid- to late-second century pieces are absent.

Sealed by the sleeper walls of granary C1

123. Small c-p. in BB1 fabric. Hadrianic–early Antonine.
124. Bowl in light grey fabric with black surface. Early-Antonine.

From the core of the west wall of granary C12

125. C-p. in BB1 fabric. Mid–late Antonine.

From the core of a sleeper wall of granary C10

126. C-p. in BB1 fabric. Mid–late Antonine.
127. Bowl in BB1 fabric. Mid–late Antonine.

From the foundation trench of granary C10

128. Dish in BB1 fabric. Early-Antonine.
129. Mortarium in hard smooth orange fabric. Early–mid Antonine.

From the foundation trench of granary C1

130. Single-handled flagon in dull purple-red fabric with brick-red core. Cream slip. Hadrianic–early Antonine.
131. C-p. in BB2 fabric. Mid–late Antonine.

132. C-p. in BB1 fabric. Early–mid third century.
133. Large bowl in polished grey fabric with decoration of burnished lines. These bowls are notoriously difficult to date unless they fall into one of a limited number of closely defined categories. This vessel has features in common with Curle, *Newstead 1911, type 46*, which may well be of mid second-century date.
134. Dish in BB2 fabric. Late second–mid third century.

The five groups, nos. 123 to 134, taken together, make up a pre-Severan assemblage, mainly late-Antonine, but with some survivals; a *terminus post quem* for both group and structure is provided by no. 134.

Sealed by a flagged floor in the north-west angle tower

135. C-p. in highly-burnished BB2 fabric.
136. Bowl or dish in highly-burnished BB2 fabric. Mid-Antonine.
137. Mortarium in hard fine yellowy-white fabric. Brown and black grit.

While nos. 135 to 137 do not form a useful group, it is not impossible that the new floor in the angle tower was contemporary with the granaries.

To sum up; in four out of the eleven groups which were sealed by the granaries, or by other structures of period III, the latest datable vessel is of a type which first emerged in the last quarter of the second century and continued on the market, with little change, until well into the third. This confirms the Severan date, already accepted on other grounds, for the granaries, and for structures of period III as a whole.

Later than period III

From the blocking of Vent 4, granary C11

138. C-p. in BB2 fabric.
139. Dish in BB2 fabric with an unusually deep chamfer. Mid-Antonine.

Nos. 138–40 are the only drawable pieces sealed by modifications to the granaries. All are of second-century date.

From the blocking of Vent 1, granary C10

140. Dish in BB2 fabric. Mid-Antonine.

From the build-up overlying the period III floor inside the west guardchamber of the north gate and its extension

141. Flagon in red fabric with cream slip.
142. Flagon in grey fabric with reddish brown surface.
143. Beaker in red fabric with reddish-brown surface. Probably rough-cast. Late first to early second century survival.
144. Beaker in white fabric with light brown colour coat. Late second century.
145. Beaker in white fabric with brown colour coat. Third century.

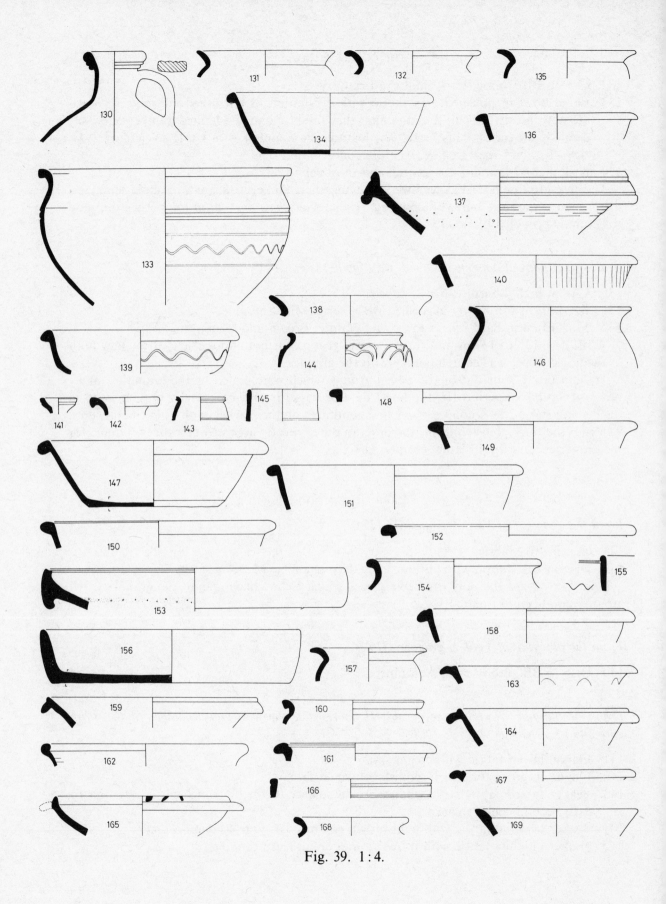

Fig. 39. 1:4.

146. C-p. in dark grey fabric with darker grey surface.
147. Bowl in BB2 fabric. Late second–mid third century.
148. Bowl or dish in light grey fabric with darker surface. Hadrianic.
149. Bowl in light grey fabric. Probably north-eastern non calcite-gritted Dalesware. Third century.
150–2. Bowls in BB2 fabric. Late second–mid third century.
153. Mortarium in hard buff fabric with reddish brown surface. Surrey/Sussex type. Late second–late third century. cf. *Hartley, 1973*, p. 42.

The usual survivals apart, nos. 141 to 153 seem to represent a third-century occupation lasting little if at all beyond the middle of the century.

From burnt material overlying the period III flags at the south end of the west portal of the north gate

154. Narrow-mouthed jar in gritty grey fabric with greyish-brown surface.
155. Bowl in BB2 fabric. Mid-Antonine.
156. Dish in grey fabric with reddish-brown surface.

Though the actual fragments are earlier or undated, the group formed by nos. 154 to 156 may be contemporary with nos. 141–53.

From material overlying the period III road to the south of the east portal

157. C-p. in grey fabric, badly burned. Mid–late third century.
158. Flanged bowl in greyish-brown fabric with smooth brown surface. Possibly a BB1 variant. Mid–late third century.
159. Flanged bowl in light grey fabric with slightly darker surface. Probably Crambeck. Fourth century.

From material overlying the period III flagged surface to the south of the east guardchamber

160. C-p. in slightly gritty grey-brown fabric with darker surface.
161. C-p. in calcite-gritted fabric. Fourth century.
162. Bowl or dish in light grey fabric.
163. Flanged bowl in BB1 fabric. Third century.
164. Flanged bowl in hard grey fabric. Crambeck. Fourth century.

From the bottom of material overlying the period III road surface in the east portal

165. Flanged dish in hard orange-yellow burnished fabric with dark blue grey core and orange-brown paint on the outside of the bead. Last three-quarters of the third century.

The three groups, nos. 157 to 165, taken together, may be part of an intentional levelling-up for the overlying walling, at the beginning of the final occupation of the fort. Some residual material is not unexpectedly present; a *terminus post quem* of very roughly the middle of the fourth century is provided by nos. 159 and 164 which are Crambeck ware, though not of post-Picts'-War types.

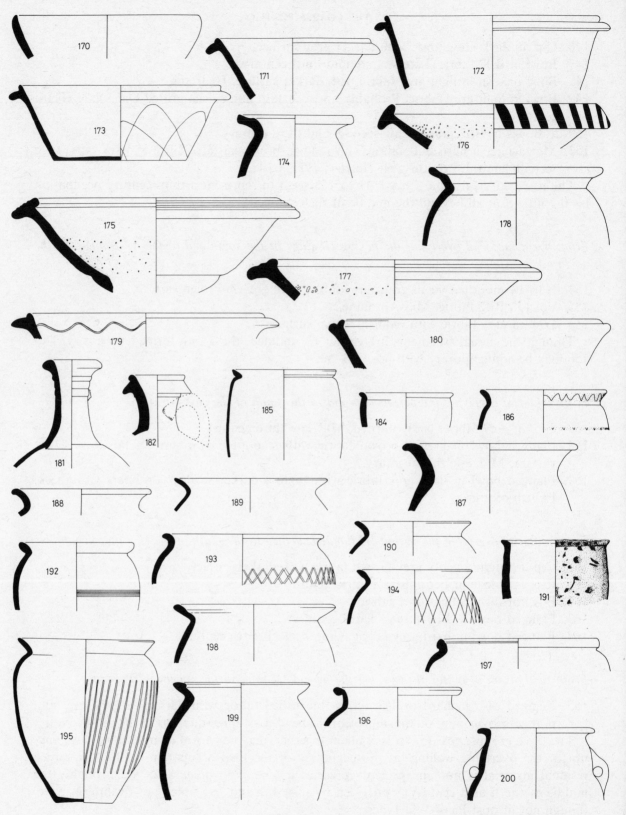

Fig. 40. 1 : 4.

From over the late flagged surface in the east portal

166. Bowl in **BB2** fabric. Late second–third century.
167. Flanged bowl in **BB1** fabric. Late third century to early fourth.

Though to different degrees nos. 166 to 167 are both residual in their context, which is that of the latest occupation deposit.

From material over late wall inside the east guardchamber of the north gate

168. C-p. in grey fabric with darker surface. Trajanic–early Hadrianic.
169. C-p. in brown shell-gritted fabric. Dalesware. Mid third century to early fourth.
170. Bowl in grey Crambeck fabric. Fourth century.
171. Small flanged bowl in grey Crambeck fabric. Fourth century.

Of nos. 168–71 two are residual while two could have been broken during the occupation which seems to have begun in about the middle of the fourth century.

From the stokehole of kiln 1 inside the period I granary

172. C-p. in hard light grey fabric with dark grey gritty surface. Mid third to mid fourth century.
173. Flanged bowl in **BB1** fabric. First half fourth century.
174. Flanged bowl in hard light grey fabric. First half fourth century.
175. Mortarium in hard sandy whitish-buff fabric. Orange slip on rim. Medium and small black grit. Third or fourth century.

Nos. 172 to 175 form the only homogeneous group of the turn of the third and fourth centuries from any part of the site. The group provides an approximate date for the operation of the tile kiln.

Sealed by late flagging over upper gravel surface which overlies the period I storehouse

176. Mortarium in white pipeclay fabric, heavily burnt. Red grit, orange-brown paint on rim. Third or fourth century.
177. Mortarium in hard off-white fabric. Black grit. Third or fourth century.
178. C-p. in hard coarse gritty dark grey fabric. Late third–early fourth century.
179. Flanged bowl in grey Crambeck fabric. Late fourth century.
180. Flanged bowl in lead grey fabric.

Nos. 176 to 178 are types which, having emerged earlier, were still on the market in the middle of the fourth century, while nos. 179 and 180 are still later types. The flagging is not related structurally to the latest occupation elsewhere on the site, though it clearly belongs to it.

To sum up; the modifications to the granaries seal three fragments of pottery, none of them later than the late second century. This would not conflict with a conclusion reached on other grounds that the conversion of the granaries to new uses took place shortly after the end of the Severan campaigns, rather than almost a century later, as has been thought. The group of four pieces from the kiln stokehole attests activity, of a kind unusual within a fort, at a time when negative ceramic evidence suggests reduced activity elsewhere within it. Of the remaining thirty-six vessels from stratified deposits later than the structures of period III, seven are not dated, five are of types which were already off the market by the time of building, in the first decade of the third century; twelve are of types which were on the market during the first three-quarters of the third century; five are of types which were on the market between then and the middle of the fourth century, though some of them might have reached the site before the last quarter of the third century, and others might have reached it after the middle of the fourth. It is difficult to establish a negative from the evidence of coarse pottery alone, but, taken with the absence of any structure later than the granaries and earlier than the mid fourth century fragments, apart from the kilns, the composition of the pottery groups strongly suggests that there was a break in the occupation of about three-quarters of a century. Seven vessels are of types which emerged around the middle of the fourth century, and thereafter had a long life. Among the stratified groups there are no examples of the Huntcliff type, or of Crambeck parchment ware, though both are present in some abundance in the topsoil.

UNSTRATIFIED MATERIAL

The following is a selection of the unstratified material recovered from the excavations of 1966, 1967 and 1973.

1966 and 1967

Flagons and narrow-mouthed jars

181. Buff, early–mid second century.
182. Reddish-pink, mid–late second century.
183. Light grey, late third–early fourth century.

Small jars and beakers

184. Grey burnished, mid–late second century.
185. Hard, fine, pinkish-brown with light grey core and black, highly-polished surface, first century survival.

Cooking-pots in black burnished 1 fabric

186. Mid second century.
187. Third century.
188. Early–mid third century.

Cooking-pots in black burnished 2 fabric

189. Mid–late second century.
190. Mid–late second century.

Cooking-pots in other fabrics

191. Hard, slightly gritty reddish-brown fabric with black core.
192. Light grey, late first–early second century.
193. Grey, early–mid second century.
194. Grey, early–mid second century.
195. Grey burnished, early–mid third century. ˙
196. Light brown.
197. Grey.
198. Hard, gritty black, mid–late third century.
199. Hard, gritty grey, mid–late third century.
200. Grey Crambeck fabric, mid–late fourth century.
201. Hard, dark grey, fourth century.
202. Hard, grey, fourth century.
203. Hard, fine, light blue-grey, with dark grey core and polished black surface, mid–late third century, a product of the Norton kilns.

Cooking-pots in calcite-gritted fabric

The nine vessels here illustrated are but a small selection of the large number of sherds, representing some 168 vessels, in calcite-gritted fabric, which were recovered from the excavations of 1966 and 1967.

204. Late third–early fourth century.
205. Late third–early fourth century.
206. Late third–early fourth century.
207. Late third–early fourth century.
208. Late fourth century.
209. Late fourth century.
210. Late fourth century.
211. Late fourth century.
212. Possibly mid–late third century. The form, with the widely flaring neck and the exaggerated bead, is similar to that of third-century cooking-pots in BB1 fabric.

Bowls

213. BB1, second century.
214. BB2, mid–late second century.
215. BB2, mid–late second century.
216. BB2, late second–mid third century.
217. Hard, gritty grey with light blue-grey core, late second–mid third century.
218. Hard, light grey, probably third century.
219. Hard, lead grey, burnished.
220. Hard, greyish-brown.
221. Light grey, possibly Crambeck, in which case fourth century.

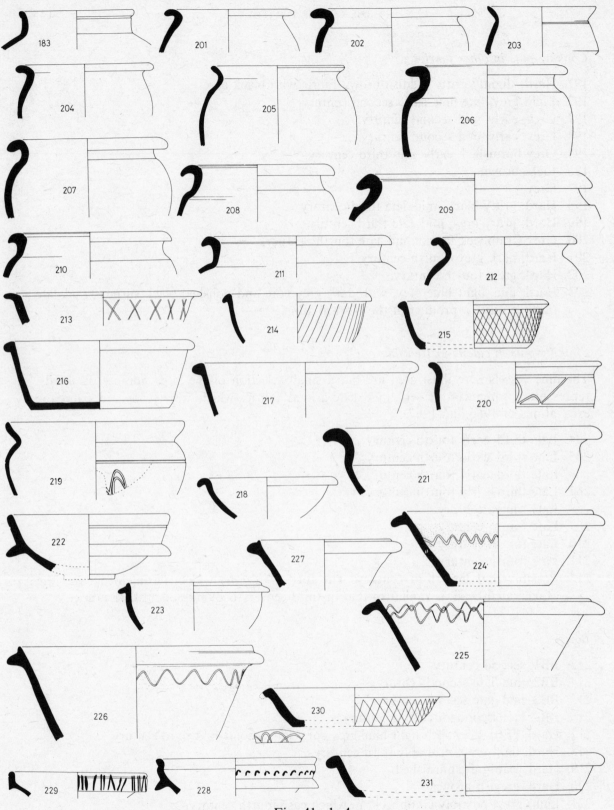

Fig. 41. 1 : 4.

222. Grey Crambeck fabric, mid–late fourth century.
223. Orange-red with dull red core.
224. Grey Crambeck fabric, late fourth century.
225. Dark grey fabric, probably Throlam, fourth century.
226. Dark grey gritty, late fourth century.
227. Light, orange-buff with black burnished surface.
228. Hard white with brown-painted decoration, late fourth century.
229. Light buff with dark brown paint, late fourth century.

Dishes

230. BB2 mid–late second century.
231. Light grey with darker surface, first century.
232. Grey.
233. White with dark grey surface, mid–late fourth century.
234. Greyish-brown, probably second century.
235. Dark grey, mid–late fourth century.
236. Grey with black burnished surface.
237. Black, calcite-gritted, fourth century.
238. Light grey grey with black burnished surface, mid–late fourth century.
239. Light buff with reddish-brown paint, no grit visible, late fourth century.
240. Cream with brown paint, late fourth century.
241. White with reddish-brown paint, late fourth century.
242. White with reddish-brown paint, late fourth century.

Mortaria

243. Reddish-pink with multi-coloured grit, early–mid second century.
244. Very heavy; reddish-buff with sparse white grit.
245. Soft, pale yellowish-white with white flint grit, early third century.
246. Reddish-buff with grey core and cream slip, black grit, third–fourth century.
247. White with black grit, third–fourth century.
248. Light buff with black grit, third–fourth century.
249. White with buff surface and large angular black grit; Crambeck type 6, third–fourth century.
250. Grey, no apparent grit, probably Crambeck, fourth century.
251. White with brown-painted decoration and small red grit, early–mid fourth century.
252. Buff, abraded, paint probably worn off, late fourth century.
253. White with brown paint, early–mid fourth century.
254. Light buff with reddish-brown paint and small black grit, late fourth century.
255. Light buff with dark brown paint and small black grit, late fourth century.

Miscellaneous

Cup: 256. White fabric with dark brown colour coat, possibly fourth century.

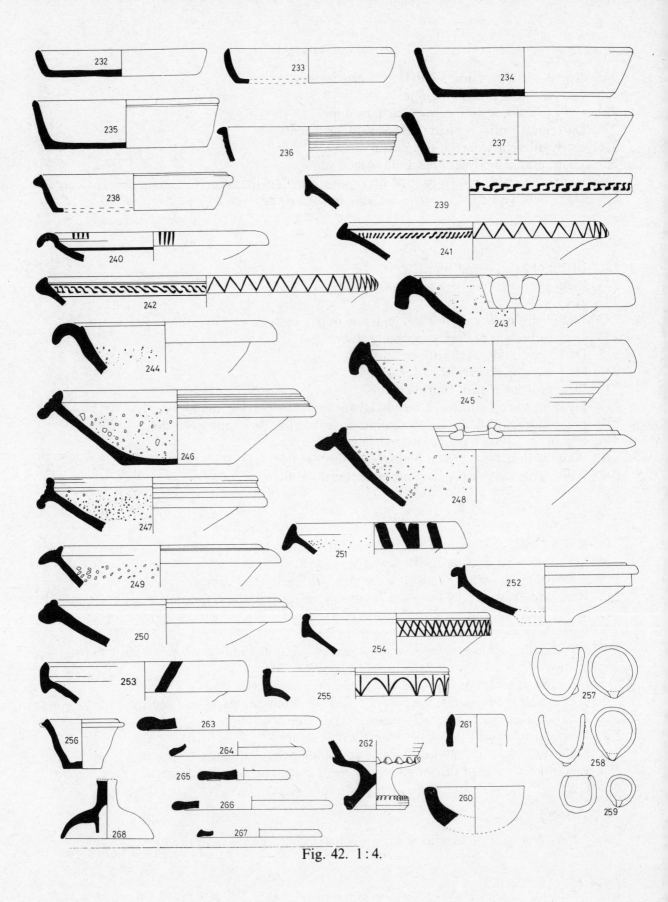

Fig. 42. 1:4.

Crucibles

257, 258 and 259. Found in the bottom of the robber trench of the south wall of the east
   guardchamber of the north gate. Brown fabric with slag fused to the outside.
260. Brown, very badly burnt. May have been used as a crucible, though there is no slag
   adhering to the outside.
261. Brown fabric with slag adhering to the outside.

Tazza

262. Hard orange-yellow fabric with buff core and smoothed surface, probably second
   century.

Lids

263. Grey, late first–early second century.
264. Grey, sandy, late first–early second century.
265. Red, gritty, second century.
266. Grey, second century.
267. Grey.
268. Hard, dirty red, possibly fourth century.

1973

Flagons and narrow-mouthed jars

269. Soft, light orange-yellow with dark blue-grey core, second century.
270. Soft, light blue-grey.
271. Hard, medium grey, burnished, possibly second century.

Small jars and beakers

272. Hard grey with black burnished surface, early–mid second century.
273. Hard, grey, burnished.
274. Hard, grey, smoothed.
275. Soft, very pale sandy-yellow with purple-grey surface; Crambeck type 12, mid–late
   fourth century.
276. White, with orange to chocolate-brown colour-coat, late second–mid third century.
277. Very hard, fine, deep jet-black with polished surface, late second–mid third century.
278. Buff with dark brown-black colour-coat, mid–late third century.
279. White with orange colour-coat, mid–late second century.
280. Hard white with orange to dark brown colour-coat, late second–mid third century.

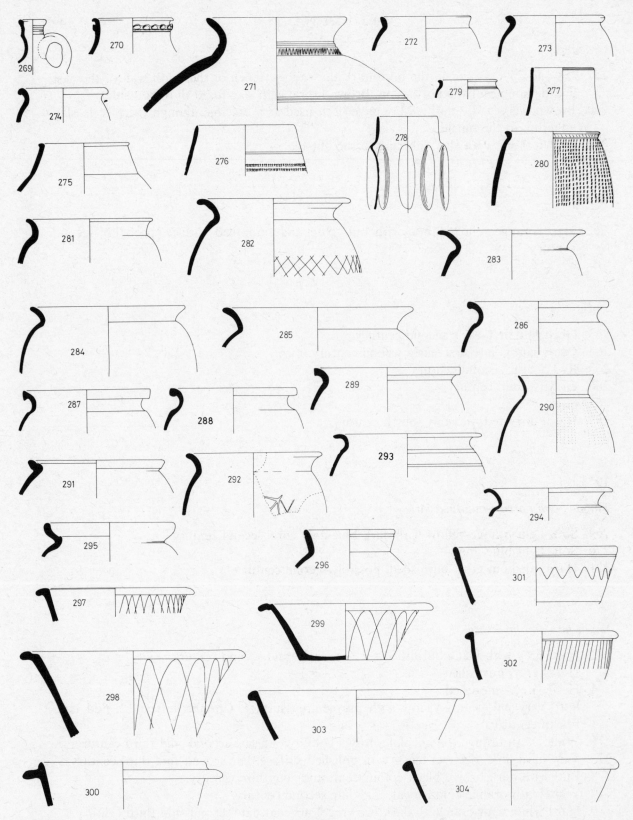

Fig. 43. 1 : 4.

Cooking-pots in black burnished fabric

281. BB1, early–mid second century.
282. BB1, mid third century.
283. BB1 mid–late third century.
284. BB2, mid–late second century.
285. BB2, early third century.

Cooking-pots in other fabrics

286. Hard, gritty grey with light blue-grey core, early–mid second century.
287. Grey, early–mid second century.
288. Hard, dull reddish-grey with sparkling grit, early–mid second century.
289. Hard, fine, off-white, early second century.
290. Hard, fine, grey-burnished, mid–late second century.
291. Hard, gritty, dull orange-red with light-grey core, mid–late second century.
292. Grey with light blue-grey core, second century.
293. Hard, fine, dull orange with black core.
294. Hard, slightly gritty grey, third century.
295. Light grey with dark grey, gritty surface, third century.
296. Grey Crambeck fabric, mid–late fourth century.

Bowls

297. BB1, second century.
298. BB1, early third century.
299. BB1, early third century.
300. BB1, mid fourth century.
301. BB2, mid–late second century.
302. BB2, mid–late second century.
303. BB2, late second–mid third century.
304. BB2, late second–mid third century.
305. BB2, late second–mid third century.
306. Light grey, gritty with dark grey core, probably fourth century.
307. Sandy, dull orange with dark grey core, mid–late fourth century.
308. Grey Crambeck fabric, mid–late fourth century.

Dishes

309. BB1, second century.
310. BB1, second century.
311. BB2, mid–late second century.
312. BB2, mid–late second century.
313. BB2, late second–mid third century.
314. Hard, coarse orange-buff with dark grey core, second century.

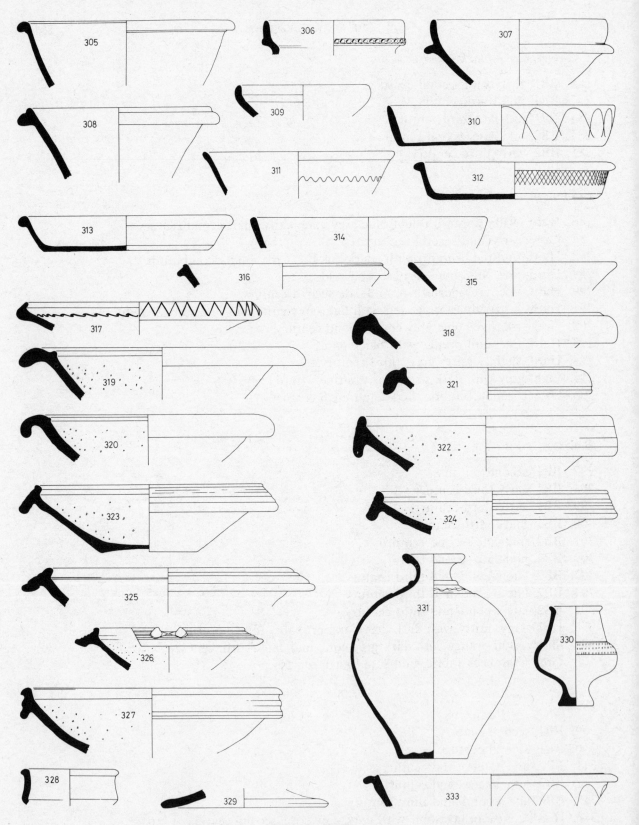

Fig. 44. 1:4.

315. Fine, hard dark grey, micaceous, burnished.
316. Coarse, hard, grey burnished, mid–late fourth century.
317. Very pale yellow with orange-brown paint, late fourth century.

Mortaria

318. Soft, pale orange-yellow with orange core and white grit extending over the flange, late first–early second century.
319. Sandy-red with grey core and white slip; white grit, early–mid second century.
320. Soft, sandy, pale yellow with multi-coloured grit, early–mid second century.
321. Dull red with dark grey core and cream slip, early–mid second century.
322. Hard, coarse white with white quartz grit, early third century.
323. Light buff with multi-coloured grit, third–fourth century.
324. White pipeclay with multi-coloured grit, third–fourth century.
325. Pale buff with trace of orange-brown paint on the rim, third–fourth century.
326. Hard pale yellow with light orange-yellow slip and black grit, third–fourth century.
327. Hard, off-white with pale yellow slip and black grit, possibly fourth century.

Miscellaneous

Cup: Grey, burnished.
Lid: 329. Hard, dark grey with light grey core, late first–early second century.

POTTERY FROM THE COLLECTION AT THE
ROMAN FORT MUSEUM AT SOUTH SHIELDS

Nos. 330–3 were from the well of the Headquarters building. With this group was a stamped Central Gaulish Dr.18/31. Cf. stamp no. 29. Roman Fort Museum.

330. Beaker in buff fabric with black polished colour coating. Fourth century.
331. Narrow-mouthed jar in lead grey fabric. Fourth century. While the cordoned narrow-mouthed jar had its origins in the pre-Roman and early Roman south-east, examples of the class are still found in deposits ranging in date from the early second century to the late fourth. While the treatment of the base differs from that of pre-Roman specimens, the rim, neck and shoulder are almost identical.
332. Large double-handled jar in grey fabric with burnished decoration. Fourth century.
333. Bowl in BB1 fabric. Mid–late third century.

Nos. 334 to 342 are cinerary urns found *c.* 1875 in the area to the south of the fort. Roman Fort Museum.

334. Jar or cooking-pot in fine, light brown sandy fabric. Soot caked. late first–early second century.
335. Wide-mouthed jar or bowl in hard white fabric with dark grey surface. Grooved

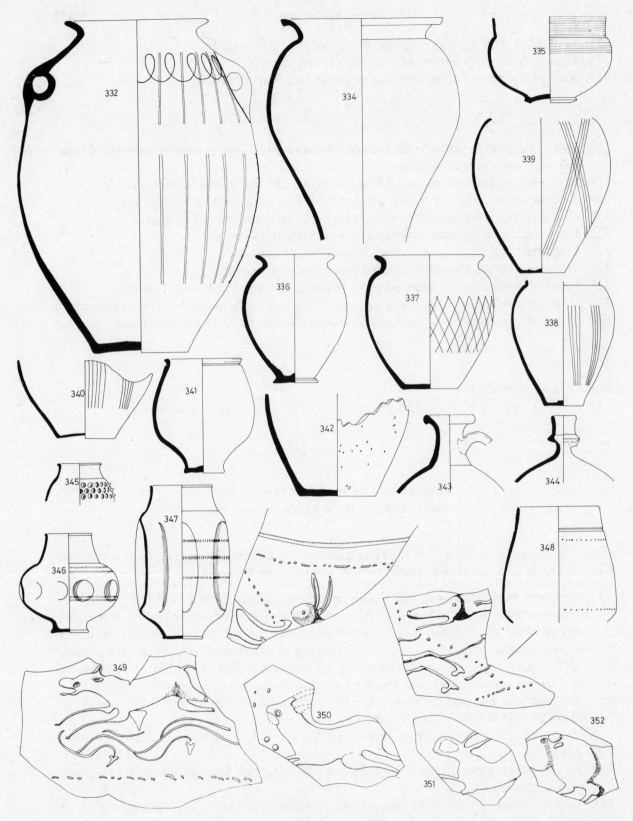

Fig. 45. 1 : 4.

decoration. Contains a wall fragment of a BB1 cooking-pot with obtuse-angle cross-hatching. Late first–early second century.

336. Small jar or cooking-pot in hard greyish white fabric with dark grey smoothed surface. Contains charcoal, bones and ash. Early–mid second century.

337. Cooking-pot in hard light grey fabric, smoothed above and below decoration. Contains a solid, homogeneous mass of burnt bone and ash, several loose scraps of burnt bone, oxidised iron and a scrap of a grey, sandy jar. Mid second century.

338. Small jar or cooking-pot in fine, hard dark grey fabric burnished on shoulder and base. Contains ash, bone, and badly rusted piece of iron and a small scrap of a grey sandy jar. Second century.

339. Jar or cooking-pot in fine light brown fabric. Contains corroded bronze object, ash, bone fragments and two lumps of charcoal. Second century.

340. Jar or cooking-pot in fine, light brown sandy fabric. Scored decoration.

341. Beaker in hard, fine greyish-white fabric with light orange, matt colour-coating. Contains bones, ashes, loose soil, charcoal and two fragments of a grey sandy jar. Early third century.

342. Jar or cooking-pot in black calcite-gritted fabric. Contains ash, bone fragments and several small wall fragments of a pinkish-buff flagon. Fourth century.

Other material

343. RFM/BF6. Single-handled flagon in hard, sandy orange fabric with blue-grey slip. Late second–early third century.

344. RFM/BF1. Single-handled flagon in white fabric with dark brown colour-coating. Mid–late third century.

Beakers

345. RFM. Hard, fine pink fabric with metallic-black, iridescent colour-coating. Unusual decoration of small horns. Possibly as early as mid second century.

346. RFM. Hard, fine pink fabric with shiny black colour-coating. Late second–mid third century. Neck and base restored.

347. RFM. Hard, fine orange-pink fabric with grey core and black metallic colour-coating. Mid–late third century. Three other examples in this fabric; one example in fabric of no. 345.

Nos. 345 and 346, and one of the examples of 347 originated in the Central Gaulish Potteries making colour-coated ware in the second and third centuries. No. 347 came from the Moselle area. Thanks are due to Dr. Greene, who identified the fabrics.

348. RFM/BC25. Pinkish-white fabric with matt-black colour-coating. Animal decoration *en barbotine*. Late second–early third century.

349. RFM/BC24. Wall fragment from vessel similar to no. 348. Dark brown fabric with reddish-brown, matt colour-coating. Animal and tendril decoration *en barbotine*. Late second–early third century.

350, 351 and 352. RFM/BC92, 32 and 34. Small fragments showing animal decoration *en barbotine*. 350 and 352: white fabric with shiny black colour-coating. 351: white fabric with bronze colour-coating.

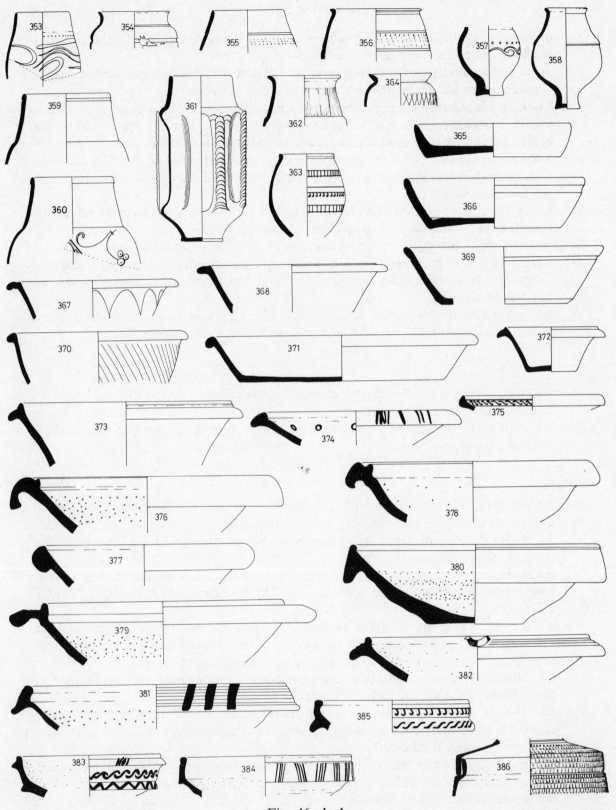

Fig. 46. 1:4.

353. RFM/BC42. White fabric with bronze colour-coating. Vegetable decoration *en barbotine*. Mid third century.
354. RFM/BC30. White fabric with matt-black colour-coating. Animal decoration *en barbotine*. Third century.
355. RFM/BC123. White fabric with dark brown colour-coating. Stuttered decoration. Early–mid third century.
356. RFM. White fabric with purplish-orange colour-coating. Stuttered decoration. Early–mid third century. One other example.
357. RFM/BC114. White fabric with metallic-grey colour-coating. Pale orange slip applied *en barbotine* over colour-coating. Third–fourth century.
358. RFM/BC15. White fabric with matt-brown to black colour-coating. Early fourth century.
359. RFM. Grey fabric with pink core and metallic-black colour-coating. Mid third–early fourth century. One other example.
360. RFM/BC89, 93. White fabric with metallic-black colour-coating. White slip applied *en barbotine* over colour-coating. Mid third–early fourth century.
361. RFM. White fabric with dark brown colour-coating. Late third–early fourth century. Drawing reconstructed from fragments. Numerous other fragments, probably representing six other vessels.
362. RFM. Dark grey fabric with burnished surface. Vertically burnished decoration. Late fourth century.
363. RFM. Fine white fabric with pale orange surface (slip?) and dull orange painted decoration. This vessel would appear to be in fine Crambeck fabric, and the decoration is certainly typical of that used on painted bowls and dishes from Crambeck.

Cooking-pots

364. RFM/BB39. Small jar or cooking-pot in grey fabric with black burnished surface. Late second–early third century.

There are very few cooking-pots in the collection of the Roman Fort Museum. One can only conclude that this is due, regrettably, to the preferences of the original excavators, who would probably have been more interested in the finer pottery. Apart from no. 364 there are four or five rim sherds similar to no. 334. Indeed, they may well be from the same vessel.

Bowls and dishes

365. RFM/BB18. Dish in BB1 fabric. Third and early fourth century.
366. RFM/BB23. Bowl in grey Crambeck fabric. One other example. Fourth century.
367. RFM/BB14. Bowl in BB1 fabric. Third century.
368. RFM/BB7. Bowl in light grey fabric with dark grey core and black surface.
369. RFM/BB19. Bowl in BB2 fabric.
370. RFM. Bowl in BB2 fabric. Late second century.
371. RFM/BB3. Bowl in BB2 fabric. Late second–early third century.

372. RFM/BB4. Small flanged bowl in pale grey fabric with dark grey burnished surface. Fourth century.
373. RFM/BB6. Flanged bowl in light grey fabric with black burnished surface. Fourth Century. Two other examples.
374 and 375. RFM. Dishes in white fabric with orange-brown paint. Late fourth century.

Mortaria

376. RFM/BJ16. Gritty buff fabric with multi-coloured grit, mainly white. Late second–early third century.
377. RFM/BJ9. Sandy buff fabric. No grit showing. Mid–late second century.
378. RFM/BJ6. Soft sandy buff fabric with sparse red and grey grit. Mid–late second century.
379. RFM/BJ15. White fabric with pale orange-yellow slip and black grit. Mid–late third century.
380. RFM/BJ1. White fabric with orange-yellow surface and small white flint grit. Third century.
381. RFM/BJ20. White pipeclay fabric with orange-brown paint and black grit. Four similar examples. Late third–mid fourth century.
382. RFM/BJ17. White fabric with black grit. Early fourth century.
383. RFM/BJ25. Hard white, smoothed fabric with orange-brown paint and black grit. Late fourth century.
384. RFM. Pinkish-white fabric with dark brown paint and black grit. Five similar examples, one without paint and possibly not a mortarium. One other example with cross-hatched painted decoration. Late fourth century.
385. White fabric with orange-brown paint. No grit showing. Two other examples. Late fourth century.
386. Castor box in white fabric with dark brown colour-coating. Stuttered decoration. Numerous other fragments, probably representing three other vessels.

Stamped amphorae (fig. 47)

1. Bruce, 1884, no. 28. Now lost. CI⚱B. *Callender, 1965*, no. 334. Dated earlier than the reign of Antoninus Pius.
2. 1966/67. On the handle of a globular amphora. LCM. *Callender, 1965*, no. 827: *Lucius Caecilius Martius* (C.I.L. ii, 3629), *Lucius Caelius Moderatus* (C.I.L. ii, 1490). South Spanish, *c.* A.D. 140–190.
3. JMN/445/1956.128.4A. Hooppell, 1878. LIVN.M/ELIS(——. *Callender, 1965*, no. 879: LIVN.M/ELISSI.P.
4. RFM. On the handle of a globular amphora. MMRCI. *Callender, 1965*, no. 1138: M. MARCI. South Spanish.
5. 1966/67. On the handle of a globular amphora. ——)ODIICE. *Callender, 1965*, no. 1302: P.CLODI ICELI. South Spanish, *c.* A.D. 110–150.
6. Bruce, 1884, no. 27. Now lost. QPPHRYXI. *Callender, 1965*, no. 1492. Probably South Spanish. *c.* A.D. 100–150.

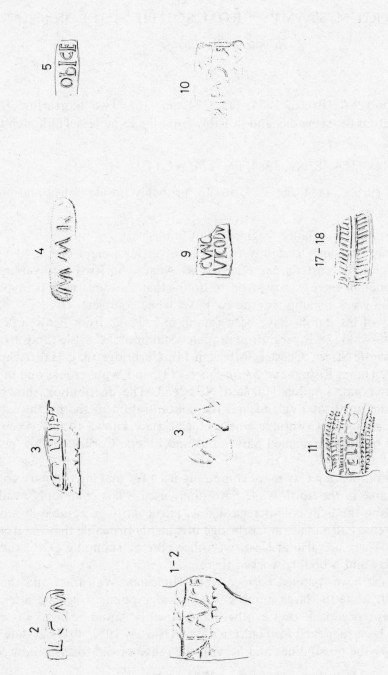

Fig. 47. Stamps on Amphora (top line) and Mortariae 1:2 (drawings by Miriam Daniels).

MORTARIUM STAMPS FROM SOUTH SHIELDS (fig. 47)

Katharine F. Hartley

1–8. Anaus.

1–2. JMN/457/1956.128A (Bruce, 1884, fac. 274, no. 16). Two mortarium fragments, each with a stamp from the same die, and possibly from the same vessel although the pieces do not join.

3. JMN/658/1956.128.115A (Bruce, 1884, fac. 274, no. 14).

4–7. Now missing. (Bruce, 1884, fac. 274, no. 13, probably upside down; and nos. 17, 20 and 21.)

8. A fragmentary stamp on a flange fragment (not published).

These eight stamps are fairly certainly from two of at least eight dies used by Anaus. Three of the dies give the potter's name clearly as Anaus, but two give variant, almost illiterate, versions though there is no reason to doubt that the same man is involved. The die used for nos. 3–8 gives a stamp reading A∕ИА˙Λ when complete.

More than eighty of his stamps have been found; in England from Benwell (at least 4); Binchester (9); Birdoswald (2); Bowes; Brough-under-Stainmore; Carlisle (2); Carrawburgh; Catterick (2); Chester-le-Street; Chesters Museum (4); Corbridge (35); Haltonchesters (2); Housesteads; Kirby Thore; Risingham; *South Shields* (8), and Watercrook; and in Scotland from Camelon; Cramond; Loudon Hill and Newstead. The distribution shows that his workshop was in the north of England and the concentration in the north-east suggests that it was there, perhaps at Corbridge where mortaria are known to have been made in the second century by a potter named Saturninus and others. Corbridge also has obvious value as a dispersal point.

Anaus used the iron-bearing clay more commonly used for making ordinary coarseware, a clay widely available in the north while Saturninus used a less commonly available one suitable for producing the light colour regarded as particularly acceptable in mortaria. If ordinary coarseware was also made at Corbridge it is highly probable that the iron-bearing clay was available. There are also at least two other potters, stamping DNC and CVSEC who used such a clay and probably worked there.

Anaus' career must have spanned periods when Hadrianic Wall forts and the Scottish forts were occupied, while the large number at Corbridge points to a date after A.D. 139 when Corbridge was reoccupied. On the other hand an early Antonine break in occupation *c.* A.D. 139–158 has been suggested for Hadrian's Wall (Hartley 1972, 40–1). A date of *c.* A.D. 140–175 would cover the possibilities and fit with the range of rim-forms produced.

9. JMN/658/1956.128.115A (Bruce, 1884, fac. 274, no. 19).

This is a broken stamp of Cunoarda, which reads when complete, CVNOARDA/ VICODVROBRI. The only other stamps of his recorded are from Ashley, Northants., and an unknown provenance in the Peterborough area. The lower line records that he worked in the *vicus* of Durobrivae, presumably the Roman town in Chesterton parish commonly known as Water Newton. The fabric, form and distribution of his mortaria fit well with manufacture there. The use of *"vicus"* in a mortarium stamp is unparalleled (cf. however, a mortarium stamp from Arentsburg reading ATTICVS.FEC/KANABIS.BON, mentioning the *canabae* at Bonn, in Holwerda 1923, pl. LXV, no. 1). There are a few instances of place-names being used on mortarium stamps, and remarkably a second instance of Durobrivae, "Sennianus Durobrivis urit", a painted inscription on another Nene Valley mortarium (*J.R.S.* XXX (1940), 190).

Nene Valley mortaria had a thin, but widespread, distribution in the third and fourth centuries and a very much thinner distribution in the second century when some of them were presumably shipped together with the popular "Castor" ware. South Shields, a fort of Hadrianic foundation, provides the only site-dating evidence for this potter's work.

10. JMN/456/1929.104 (Bruce, 1884, fac. 274, no. 22).

This is a retrograde stamp of Regalis. Stamps of his have now been noted from Brundall, Norfolk; Caistor-by-Norwich (4); Colchester (7); Ellingham, Norfolk (several); Great Chesterford; Grimstone End (2); Scole, Norfolk (2); *South Shields*, and Stebbing?, Essex. Regalis worked at Colchester (Hull, 1963, 110), but a kiln also used by him has recently been excavated at Ellingham in Norfolk (information kindly supplied by Andrew Rogerson of the Norfolk Archaeological Unit). There is evidence for export on a small scale from Norfolk to the north-east, and abundant evidence of export from Colchester to north-east England and especially to Antonine Scotland in the second century (*ibid.* 114–16). Indeed the best dating evidence for the Colchester mortaria comes from Antonine Scotland, but it is notable that despite the many Colchester mortarium stamps in Scotland only one gives a name, MESSOR, the rest being herringbone stamps. However, a few named Colchester potters including Regalis often used wall-sided or allied forms which are also virtually absent from Scotland. These named potters may well have started working when the trade with Scotland was coming to a close and a date within the period A.D. 160–200 seems reasonable for them.

11. JMN/456/1956.128.27A (Bruce, 1884, fac. 274, no. 24).

When complete the stamp reads FELICIOLES (with S reversed and the lower bar of the F omitted). Stamps of his have now been recorded from Ambleside; Benwell; Birdoswald; Chesters Museum; Corbridge (6), and *South Shields*. The distribution shows that he was serving the military zone, centred on the Hadrianic frontier and manufacture somewhere in this area is likely. The site-dating evidence, including as it does Corbridge (thought to have been unoccupied *c.* A.D. 125–139) and forts on Hadrian's Wall, would accord either with Hadrianic–Antonine date or with a date later in the Antonine period, after A.D. 158 when Corbridge and the Hadrianic Wall forts were held simultaneously. The former seems more likely to judge from the rim-forms.

12. Now missing. (Bruce, 1884, fac. 274, no. 15.)

It is not possible to identify the potter from the drawing of the stamp, which appears to be retrograde and to read MARTIIV[. It may be that Bruce misinterpreted the stamp but since all the other stamps which he published from South Shields can be readily identified from the drawings it is perhaps more likely that it is a true record of a stamp otherwise unknown.

13. Now missing. (Bruce, 1884, fac. 274, no. 18.)

The drawing published by Bruce is upside down but it can be identified with certainty as a retrograde stamp of Aesico, who frequently impressed his dies twice close together as in this example.

A group of mortaria which are clearly from a kiln used by Aesico was found early in this century in Lincolnshire, probably north-west of Lincoln itself. His mortaria are identical in every way with those of Crico who worked at South Carlton, north-west of Lincoln, and there can be little doubt that his kiln was in this vicinity. Stamps of Aesico have now been noted from Aldborough; Benwell; Brough-on-Humber (2); Elslack; *South Shields*; Thealby; Winterton; York (3); Yorkshire Museum (unknown provenance), and kiln-site (4 stamps and 15 unstamped rim-fragments).

The samian evidence from Elslack along with that from Ilkley and Bainbridge indicates a break in occupation *c.* A.D. 125–160 (information kindly supplied by Brian Hartley). This being so, the mortarium at Elslack should have reached there after A.D. 160 as his mortaria are identical with those made at South Carlton, none of which could be very early second century. Aesico, like another South Carlton potter Vorolas lacks any stamps in Antonine Scotland, although this area formed the main market for another South Carlton potter, Crico, making similar mortaria. Various factors might account for this, such as a difference in the date of their initial production. A mid- or late-Antonine date for Aesico seems likely.

14. Now missing. (Bruce, 1884, fac. 274, no. 25, upside down.)

This stamp when complete reads LOCCI.PRO retrograde, for some such name as Loccius Probus or Loccius Proculus. Stamps of his are known from Alcester; Aldborough; Ambleside; Benwell; Binchester; Cirencester; Kenchester; Leicester (2); Little Chester; Mancetter (5); Orton Longueville; Ribchester; Sawtry, Hunts.; Shenstone; *South Shields*; Thistleton, Rutland; and Wall in England; and from Balmuildy (4); Bar Hill; Birrens; Mumrills; Newstead; Old Kilpatrick and Rough Castle in Scotland.

This potter's work is dated primarily by the stamps at forts on the Antonine Wall and his rim-forms fit with manufacture *c.* A.D. 135–165. He worked at Mancetter (*Manduessedum*), Warks., his activity overlapping with two other potters Loccius Vibius and Iunius Loccius to whom he was surely related.

15. Now missing. D.T. 28/9/4.

No other examples of this stamp are known but the deliberate dents in the ends of the spout are characteristic of some mortaria made in the second century in northern England, especially at Corbridge by Bellicus. A Hadrianic or Antonine date seems generally probable.

16. Now missing. (Bruce, 1884, fac. 274, no. 23.)

This is a stamp from one of ten dies giving the name Viator, but up to three different potters could have been involved in their use. Other stamps from the same die are from Brough-on-Noe; Melandra Castle and Templeborough (8 recorded, but 7 now missing), and stamps from a second die probably used by the same potter are from Castleford (2) and Corbridge (2).

The mortaria concerned are all second century and the South Shields one cannot be much earlier than *c.* A.D. 120. One of the Castleford examples is from a deposit dated to the first half of the second century, and since Melandra was abandoned *c.* A.D. 140 a date *c.* A.D. 110–140 may be suggested. The fabric used is not typical of any of the major potteries and could perhaps be from the Little Chester kilns, where the full range of mortaria produced is probably not yet known.

17–18. 1929.104 and a flange fragment thought to be from a different vessel in Box 457, 14/50. L3.12.77.

These stamps are from a herringbone type die used in the second-century potteries at Colchester (Hull, 1963, fig. 60, no. 230). This is from one of the most commonly used herringbone dies and stamps from it have been noted from Braughing; Chelmsford; Colchester (Hull records 18 examples from the kilns and ten in the Museum)[1]; Corbridge (3); Eccles, Kent; Great Chesterford (4); London; Lower Hacheston, Suffolk (2); Reculver; Richborough (3); Rochester (4); Springhead, Kent; *South Shields* (2); Verulamium (4); West Mersea, Essex and Wilderspool in England; and in Scotland from Ardoch; Cadder; Camelon (5); Castlecary; Inveresk; Mumrills (6); Newstead; Rough Castle (2), and Strageath.

The date of this potter and others producing herringbone stamps at Colchester is attested by the large number of stamps from forts on the Antonine Wall in Scotland (*ibid.* 114, fig. 62). The absence of stamps of those named Colchester potters who made wall-sided and allied forms must be regarded as significant. It seems highly probable that the herringbone stamps appearing in Scotland largely pre-date potters like Regalis, Martinus and Acceptus and should therefore be dated *c.* A.D. 140–165.

[1] My totals differ from the late M. R. Hull's and are 8 from the kiln and 7 in the Museum. There could perhaps be stamps which I have not seen but fragmentary herringbone stamps are often difficult to assign to a die and this could well account for different totals being reached by different people.

THE LEAD SEALS

1. At left, head of Geta facing right towards heads of Severus and Caracalla, facing left. Superscribed: AVGG. JMN. Richmond nos. 1–3 or 5, CB. no. 1.
2. As 1. Superscribed: ——)GG. JMN. Richmond no. 4.
3. As 1. Superscribed: /VGG. JMN. Richmond nos. 1–3 or 5.
4. As 1. Superscribed: AVGG. JMN. Richmond nos. 1–3 or 5.
5. As 1. Superscribed: AVG(—— RFM. Richmond nos. 6–15.
6. As 1, but left head and legend missing. Richmond no. 6. JMN.
7. As 1, but legend missing. RFM. Richmond nos. 6–15.
8. As 1, but legend now illegible. JMN. Richmond nos. 1–3 or 5. CB. no. 7.
9. At left, male head looking right towards, at right, female head looking left. Richmond was of the opinion that these were the heads of Caracalla and Julia Domna. JMN. Richmond no. 24. CB. no. 3. A.D. 212–218.
10. Obv. LVI. Rev. blank. JMN.
11. Obv. LVI. Rev. AVO retro. RFM. Richmond no. 23. CB. no. 8.
12. Obv. CVG retro., over bird looking right. Rev. CAL/VEN and centurion's stick. JMN. Richmond no. 16.
13. Obv. CVG (the G reversed). Rev. FL*/——)V. JMN. Richmond no. 18. CB. no. 9.
14. Obv. CV̄ G. Rev. NÊM/*FL* (the L reversed). JMN. Richmond no. 17. CB. no. 11.
15. Obv. CVG. Rev. illegible. JMN. Probably Richmond no. 21.
16. Obv. A(——/VG(—— (?). Richmond was of the opinion that this should be read (C)VG. This must now be regarded as highly unlikely. Rev. ÂLSA. JMN. Richmond no. 19. CB. no. 10.
17. PAV RFM. Richmond no. 25. CB. no. 2.
18. Impression of a signet ring. Probably Bonus Eventus. Figure standing front, facing left; right hand extended, left hand on hip. RFM. Richmond nos. 26–9. CB. no. 4.
19. Impression of a signet ring. Probably Mars. Helmeted figure standing front, facing left; right hand, extended, holds a spear or sword; left hand holds a transverse spear (?). RFM. Richmond nos. 26–9. CB. no. 5.
20. Plaster impression, original seal now missing. Both obv. and rev.: head to right. Possibly the head of Constantine. RFM. Richmond nos. 26–9. CB. no. 6.

21–24. JMN collection and 25–6, RFM collection blank.

Seals which are figured in Collingwood Bruce but are now missing:

   CB. 12. Obv. CV̄ G Rev. ——)EA (?)/*(——.
   CB. 13. Obv. CVG (?) Rev. MV/——)DO (?). = Richmond no. 20.
   CB. 14. Obv. HA. Rev.——)IVI (?).

Seals which are figured in Richmond, but are now missing:
   Eight from the imperial seals, nos. 6–15.

Richmond 20. Obv. $\overline{CV}$ G Rev.——)V/——)D (Richmond's reading) = CB. no. 20.

Richmond 22. Obv. $\overline{CV}$ (G) retro Rev. L.

One out of the signet type seals, nos. 26–9.

Abbreviations

Richmond   =   Richmond, 1934, pp. 101–2.
CB.   =   Collingwood Bruce, 1884, p. 274.
Full references will be found in the bibliography on p. 168.

GLASS FROM THE EXCAVATIONS OF 1966, 1967 AND 1973 (fig. 48)

D. Charlesworth, M.A., F.S.A.

Stratified pieces

1. From the lower levels of the earth backing of the fort wall, to the west of the north gate. Corner fragment of a moulded window pane; blue-green metal. First–second century. Not illustrated.
2. From the upper clay floor, inside the east guardchamber of the north gate. Edge fragment of a moulded window pane; blue-green metal. First–second century. Not illustrated.
3. From the period I drain at the west side of the praetentura. Small fragment of the base of a small flask or beaker; greenish. Not illustrated.
4. Sealed by the period II gravel overlying the storehouse. Base of a beaker in thick, colourless glass, with a "pie crust" decoration at the junction of the straight side and the incurving base, apparently formed with pincers. Only the lowest element of the side decoration, which could be a honeycomb or ribbing, survives. Pad foot-ring in thinner metal added. Second century. Illustrated.
5. Sealed by the period III flagging to the south of the east guardchamber of the north gate. Small fragment of a square bottle in green metal. *c.* A.D. 60–130. Not illustrated.

Unstratified pieces—1966/67

6. Part of the shoulder of a square bottle. The angle is not sharply made and suggests that the bottle was free-blown and flattened, not moulded. *c.* A.D. 60–130. Illustrated.
7, 8 and 9. Three fragments of square bottles. *c.* A.D. 60–130. Not illustrated.
10. Infolded and flattened rim of a large jar or bottle; green metal. Illustrated.
11. Lower sticking part of a three-ribbed handle in blue-green glass. The type of vessel cannot be determined. It may be a flagon. *c.* A.D. 70–130. Illustrated.
12. Fragment of beaker rim, colourless glass, beaded, slightly thickened round the rim, straight side. Similar example from Housesteads, cf. *Journal of Glass Studies*, xiii (1971), p. 35, fig. 5. Second century. Illustrated.
13. Rim of a beaker in colourless glass, tip of the rim rounded, curvilinear shallow cut design. The lines of the cutting wheel can be seen as short strokes running parallel with the rim of the vessel. This type of decoration is generally attributed to the fourth century. Illustrated.
14 and 15. Two rounded lumps of green glass which seem to be attempts at bead making, but could be beads subsequently distorted by fire. Not illustrated.
16 and 17. Two small fragments distorted by fire. Not illustrated.

Unstratified pieces—1973

18 and 19. Two small fragments of square bottle(s) in green glass. First century. Not illustrated.

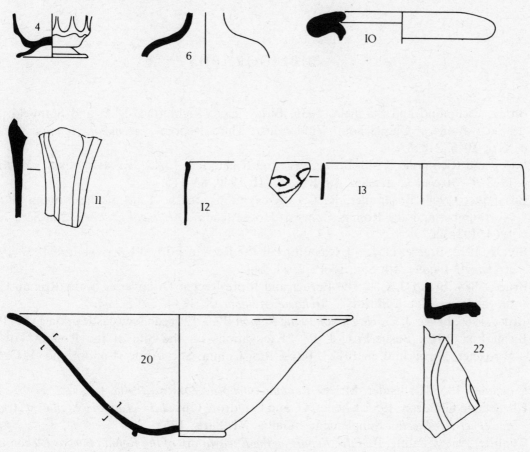

Fig. 48. Glass 1 : 2.

20. Two fragments, apparently from the same vessel in good quality colourless glass, with cloudy weathering, and polished surface. The shallow base ring was probably formed by cutting. Pontil mark in centre of base. The outsplayed rim is thickened and rounded at the tip. The metal suggests a mid first–early second century date. Illustrated.

21. Rim of bottle similar to no. 10. Not illustrated.

22. Fragment of base of square bottle in green glass. Illustrated.

BIBLIOGRAPHY

Birley, Richmond and Stanfield, 1936: Birley, Eric, Richmond, I. A. and Stanfield, J.A., "Excavations at Chesterholm–Vindolanda: Third Report", *Archaeol. Aeliana*, 4th Ser., XIII, 1936, 218–57.

Birley and Richmond, 1940: Birley, Eric and Richmond, I. A., "Excavations at Corbridge, 1938–9", *Archaeol. Aeliana*, 4th Ser., XVII, 1940, 85–115.

Bosanquet, 1904: Bosanquet, R. C., "Excavations on the Line of the Roman Wall in Northumberland–the Roman Camp at Housesteads", *Archaeol. Aeliana*, 2nd Ser., XXV, 1904, 193–300.

Breeze, 1972: Breeze, D. J., "Excavations at the Roman Fort of Carrawburgh 1967–1969", *Archaeol. Aeliana*, 4th Ser., L, 1972, 81–144.

Bruce, 1884: Bruce, J. C., "The Earlier and More Recent Discoveries in the Roman Camp on the Lawe, South Shields", *Archaeol. Aeliana*, X, 1884, 233 *et seq.*

Bruce, 1966: Bruce, J. C., *Handbook to the Roman Wall*, 12th ed., Newcastle upon Tyne, 1966.

Bushe-Fox, 1913: Bushe-Fox, J. P., "Excavations on the Site of the Roman Town at Wroxeter, Shropshire, in 1912", Reps. Res. Comm. Soc. Antiq. London, no. 1, Oxford, 1913.

Callender, 1965: Callender, M. H., *Roman Amphorae*, Oxford, 1965.

Chenet and Gaudron, 1955: Chenet, G. and Gaudron, Guy, *La Céramique Sigillée d'Argonne des IIe et IIIe Siecles*, Supplément a Gallia, VI, Paris, 1955.

Cunliffe, 1968: Cunliffe, B., *Fifth Report on the Excavations of the Roman Fort at Richborough, Kent*, Reps. Res. Comm. Soc. Antiq. London, no. XXIII, Oxford, 1968.

Cunliffe, 1971: Cunliffe, B., *Excavations at Fishbourne, 1961–1969*, Reps. Res. Comm. Soc. Antiq. London, Leeds, 1971.

Curle, 1911: Curle, J., *A Roman Frontier Post and its People. The Fort of Newstead in the Parish of Melrose*, Glasgow, 1911.

Déchelette, 1904: Déchelette, J., *Les Vases Céramiques Ornés de la Gaule Romaine*, Paris, 1904.

Dore, 1976: Dore, J. N., "Excavations at South Shields, 1975", *Archaeol. Aeliana*, 5th Ser., IV, 1976, 185.

Dore and Greene, 1976: Dore, J. and Greene, K., "North African Pottery from South Shields", *Archaeol. Aeliana*, 5th Ser., IV, 1976, 186–9.

Fölzer, 1913: Fölzer, E., *Die Bilderschüsseln der Ostgallischen Sigillata-manufakturen*, Bonn, 1913.

Gillam, 1976: Gillam, J. P., "Coarse Fumed Ware in Britain and Beyond", *Glasgow Archaeol. J.*, 4, 1976, 57–80.

Hartley, 1972: Hartley, B. R., "The Roman Occupation of Scotland: the evidence of the samian ware", *Britannia*, III, 1972, 1–55.

Hartley, 1973: Hartley, K. F., "The Marketing and Distribution of Mortaria", in

Detsicas (ed.) *Current Research in Romano–British Coarse Pottery*, C.B.A. Res. Rep. no. 10, London, 1973.

Hayes, 1972: Hayes, J. W., *Late Roman Pottery*, London, 1972.

Hogg, 1965: Hogg, R., "Excavation of the Roman Auxiliary Tilery, Brampton", *Trans. Cumberland Westmorland Antiq. Archaeol. Soc.*, New Ser., LXV, 1965, 133–68.

Holwerda, 1923: Holwerda, J. H., *Arentsburg: een Romeinsch Militair Vloorstation bij Voorburg*, Leiden, 1923.

Hooppell, 1878: Hooppell, Rev. R. E., "On the Discovery and Exploration of Roman Remains at South Shields", *Natur. Hist. Trans. Northumberland, Durham and Newcastle upon Tyne*, VIII, 1878, 126–67.

Hull, 1963: Hull, M. R., *The Roman Potters Kilns of Colchester*, Rep. Res. Comm. Soc. Antiq. London, no. XXI, Oxford, 1963.

Kewley, 1973: Kewley, J., "Inscribed Capitals on Roman altars from Northern Britain", *Archaeol. Aeliana*, 5th Ser., I, 1973, 129–32.

Knorr, 1919: Knorr, R., *Töpfer und Fabriken Verzierter Terra-sigillata des ersten Jahrhunderts*, Stuttgart, 1919.

Leland, 1715: Leland, J., *De Rebus Britannicis Collectanea*, Oxford, 1715.

Margary, 1967: Margary, I. D., *Roman Roads in Britain*, London, 1967.

Oelmann, 1914: Oelmann, F., *Die Keramik des Kastells Niederbieber*, Frankfurt, 1914.

Oswald, 1936–37: Oswald, F., *Index of Figure Types on Terra Sigillata*, Liverpool, 1936–7.

Oswald and Pryce, 1920: Oswald, F. and Pryce, T. D., *An Introduction to the Study of Terra Sigillata*, London, 1920.

Petrikovits, 1975: Petrikovits, Harald von, *Die Innenbauten römischer Legionslager während der Principatszeit*, Opladen, 1975.

Rae, 1974: Rae, Alan and Viola, "The Roman Fort at Cramond, Edinburgh: excavations 1954–66", *Britannia*, V, 1974, 163–224.

Richmond Guidebook: Richmond, I. A., *The Roman Fort at South Shields, A Guide*, Undated.

Richmond, 1934: Richmond, I. A., "The Roman Fort at South Shields", *Archaeol. Aeliana*, 4th Ser., XI, 1934.

Richmond, 1936: Richmond, I. A., "Roman Lead Sealings from Brough under Stainmore", *Trans. Cumberland Westmorland Antiq. Archaeol. Soc. New Ser.*, XXXVI, 1936, 104–26.

Richmond, 1958: Richmond, I. A., *Roman and Native in North Britain*, Nelson, 1958.

Richmond and Birley, 1930: Richmond, I. A. and Birley, E., "Excavations on Hadrian's Wall in the Birdoswald—Pike Hill Sector, 1929", *Trans. Cumberland Westmorland Antiq. Archaeol. Soc. New Ser.*, XXX, 1930, 169–205.

Richmond and Gillam, 1950: Richmond I. A. and Gillam, J. P., "Excavations on the Roman Site at Corbridge, 1946–49", *Archaeol. Aeliana*, 4th Ser., XXXIII, 1950, 152–201.

Richmond and Gillam, 1952: Richmond, I. A. and Gillam, J. P., "Further Exploration of the Antonine Fort at Corbridge", *Archaeol. Aeliana*, 4th Ser., XXX, 1952.

Ricken, 1934: Ricken, Heinrich, "die Bilderschusseln der Kastelle Saalburg und Zugmantel", *Saalburg Jahrbuch*, VIII, 1934, 130–82.

Ricken and Ludowici, 1948: Ricken, H. and Ludowici, W., *Katalog VI meiner Ausgrabungen in Rheinzabern 1901–1914*, Speyer, 1948.

Ricken and Fischer, 1963: Ricken, H. and Fischer, C., *die Bilderschusseln der Römischen Töpfer von Rheinzabern*, Bonn, 1963.

Rogers, 1974: Rogers, G., *Poteries Sigillées de la Gaule Centrale: I—Les Motifs non figurés*, XXVIIIe supplément a "Gallia", Paris, 1974.

Savage, 1898: Savage, Rev. H. E., "Abbess Hilda's First Religious House", *Archaeol. Aeliana*, 2nd Ser., XIX, 1898, 47–88.

Schönberger and Simon, 1976: Schönberger, Hans and Simon, Hans-Gunter, *Römerlager Rödgen*, Limesforschungen Band 15, Berlin, 1976.

Seeck, 1962: Seeck, Otto (ed.), *Notitia Dignitatum accedunt Notitia Urbis Constantinopolitanae et Latercula Provinciarum*, Frankfurt, 1962.

Shotter, 1973: Shotter, D. C. A., "Numeri Barcariorum, A Note on RIB 601", *Britannia*, IV, 1973, 206–9.

Simpson and Richmond, 1941: Simpson, F. G. and Richmond, I. A., "The Roman Fort on Hadrian's Wall at Benwell", *Archaeol. Aeliana*, 4th Ser., XIX, 1941, 1–43.

Smith, 1959: Smith, David, "A Palmyrene Sculptor at South Shields?", *Archaeol. Aeliana*, 4th Ser., XXXVII, 1959, 203–11.

Stanfield and Simpson, 1958: Stanfield, J. A. and Simpson, Grace, *The Central Gaulish Potters*, London, 1958.

Thornborrow, 1959: Thornborrow, J. "Report on the Excavations at Beacon Street, South Shields, 1959", *Papers of the South Shields Archaeol. Hist. Soc.*, Vol. I, no. 7, 1959, 8–25.

Thornborrow, 1960: Thornborrow, J., "Report on the Excavations at Beacon Street, South Shields, 1960", *Papers of the South Shields Archaeol. Hist. Soc.*, Vol. I, no. 8, 1960, 9–10.

Thornborrow, 1961: Thornborrow, J., "Report on the Excavations at Pearson Street, South Shields, 1961", *Papers of the South Shields Archaeol. Hist. Soc.*, Vol. I, no. 9, 10–12.

Thornborrow, 1964: Thornborrow, J., "Excavations on the Lawe, South Shields, 1962", *Papers of the South Shields Archaeol. Hist. Soc.*, Vol. II, no. 1, 15–18.

Wilkes, 1961: Wilkes, J. J., "Excavations in Housesteads Fort, 1960", *Archaeol. Aeliana*, 4th Ser., XXXIX, 1961, 279–301.